Bargain Hunters' London

Andrew Kershman

Bargain Hunters' London

Written by Andrew Kershman
Additional research and writing by
Daisy Wyatt, Lesley Gilmour and Vanesa Rodriguez
Photography by Andrew Kershman
Edited by Tony Whyte
Maps designed by Lesley Gilmour
Book design by Susi Koch and Lesley Gilmour

Published in 2008 by
Metro Publications
PO Box 6336
London
N1 6PY

Printed and bound in India

© 2008 Andrew Kershman
British Library Cataloguing in Publication Data.
A catalogue record for this book is available from the
British Library.

ISBN 9781902910277

Octavia Charity Shop

Unto this Last

www.bargainhunterslondon.com

Rokit

Wow Retro

1 **Introduction**

3 **Shopping Areas**

Map 1 Central London
Map 2 Camden
Map 3 Islington
Map 4 Kilburn
Map 5 Hammersmith
Map 6 Portobello
Map 7 Kensington High Street
Map 8 Wandsworth & Putney
Map 9 Fulham
Map 10 Finchley
Map 11 Golders Green
Map 12 Brick Lane
Map 13 Tottenham Court Road

19 **BARGAIN HUNTING BY ITEM**

20 **How to Use this Book**
21 **Fashion**
22 Street Fashion
36 Classic & Retro Clothing
64 Designer Sale Shops
67 Designer Warehouse Sales
76 Dress Agencies
90 Shoes, Boots & Bags

99 **Electronics**
100 Computers
103 Computer Fairs & Auctions
105 Computer Games & Consoles
107 Hifi, DVD & TV
112 Miscellaneous
115 Tottenham Court Road

117 **Health & Beauty**
118 Contact Lenses & Glasses
125 Haircare & Cosmetics
128 Hairdressing

135 **Home**
136 Bathroom
143 Beds & Bedding
151 Carpets, Rugs & Tiles
160 Curtains
167 DIY & Equipment
175 Domestic Appliances
181 Fabrics & Haberdashers
191 Furniture
200 Kitchenware & Cutlery
205 Picture Frames & Mirrors

207 **Kids**

213 **Leisure**
 214 Bikes
 225 Books
 236 CDs, Records, Tapes & DVDs
 248 Photography
 259 Travel

271 BARGAIN HUNTING BY OUTLET

272 **Architectural Salvage**

276 **Auctions**
 277 General Auctions
 285 Car Auctions
 286 Property Auctions

287 **Charity Shops**

323 **Factory Shops**
 324 Clothing
 325 Household Goods
 327 Out of Town Shopping Villages

329 **Independent Designers**
 330 Fashion & Textiles
 332 Ceramics
 332 Lighting
 333 Furniture
 334 Clocks
 334 Accessories
 335 Workshop Open Days

339 **Junk Shops & Second Hand Furniture**

351 **Markets**

357 **Car Boot Sales**

361 **Pawnbrokers**

366 **Index**

Acknowledgments

This book has been researched over six months and would have taken considerably longer were it not for the help of an enthusiastic and skilled group of researchers and writers. Daisy Wyatt did sterling work visiting and writing about over 150 charity shops, while Vanessa Rodreguez did a good deal of fact checking and updating of the household and leisure sections. Lesley Gilmour deserves special mention for her research and writing about fashion and retro clothing as well as for the detailed maps she has created from my clumsy cartography. Susi Koch has my thanks for the imagination and skill applied to the layout and design of Bargain Hunters' London. My editor, Tony Whyte, has applied care and patience in correcting my many mistakes and helping to make this book easy and clear to read.

My thanks also go to the people working in the businesses featured in this book who have volunteered information, answered my questions and in some cases posed for photographs. Their help and support has made the writing and researching of this book a lot easier and a great deal more enjoyable. I am indebted to the many readers of the last edition of the book who contacted me with suggestions and information, a great deal of which has been incorporated into this new edition.

Introduction

There are many people who think that hunting for bargains is a disreputable and squalid activity. One of the reasons for this attitude is the belief that goods bought cheaply will be inferior and that the more you pay for something the better it must be. A brief look through this greatly expanded fourth edition of Bargain Hunters' London will confound this prejudice with details of warehouse sales, retro clothing shops, furniture discount stores, factory shops and many more London outlets which sell high quality goods at considerable discounts. With the help of this book it is possible to find a beautiful three-seater leather sofa for £700 that would cost over £2000 in some more obvious high street retailers or a new Yamaha midi-system for £130, compared with over £170 in a leading electrical store. With very little fuss this book makes it possible to save money on all kinds of top quality goods without having to accept second-best.

If, like me, you regard shopping as a pleasure rather than a chore, then minimising the 'fuss' is not part of your shopping strategy. This book understands the pleasure derived from shopping for second-hand things and aims to provide shopping adventurists with plenty of new regions for exploration – from eccentric junk shops to over 150 of London's best charity shops. The great expansion in the number of retro clothing stores in the capital in recent years shows that shopping is just as much about the experience of finding unique things as it is about price. Occasionally there is a conflict between shopping for pleasure and finding the cheapest price. This book has remained neutral on the matter – listing both cheap high street stores as well as funky independent outlets and allowing readers to mix and match as they see fit.

Probably the greatest change to this new edition of Bargain Hunters' London is the launch of an accompanying website – www.bargainhunterslondon.com. The website is not a replacement for this publication but a way of informing readers about new bargain stores and events, getting their feedback and news and in this way collecting information for inclusion in the next edition of the Bargain Hunters' London. A great deal of effort has been made so that this book contains all the information you will need to find great bargains in London – I hope it also helps you enjoy the experience.

Rellik

Deuxieme

Past Caring

Rokit

£3 OR 2 FOR £5 VINTAGE FOR LESS

map 4

£2

Maps

map 1 Central London, p.4

map 2 Camden, p.6

map 3 Islington, p7

map 4 Kilburn, p.8

map 5 Hammersmith, p.9

map 6 Portobello, p.10

map 7 Kensington High Street. p.11

map 8 Wandsworth & Putney, p.12

map 9 Fulham, p.13

map 10 Finchley, p.14

map 11 Golders Green, p.15

map 12 Brick Lane, p.16

map 13 Tottenham Court Road, p.17

map 1 Central London

1. Beyond Retro, p.36
2. Blackout II, p. 36
3. Kingly Court,
   Marshmallow Mountain, p.38
   Sam Greenberg, p.42
   Twinkled, p.43
   Love Vintage, p.37
4. Pop Boutique, p.38
5. Rokit, p.40
6. WOW Retro, p.46
7. WOW Retro, p.46
8. Paul Smith Sale Shop, p.64
9. Bang Bang, p.77
10. The Loft, p.80
11. Office, p.90
12. Shoe Express, p.91
13. Apricot, p.22
14. Lillywhites, p.23
15. Morgan, p.251

16. Richer Sounds, p.107
17. Musical Images, p.108
18. Spex in the City, p.118
19. Sally Hair & Beauty, p.125
20. The Linen Cupboard, p148
21. Russell & Chapple, p.181
22. Berwick St Fabric Stores, p.182
23. Denny's, p.200
24. Leon Jaeggi & Sons, p.200
25. Pages, p.200
26. Cass Art
27. Any Amount of Books, p.225
28. Bookends, p.225
29. Book Warehouse, p.226
30. Book Warehouse, p.226
31. Henry Pordes Books, p.228
32. Soho Original Bookshop, p.229
33. Borders Books & Music, p.236
34. Borders Books & Music, p.236

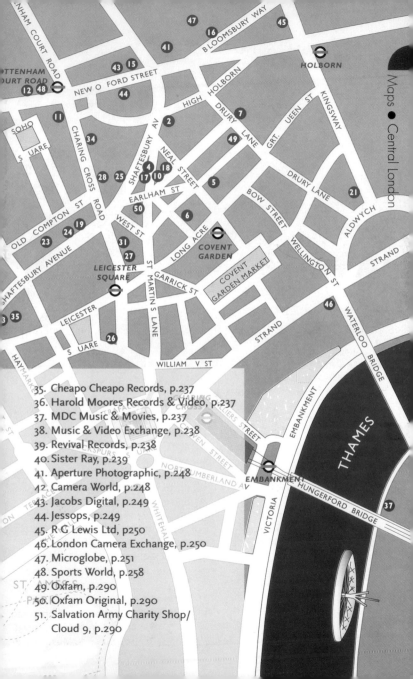

35. Cheapo Cheapo Records, p.237
36. Harold Moores Records & Video, p.237
37. MDC Music & Movies, p.237
38. Music & Video Exchange, p.238
39. Revival Records, p.238
40. Sister Ray, p.239
41. Aperture Photographic, p.248
42. Camera World, p.248
43. Jacobs Digital, p.249
44. Jessops, p.249
45. R G Lewis Ltd, p250
46. London Camera Exchange, p.250
47. Microglobe, p.251
48. Sports World, p.258
49. Oxfam, p.290
50. Oxfam Original, p.290
51. Salvation Army Charity Shop/
    Cloud 9, p.290

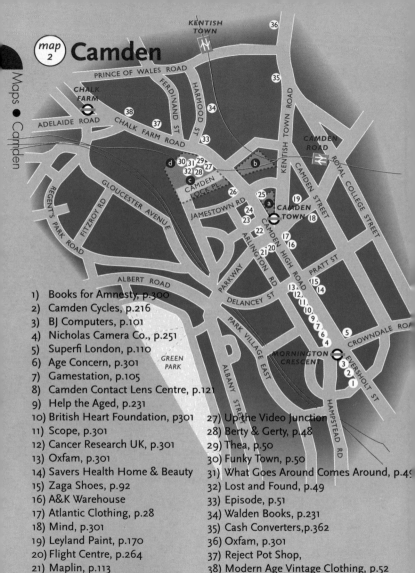

map 2 Camden

1) Books for Amnesty, p.300
2) Camden Cycles, p.216
3) BJ Computers, p.101
4) Nicholas Camera Co., p.251
5) Superfi London, p.110
6) Age Concern, p.301
7) Gamestation, p.105
8) Camden Contact Lens Centre, p.121
9) Help the Aged, p.231
10) British Heart Foundation, p301
11) Scope, p.301
12) Cancer Research UK, p.301
13) Oxfam, p.301
14) Savers Health Home & Beauty
15) Zaga Shoes, p.92
16) A&K Warehouse
17) Atlantic Clothing, p.28
18) Mind, p.301
19) Leyland Paint, p.170
20) Flight Centre, p.264
21) Maplin, p.113
22) ALDO Sale Shop, p.91
23) Out On The Floor, p.243
24) Rokit, p.51
25) Music & Video Exchange, p.242
26) Music & Video Exchange, p.242

27) Up the Video Junction
28) Berty & Gerty, p.48
29) Thea, p.50
30) Funky Town, p.50
31) What Goes Around Comes Around, p.49
32) Lost and Found, p.49
33) Episode, p.51
34) Walden Books, p.231
35) Cash Converters, p.362
36) Oxfam, p.301
37) Reject Pot Shop,
38) Modern Age Vintage Clothing, p.52

a) Camden Market
b) Canal Market
c) Camden Lock Market
d) Stables Market

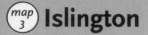

map 3 Islington

1) Dress for Less, p.79
2) Oxfam, p.294
3) Pandora's Box, p.201
4) Cancer Research UK, p.294
5) Blue Audio Visual, p.109
6) Cass Art
7) Bargain Centre, p.184
8) Seconda Mano, p.83
9) Flashback, p.240
10) Past Caring, p.343
11) Sue Ryder, p.294
12) Sew Fantastic, p.185
13) Handmade & Found
14) Haggle Vinyl, p.240
15) Salvation Army Charity Shop, p.294
16) Computer Precision, p.101
17) Marie Curie Cancer Research, p.294

a) Chapel Market
b) Camden Passage

HIGHBURY &
ISLINGTON

ISLINGTON PAR RD

ARNS URY ST

UPPER STREET

AL EI DA ST

CROSS ST

ESSEX ROAD

RITANNIA ROW

THE ERTON RD

GAS IN ST

PAC INGTON ST

LIVERPOOL ROAD

ARNS URY ROAD

UPPER STREET

ST PETER'S ST

CHAPEL ST

ANGEL

COLE ROO ROW

WHITE LION ST

PENTONVILLE RD

CITY RD

GOSWELL RD

ST OHN ST

ROSE ERY RD

EX OUTH T

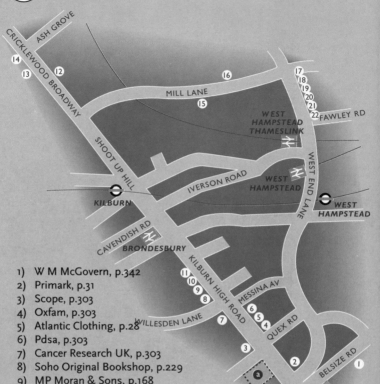

(map 4) **Kilburn**

1) W M McGovern, p.342
2) Primark, p.31
3) Scope, p.303
4) Oxfam, p.303
5) Atlantic Clothing, p.28
6) Pdsa, p.303
7) Cancer Research UK, p.303
8) Soho Original Bookshop, p.229
9) MP Moran & Sons, p.168
10) Cash XChange, p.363
11) Cash Converters, p.362
12) Satellite Electronics, p.110
13) TV4U, p.111
14) Boznia Herzegovina Community Charity Shop, p.303
15) The Community Charity Shop, p.303
16) Farz Design, p.25
17) Oxfam, p.303
18) The Children's Society, p.302
19) Cancer Research Society, p.302
20) All Aboard, p.302
21) Marie Curie Charity Shop, p.303
22) Scope, p.303
a) Kilburn Market

Hammersmith & Shepherd's Bush

1) FARA, p.312
2) Age Concern, p.312
3) Travel Zone, p.94
4) Games Planet, p.106
5) Traid, p.312
6) Shepherd's Bush Eye Centre
7) MK One, p.31
8) Gray & Lowe
9) Classic Textiles, p.187
10) A-One Fabrics, p.187
11) Cash Converters, p.362
12) UK Textiles, p.187

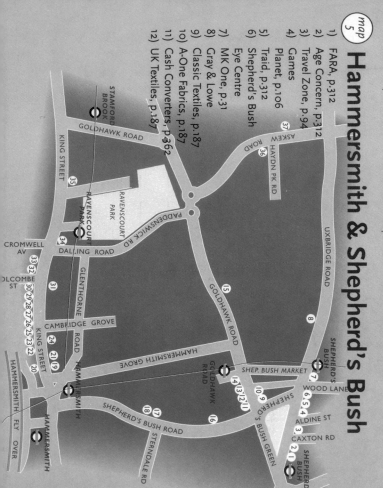

13) Toni Textiles, p.187
14) A to Z Fabrics, p.187
15) The Carpetstore, p.154
16) Super Design Ltd, p
17) The Furniture Gallery, p.344
18) Red Cross Shop, p.313
19) Dreamsport
20) TK Maxx, p.32
21) Atlantic, p.28
22) Oxfam, p.313
23) Jessops, p.249
24) Primark, p.31
25) The Book Warehouse, p.226
26) Traid, p.312
27) Cancer Research UK, p.313
28) X Electrical, p.111
29) British Heart Foundation, p.313
30) Books For Amnesty, p.313
31) Maplin, p.113
32) Kitchen Tech, p.178
33) The Carpetstore, p.154
34) Cash Converters, p.362
35) Mac's Cameras
36) Askew Paint Centre, p.171
37) Octavia, p.312

map 6 Portobello

1) Traid, p.311
2) Lords Home Care, p.202
3) Oxfam, p.312
4) 20th Century Theatre (On the QT), p.72
5) Oxfam Bookshop, p.312
6) Nu-Line Builders Merchants, p.169
7) Intoxica Records, p.244
8) Pili & Mili, p.31
9) Marie Curie, p.312
10) Buyers & Sellers, p.177
11) Crazy Clothing Connection, p.55
12) L. H. Cook Furnishers, p.344
13) Honest Jon's Records, p.244
14) 295, p.57
15) The Cloth Shop, p.163
16) Golborne Furniture, p.344
17) London Camera Shop, p.255
18) Ollies, p.346
19) Les Couilles du Chien, p.346
20) Hot & Cold Inc, p.178
21) Rellik, p.56

 map 7 Notting Hill Gate

1) Factory Outlet, p.29
2) Purple Bee, p.32
3) Uttam London Ltd, p.32
4) Retro Man
   (32 & 34 Penbridge Rd), p.57
5) Retro Home & Jewellery
6) Retro Clothing, p.57
7) Retro Woman. p.57
8) Book & Comic Exchange, p.232
9) The Book Warehouse, p.226
10) Retro Clothing & Home Accessories
11) Soul & Dance Exchange, p.245
12) Computer Games Exchange, p.245
13) Music & Video Exchange, p.245
14) Classical Music Exchange, p.245
15) Stage & Screen, p.245
16) Trinity Hospice Shop p.311
17) Oxfam, p.311
18) Octavia, p.311
19) Octavia, p.310
20) Trinity Hospice Shop, p.310

⓶ Wandsworth & Putney

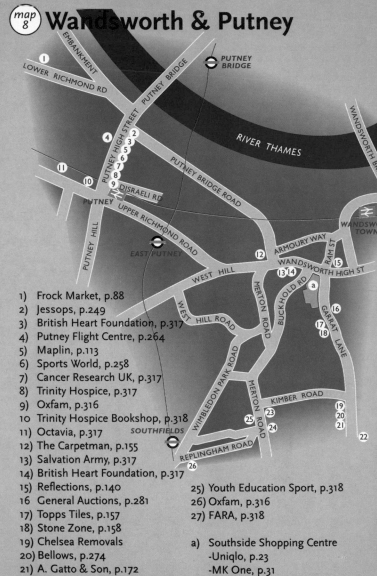

1) Frock Market, p.88
2) Jessops, p.249
3) British Heart Foundation, p.317
4) Putney Flight Centre, p.264
5) Maplin, p.113
6) Sports World, p.258
7) Cancer Research UK, p.317
8) Trinity Hospice, p.317
9) Oxfam, p.316
10 Trinity Hospice Bookshop, p.318
11) Octavia, p.317
12) The Carpetman, p.155
13) Salvation Army, p.317
14) British Heart Foundation, p.317
15) Reflections, p.140
16 General Auctions, p.281
17) Topps Tiles, p.157
18) Stone Zone, p.158
19) Chelsea Removals
20) Bellows, p.274
21) A. Gatto & Son, p.172
22) 331, p.34
23) Villeroy & Boch, p.326
24) Chomette, p.325

25) Youth Education Sport, p.318
26) Oxfam, p.316
27) FARA, p.318

a) Southside Shopping Centre
   -Uniqlo, p.23
   -MK One, p.31
   -Primark, p.31
   -RSPCA
   -Shoe Zone, p.92

map 9 Fulham

1) Fulham Pot Shop
2) Hansens Cookware, p.202
3) Richer Sounds, p.107
4) Octavia, p.308
5) Oxfam, p.308
6) Cancer Research UK, p.308
7) Trinity Hospice Shop, p.308
8) World's End Bookshop, p.
9) Leyland SDM, p.
10) Lots Road Auctions, p.170
11) Lombok Clearance Store, p.280
12) Criterion #2 Tiles, p.194
13) Thames Motor Auction, p.158
14) Topps Tiles, p.285
15) Bathstore, p.157
16) FARA, p.138
17) Deuxieme, p.308
18) Colourwash, p.84
19) Old Hat, p.137
20) Shaya, p.56
21) Ideabright, p.172
22) Swim, Bike, Run, p.218
23) Mend-a-Bike, p.216
24) FARA, p.308

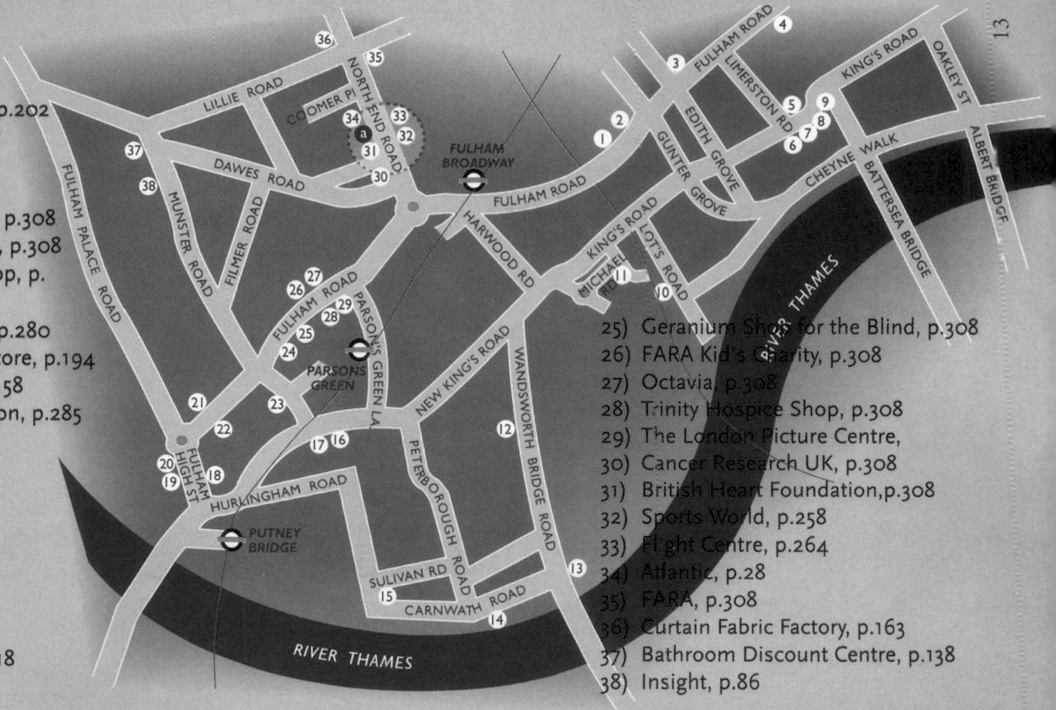

25) Geranium Shop for the Blind, p.308
26) FARA Kid's Charity, p.308
27) Octavia, p.308
28) Trinity Hospice Shop, p.308
29) The London Picture Centre,
30) Cancer Research UK, p.308
31) British Heart Foundation,p.308
32) Sports World, p.258
33) Flight Centre, p.264
34) Atlantic, p.28
35) FARA, p.308
36) Curtain Fabric Factory, p.163
37) Bathroom Discount Centre, p.138
38) Insight, p.86

a) North End Road Market

13

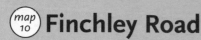

Finchley Road

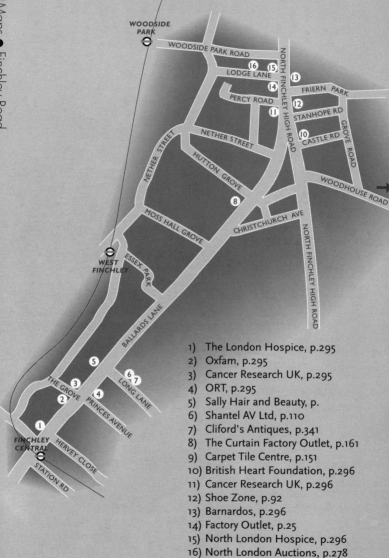

1) The London Hospice, p.295
2) Oxfam, p.295
3) Cancer Research UK, p.295
4) ORT, p.295
5) Sally Hair and Beauty, p.
6) Shantel AV Ltd, p.110
7) Cliford's Antiques, p.341
8) The Curtain Factory Outlet, p.161
9) Carpet Tile Centre, p.151
10) British Heart Foundation, p.296
11) Cancer Research UK, p.296
12) Shoe Zone, p.92
13) Barnardos, p.296
14) Factory Outlet, p.25
15) North London Hospice, p.296
16) North London Auctions, p.278

Golders Green

1) All Aboard, p.297
2 Cancer Research UK, p.297
3) Peter Jude, p.162
4) The Flight Centre, p.264
5) Husen Moda
6) North London Hospice, p.297
7) Next To Choice, p.27
8) Book Warehouse, p.226
9) Sally Hair & Beauty, p.125
10) North London Hospice Shop, p.297
11) Norwood Ravenswood (84), p.297
12) Norwood Ravenswood (87), p.297
13 Jami, p.297
14) Golds Factory Outlet, p.26
15) All Aboard, p.296
16) Oxfam, p.297
17) All Aboard, p.296
18) Jo Jo Maman Bébé, p.208

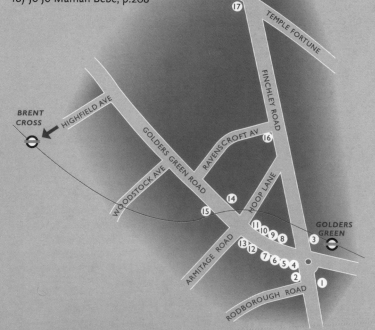

(map 12) Brick Lane

1) Torpedo Blue, p.62
2) Mordex, p.35
3) Moda, p.35
4) The Furniture Café, p.351
5) Truth Trading, p.35
6) Open Space, p.35
7) Brick Lane Bikes, p.221
8) Bacon St (16-22) Junk Shop, p.348
9) Bacon St (14) Junk Shop, p.348
10) Kitchen Warehouse, p.204
11) A.M. Leather Fashion, p.34
12) Beats Workin', p.247
13) Dublin Jim, p.350
14) The Shop, p.62
15) Burt & Mary, p.60
16) The Shop II. p.62
17) Kojak, p.34
18) Blackmans Shoes, p.95
19) Beyond Retro, p.36

20) Lost and Found, p.349
21) Rokit, p.60
22) Laden Showroom, p.66
23) Rokit, p.62
24) Truman Brewery, p.74
25) Absolute Vintage, p.59
26) Blondie, p.59
27) Bhopal Fabrics, p.188
28) Epra Fabrics, p.189
29) Z. Butt Textiles, p.189
30) KVJ, p.112

a) Spitalfields Market, p.356
b) Brick Lane Market, p.352

16

Tottenham Court Road

see page 115 & 116 for details

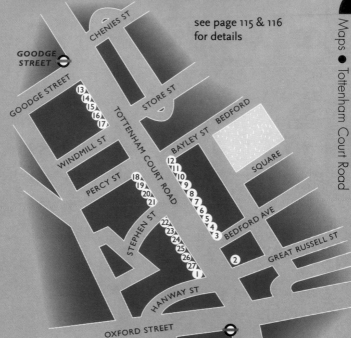

1) Micro Anvika
2) Hi-Fi Surplus Store
3) MBA
4) Microworld 2000
5) Kamla
6) ask
7) Shyamtronics
8) Micro Anvika
9) MBA
10) Shasonic
11) n-genious
12) Harp Electronics
13) Micro Anvika
14) Gultronics
15) Epsilon Computers
16) Sunrise Digital
17) GHS Technology
18) The Digital Centre
19) C&A Electronics
20) Spatial Audio & Video
21) PNR Audiovision
22) Samuel King
23) Microworld
24) Sony Centre
25) Musical Vision
26) Brains
27) Arena Electronics

Bargain Hunting by Item

Fashion 21
Electronics................. 90
Health & Beauty 117
Home 135
Kids 207
Leisure..................... 213

How to Use this Book

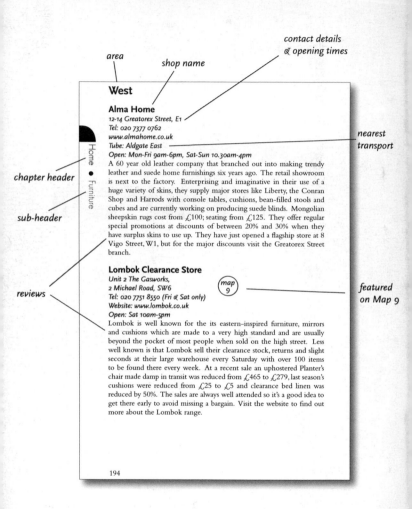

area

shop name

contact details
& opening times

West

Alma Home
12-14 Greatorex Street, E1
Tel: 020 7377 0762
www.almahome.co.uk
Tube: Aldgate East
Open: Mon-Fri 9am-6pm, Sat-Sun 10.30am-4pm
A 60 year old leather company that branched out into making trendy
leather and suede home furnishings six years ago. The retail showroom
is next to the factory. Enterprising and imaginative in their use of a
huge variety of skins, they supply major stores like Liberty, the Conran
Shop and Harrods with console tables, cushions, bean-filled stools and
cubes and are currently working on producing suede blinds. Mongolian
sheepskin rugs cost from £100; seating from £125. They offer regular
special promotions at discounts of between 20% and 30% when they
have surplus skins to use up. They have just opened a flagship store at 8
Vigo Street, W1, but for the major discounts visit the Greatorex Street
branch.

nearest
transport

chapter header

Home

Furniture

sub-header

reviews

Lombok Clearance Store
Unit 2 The Gasworks,
2 Michael Road, SW6
Tel: 020 7751 8550 (Fri & Sat only)
Website: www.lombok.co.uk
Open: Sat 10am-5pm

(map 9)

featured
on Map 9

Lombok is well known for the its eastern-inspired furniture, mirrors
and cushions which are made to a very high standard and are usually
beyond the pocket of most people when sold on the high street. Less
well known is that Lombok sell their clearance stock, returns and slight
seconds at their large warehouse every Saturday with over 100 items
to be found there every week. At a recent sale an uphostered Planter's
chair made damp in transit was reduced from £465 to £279, last season's
cushions were reduced from £25 to £5 and clearance bed linen was
reduced by 50%. The sales are always well attended so it's a good idea to
get there early to avoid missing a bargain. Visit the website to find out
more about the Lombok range.

194

Fashion

22.....Street Fashion
36.....Classic & Retro Clothing
64.....Designer Sale Shops
67.....Designer Warehouse Sales
76.....Dress Agencies
90.....Shoes, Boots & Bags

Street Fashion

Street Fashion is a catch-all phrase we have used to describe any clothing that does not carry a designer label and is not a classic or retro garment – in other words, everyday essentials like T-shirts, jeans and underwear. London is a great place to shop for this kind of casual clothing as it still has a fairly vibrant rag trade and clever designer copies from Eastern Europe and the Far East regularly feature in London shops, many of which are reviewed here. This book generally favours small independent retailers, but in this chapter it has to be conceded that many high street names offer great value and the best of these are featured below.

Central

Apricot

40 Shaftesbury Avenue, W1D
Tel: 020 7287 8043
Tube: Piccadilly
Open: Mon-Wed 10am-9pm, Thurs-Sat 10.30am-10pm, Sun 12noon-5pm
This shop has a few designer labels on its rails, but most of the clothing is good value street fashion. Among the recent bargains at their central London branch were dresses and skirts for £14–20, jeans for £20, combat trousers for £19 and leather handbags for only £10. The Birkenstock sandals were great value for £34 as was the Ralph Lauren Polo Jacket for £59.
Also at:
67-68 Whitgift Centre, Croydon, CR0 Tel: 020 8649 8792

Lillywhites

24-36 Lower Regent Street, SW1
Tel: 0870 333 9600
www.lillywhites.co.uk
Tube: Piccadilly
Open: Mon-Sat 10am-9pm, Sun 12noon-6pm

map 1

The policy of 'pile it high, sell it cheap' is rather at odds with the grand panelled staircase of Lillywhites sports store, but since the shop's take over by the Sports World chain it has become a great place for cheap clothing and sportswear. The emphasis now is on discount retailing and the store has diversified into clothing for the whole family. Recent bargains included Karrimor walking shoes for only £14.99 (reduced by 70%), a Karrimor Airspace 25L rucksack for £13.49 and YSL men's slip-on dress shoes again reduced by 70% to £29.99. YSL T-shirts, jackets and jeans were all reduced by between 70-80%. Traditionalists may be upset by the store's transformation, but for clothing bargains it is now a great place to visit.

Primark

499-517 Oxford Street, W1
Tel: 020 7495 0420
See the main entry in West London (page 31) for full details.

Uniqlo

75 Brompton Road, SW3
Tel: 020 7591 0439
Tube: Knightsbridge
Open: Mon-Wed 10am-7pm, Thurs-Sat 10am-8pm, Sun 12noon-6pm

This fantastic Japanese retailer has expanded its operation in the UK in recent years and now has eight stores in the London area. The success of the business is easy to understand with basic street fashion for men, women and children at very competitive prices. Uniqlo is a great place to stock up on basics like jeans, T-shirts, jackets, tops and accessories with plenty of savings compared with most high street retailers.
Branches at:
The Plaza Shopping Centre, 188 Oxford Street, W1N Tel: 020 7734 5369
84-86 Regent Street, W1 Tel: 020 7434 9688;
1 Lower George Street, Richmond TW9 Tel: 020 8948 6155
Unit 2, 51 The Broadway, Wimbledon SW19 Tel: 020 8944 8836
Unit 68 Southside Shopping Centre, Wandsworth, SW18 Tel: 020 8812 4803
54-58 Kensington High Street, W8 Tel:020 7376 0054
93-97 Clarence Street, Kingston Upon Thames, Surrey KT1 Tel: 020 8546 6663

North

Central Park
152 Muswell Hill Broadway, N10
Tel: 020 8883 9122
Tube: Highgate (then bus)
Open: Mon-Sat 9.30am-6pm, Sun 11am-5pm
See main entry in West London (page 28).

David Oliver Designer Outlets
16 Sussex Ring, Woodside Park,
Finchley N12
Tel: 020 8343 8343
Tube: Woodside Park
Open: Daily 10am-6pm
This established outlet has a professional team of buyers sourcing quality women's labels from manufacturers in France, Italy and Germany and sells direct to the public in the UK for up to 80% discount. The garments are all new and in perfect condition and the shop also sources bankrupt stock from the domestic market which is also sold at a considerable discount. One of the most impressive aspects of shopping here is the range of sizes available (6-24), so people of all shapes and sizes will find something of interest. The rails contain all kinds of garments from casual to evening wear.

Decoy
170 Muswell Hill Broadway, N10
Tel: 020 8815 0808
Tube: Highgate (then Bus)
Open: Mon-Sat 9am-6pm, Sun 11am-5pm
This modern boutique manages to cram a good selection of contemporary women's street fashion into a narrow retail outlet. The clothing is seasonal with plenty of bright coloured summer gear predominating on a recent visit with discounts such as cotton slacks reduced from £22.99 to £15, T-shirts reduced to £5 and a good selection of jeans for £10-25. A great little shop and next door to two other discount outlets.

Factory Monaco

426 Muswell Hill Broadway, N10
Tel: 020 8883 5501
Tube: Highgate (then Bus)
Open: Mon-Sat 10am-6.30pm, Sun 12noon-5.30pm

This large boutique offers a great selection of street fashion with many items imported from Spain and Italy and most garments sold for between £10-15. Among the recent deals was an Indian style top for £40 (reduced from £79), funky belts and bags for between £5-45 and a great selection of colourful jewellery from Barcelona for around £15. The store is worth repeated visits as the stock regularly changes.

Factory Outlet

805 High Road,
North Finchley, N12
Tel: 020 8445 2737
Tube: Woodside Park
Open: Mon-Sat 9.30am-6pm

Women's street fashion with 'extras' and overstock from Gap, Topshop, French Connection and other high street names with tops from £5, trousers from £10 and a good selection of jogging gear. The stock is always up-to-date in terms of style and colour and is aimed at the young and fashion-conscious. A great place to get street fashion on a budget.
Also at: 26 Topsfield Parade, Crouch End N8, Tel: 020 8341 9598

Farz Design

51 Mill Lane, NW1
Tel: 020 7317 8144
Tube: West Hampstead Thameslink
Open: Mon-Sat 11am-7pm

This small boutique offers well made and colourful ladies fashion imported from Italy, France and India. On a recent visit there was a great selection of summer dresses, a stylish French box jacket and large leather handbags all priced at £20. The shop is a little isolated on a quiet shopping street in West Hampstead, but with so many great deals it is well worth going out of your way to visit.

Golds Factory Outlet

110-114 Golders Green Road, NW11
Tel: 020 8905 5721
Tube: Golders Green
Open: Sun-Fri 10am-6pm

(map 11)

This large outlet occupies three shop fronts on Golders Green Road and offers hundreds of ready-made men's suits at very competitive prices. The emphasis is upon quality rather than fashion and is certainly aimed at the more conservative dresser rather than those looking for the latest designs. If you are looking for a new suit this is a good place to look with offers such as two suits for £150 and cashmere coats for £99.

Lotus Leaf

470 Holloway Road, N7
Tel: 020 7561 1114
Tube: Holloway Road
Bus: 43, 153, 271
Open: Mon-Sat 9.30am-6pm, Sun 11am-5pm

Lotus Leaf sells smart ladies clothing with names like Fenn Wright Mason, Progressive and Resources. The prices are very competitive with most garments falling in the £60-£100 range. This is a great place to find an outfit for a special occasion on a budget. They also have their own label, Lotus Leaf, and offer reasonably priced linens.
Also at:
146 Crouch Hill, N8 Tel: 020 8348 7038
6 St Christopher's Place, W1 Tel: 020 7168 7731

Matalan

279 Edgware Road, Cricklewood, NE2
Tel: 020 8450 5667
Website: www.matalan.co.uk
Tube: Kilburn
Bus: 16, 32, 89, 316
Open: Mon-Fri 9am-6pm, Sat 9am-6pm, Sun 11am-5pm

Matalan is a large chain of discount stores offering very low prices on a wide range of fashion and homeware. The stores cater for the whole family and stock brand names such as Farah, Wolsey, Playtex, Gossard and Jeffrey Rogers at up to 50% off the usual high street price. They also have a great choice of jeans with top names like Wrangler at well below the usual price. It costs £1 for lifetime membership and this means you are sent information about current offers. On the next page are the main London branches – the website has a full listing.

Branches at:
Beckton Alps Retail Park E6, Tel: 020 7473 9780
Bugsby's Way, Charlton SE7, Tel: 020 8269 4290
The Brand Centre, Enfield EN3, Tel: 020 8344 9620
Pump Lane, Hayes, Middlesex UB3, Tel: 020 8606 6700
Thurston Road, Lewisham SE13, Tel: 020 8463 9830
High Road, Leytonstone E11, Tel: 020 8988 8630
Great Western Industrial Retail Park, Southall UB2, Tel: 020 8574 0660
Lakeside Retail Park, West Thurrock RM16, Tel: 01708 864 350

Maxx Outlet

168 Muswell Hill Broadway, N10
Tel: 020 8444 5748
Tube: Highgate (then Bus)
Open: Mon-Sat 9.30am-6pm, Sun 12noon-5pm
Maxx Outlet is next to two other discount clothing outlets (Central Park and Decoy) and offers a similar mix of women's street fashion at bargain prices. The atmosphere is similar to a smart boutique, but the pricing is bargain with all garments sold for £5. At these prices the quality is not high, but for simple seasonal items this is a great place to shop.

Monica

37-39 South End Road, NW3
Tel: 020 7794 3737
Tube: Belsize Park
Open: Mon-Sat 10am-5.45pm, Sun 12noon-4.45pm
Monica has been trading from this store near Hampstead Heath for over 20 years, selling smart casual clothing mostly in linens and cottons with the emphasis on quality and value. Everything is reasonably priced with a linen two-piece outfit for £70 and trousers starting from £35 for a lightweight summer linen. A great place for casual women's wear.

Next to Choice

67 Golders Green Road, NW11
Tel: 020 8458 8247
Tube: Golders Green
Open: Mon-Sat 9am-6pm, Sun 11am-5pm
End of season Next stock from shops and the Directory sold at half-price, with new stock arriving daily. Clothes and footwear for men, women and children.
See the main entry in West London (page 29) for other branches of Choice.

West

Atlantic
260 North End Road, SW6
Tel: 020 7381 5566
Tube: Fulham Broadway
Open: Mon-Sat 9am-6pm, Sun 11am-5pm

map
5

This chain of stores offers fashionable clothing, bought in bulk and sold at very low prices to ensure a fast turnover. Trousers, tops and jackets from £10 and plenty to choose from for under £20. Well worth a visit for those looking for high street fashion on a budget.

Branches all over London, including:
Ground Floor, 162 Camden High Street, NW1
174 Kilburn High Road NW6;
32 High Road, Wood Green N22;
47 High Street, East Ham E6;
26 Rye Lane, Peckham SE15;
15 North Square, Lewisham SE13;
32 King's Mall, Hammersmith W6
Unit 2, 464-466 Brixton Road, SW9
Unit 16B, Kingsland Shopping Centre, Kingsland High Street, E8

Central Park
67 The Mall, W5
Tel: 020 8567 2250
Tube: Ealing Broadway
Open: Mon-Sat 10am-7pm; Sun 11am-5pm

This chain of stores sell their 'own-label' budget versions of top fashion at rock-bottom prices courtesy of production lines in the Far East and Eastern Europe. Knitwear, linen, jackets, jeans and whatever else is selling on the high street, all priced at £10 or £15. The atmosphere is smart with bright lighting, stone floors and glass shelving but the prices are some of the best in town.

Branches at:
9 Ealing Broadway, W5
152 Muswell Hill Broadway, N10 (details on page 24)
10 London Road, Enfield, EN2

Choice

Unit 11, Arcadia Centre, Ealing Broadway, W5
Tel: 020 8567 2747
Website: www.choice-discount.co.uk
Tube: Ealing Broadway
Open: Mon-Sat 9.30am-6pm (Thurs till 7pm), Sun 11am-5pm
End of season Next stock from Next Stores and Next Directory sold at half the usual price. Stock includes fashion, footwear and accessories for women, men and children. New stock arrives daily.
Branches at:
67 Golders Green Road, NW11 Tel: 020 8458 8247 (see page 27)
Unit 20 The Broadwalk Shopping Centre, Station Road, Edgware, HA8 Tel: 020 8905 6511
26-28 High Street, Barkingside, Ilford, Essex, IG6 Tel: 020 8551 2125
Hatfield Galleria, Comet Way, Hatfield, Herts, AL10 Tel: 01707 258 545

Factory Outlet

15a Portobello Road, W11
Tube: Notting Hill Gate
Open: Daily 9.30am-6.30pm

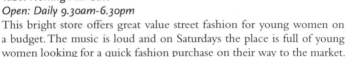

This bright store offers great value street fashion for young women on a budget. The music is loud and on Saturdays the place is full of young women looking for a quick fashion purchase on their way to the market. All the garments are sold for between £10–25 and there are usually a few clearance items to tempt the bargain hunter.

L.A.

11 Turnham Green Terrace, W4
Tel: 020 8995 4609
Tube: Turnham Green
Open: Mon-Sat 10am-6pm, Sun 11am-5pm
A long-established and great value shop which is popular with local men looking for good value casual clothing (lots of French Connection and other high street labels). They also sell end–of-lines with tops starting from £10 and trousers from £20 and have a range of shoes, bags and accessories all sold at well below the usual high street price.

The latest fashions for less, at **NEXT** to nothing prices

Choice

EDGWARE	**GOLDERS GREEN**	**BARKINGSIDE**	**EALING**	**HATFIELD**
Unit 20, Broadwalk	67, Golders Green Road	26/28 High Street,	Unit 11,	The Galleria
Shopping Centre	020 8458 8247	Ilford	Arcadia Centre	01707 258545
Tel: 020 8905 6511		020 8551 2125	020 8567 2747	

For opening times and special offers and other stores throughout
the South East visit our website at **www.choice-discount.co.uk**

MK One

28 Queensway, W2
Tel: 020 7229 2847
Website: www.mkone.co.uk
Tube: Bayswater
Open: Daily 10am-10pm

Up-to-date fashion for women at the lowest possible prices from £5 to £25 for tops, trousers and jackets. The stock is fast changing with a stylish range of clothes for larger women (14-18) and a great selection of fashion basics for teenagers. MK One also offer 15% student discount.

Branches at: 295 Walworth Road, SE17; 420 Brixton Road, SW9; Aylesham Centre, Peckham, SE15; 468 Holloway Road, N7; 66 Kingsland High Street, E8; 192 Uxbridge Road, W12; Southside Shopping Centre, Wandsworth Road, SW18; The Riverdale Centre, SE13

Pili & Mili

230 Portobello Road, W11
Tel: 020 7243 6424
Open: Mon-Thurs 10am-6pm, Fri-Sat 10am-6.30pm, Sun 12noon-5pm

This bright fashion outlet stocks lots of cheap girls' street fashion with full-length summer dresses for £25, and large leather bags for £30. The stock is regularly changed and items that don't sell are reduced to clear as were the pink mini-skirts reduced from £19.99 to £9.99

Primark

1 King's Mall, King Street, W6
Tel: 020 8748 7119
Website: www.primark.co.uk
Tube: Hammersmith
Open: Mon-Sat 9am-6pm, Sun 11am-5pm

One of the newest and largest branches of this chain of stores providing good value clothing for the whole family. The company now has stores UK-wide and has made a great success of selling everyday fashion at incredibly low prices. As well as their own label some brands like Umbro, Dunlop and Puma are also stocked.

Other branches at:
51 High Street, East Ham, E6; 365-371 Mare Street, Hackney E8; 52a-54 High Street, Kilburn NW6; 650-652 High Road, Leytonstone E11; 499-517 Oxford Street, W1; 11-19 Tooting High Street, SW17; 32-34 Southside, Wandsworth SW18; 51-57 Rye Lane, Peckham SE15; 18-28 Hare Street, Woolwich, SE18

Purple Bee

57 Pembridge Road, W11
Tube: Notting Hill Gate
Open: Daily 9.30am-7.30pm

This little shop offers a good selection of girl's teenage fashion with fashionable pumps for £10 and lots of bright summer dresses for £15. A great place to hunt down cheap seasonal throw-away fashion.

TK Maxx

45-63 King Street, W6
Tel: 020 8563 9200
Website: www.tkmaxx.com
Tube: Hammersmith LU
Open: Mon-Fri 8am-9pm, Sat 9am-7pm, Sun 11am-5pm

TK Maxx offers current season's stock of high street names and top designer labels at discounts of up to 60%. Each store has around 50,000 items in stock with some 10,000 more arriving weekly. We visited the Kingston branch where clothes were squashed up in rails, allocated to men, women and children. Good prices on suede and leather jackets, but you have to be good at searching to find what you want. There are also bargains to be had in lingerie, accessories, housewares and gifts. A new designer jewellery department is now available in selected stores along with a children's department selling clothing, furniture, toys, soft furnishings and nursery equipment. Visit their website for further information.

Other branches at:
The Galleria, Hatfield, AL10 Tel: 01707 260 066
Wood Green Shopping Centre N22 Tel: 020 8888 8803
2 Clarence Street, Kingston, KT1 Tel: 020 8974 6296
The Arcadia Centre, The Broadway, Ealing, W5 Tel: 020 8566 0447
The Drummond Centre, Croydon, CR0 Tel: 020 8686 9753

Uttam London Ltd

45 Pembridge Road, W11
Tel: 020 7727 9771
Open: Mon-Fri 9.30am-6pm, Sat 8.30am-6.30pm, Sun 10am-6pm

Unlike many of the teen fashion shops on this road, Uttam caters for women from 20 to 40 with lots of colour patterned dresses for £20 and skirts for the same price. On a recent visit a glamorous customer was compiling a cheap summer wardrobe and she assured me that the place was good value.

331

Central Park

Open Space

Factory Monacu

South

331

331 Garrett Lane, SW18
Tel: 020 8870 6638
email: elizabethburrows331@hotmail.com
Rail: Earlsfield
Open: Mon-Sat 11am-7pm, closed Wed

(map 8)

331 make and sell quality leather jackets, coats and trousers to their own designs. New leather jackets start from £95, new leather trousers from £75 and full-length leather and buckskin coats from £180. They also offer great value vintage and recycled leathers and sheepskins and a good stock of Hawaiian shirts based on original 1940s designs. 331 have a made-to-measure, repair and alterations service. On Saturday and Sunday they run a stall in Camden Lock Market.

East

A.M. Leather Fashion Ltd

137 Brick Lane, E1
Tel: 020 7729 3367
Tube: Aldgate East or Liverpool Street
Open: Mon-Fri 10.30am-6.30pm, Sun 10am-2pm

(map 12)

This shop sells anything in leather from boxing gloves to leather jackets with jackets starting from as little as £35 and going up to £125. The store is largely a wholesale outlet and little effort is made to display the goods, but the prices are cheap and they welcome individuals visiting the store.

Kojak

28 Cheshire Street, E2
Tel: 020 7729 3617
Tube: Aldgate East or Liverpool Street
Open: Mon-Sat 10am-6pm, Sun 9am-3pm

(map 12)

Kojak offer a good range of quality street fashion at the usual price, but also have discounts on certain items. All their Diesel clothing is sold at a considerable discount with authentic Diesel jeans for £70-80 which would sell for over £120 in the West End. They also do a very good line in KDK cotton summer dresses which were on a rail outside for only £20. Kojak also wholesale a range of stylish leather jackets which they retail at their store for around £70. A great little fashion outlet which is well worth visiting when in the Brick Lane area.

Moda

220 Brick Lane, E1
Tel: 020 7739 5010
Tube: Aldgate East or Liverpool Street
Open: Daily 10am-7pm, Sun 10am-3pm

Moda is a leather wholesaler that welcomes individual enquiries and sells at considerable discounts. Among the recent deals was a very fine leather jacket for £175 (reduced from £295) and a beautiful leather handbag that had been reduced several times from the original price of £250 and was on sale for £99.

Mordex

222 Brick Lane, E1
Tel: 020 7729 7550
Tube: Aldgate East or Liverpool Street
Open: Mon-Fri 10am-6pm, Sun 10am-3pm

Another good outlet along Brick Lane offering great value leathers at considerable discounts to members of the public. A basic leather box jacket can be found here for £90-£130 and leather trousers for £90.

Open Space

200 Brick Lane, E1
Tel: 020 7729 3367
Tube: Aldgate East or Liverpool Street
Open: Daily 10am-6pm

Open Space is one of the best and most welcoming leather retailers on Brick Lane. If you fancy a pair of leather trousers this is a great place to visit with prices starting from £75 and excellent biker jackets for £75 (reduced from £175). Another good bargain were the leather handbags which sell for £65 in Camden, but were sold here for a mere £25.

Truth Trading Ltd

151 Brick Lane, E1
Tel: 020 7729 0825
Tube: Aldgate East or Liverpool Street
Open: Daily 10.30am-6pm

This is a no-nonsense family wholesale outlet that specialises in all kinds of leather jackets and is prepared to sell direct to the public. There are lots of leathers to choose from with short boxy leather jackets starting from £50. Their main line is Tuscan sheepskin coats with fur lining, the full-length version of which sells for £1,200 in West End stores, but can be bought here for only £450.

Classic & Retro Clothing

Shopping for vintage and retro clothing has never been more popular! This current vogue for vintage can be seen in the ever increasing numbers of vintage shops opening in the capital and the vintage concessions in stores such as Selfridges and Topshop. Why vintage? With so much cheap mass-produced clothing on the high street these days and inspired by the likes of Kate Moss, shoppers are looking for something a little different, something unique and individual. But the advantages don't stop there. The quality of garments are often infinitely superior to today's clothing, and for the environmentally aware, 'recycling' is one of the greenest ways to shop!

The cheaper retro stores tend to buy in bulk leaving the customers to sift through for the occasional gem, whilst others have a smaller collection of carefully chosen garments, dry cleaned and well displayed and this will be reflected in the price. Also, it's always a good idea to check the seams, collars and cuffs – where the garments might show wear and tear. As long as you're careful and keep your eye out for discount racks you should be able to bag a few retro bargains.

Central

Beyond Retro

58-59 Great Marlborough Street, W1
Tel: 020 7434 1406
Website: www.beyondretro.com
Transport: Oxford Circus LU
Open: Mon-Wed and Sat 10.30am-7.30 pm, Thurs and Fri 10.30am-8.30pm, Sunday 12noon-6pm

This established retro retailer has opened this new store in what was once a car park in the heart of Soho. The space has been transformed into a glorious riot of fashion from Victoriana to 80s techno chic with chandeliers and some strange examples of taxidermy giving the place a unique atmosphere. For more about the range of clothing take a look at the review of their flagship store just off Brick Lane (page 60).

Blackout II

51 Endell Street, WC2
Tel: 020 7240 5006
Website: www.blackout2.com
Tube: Covent Garden
Open: Mon-Fri 11am-7pm, Sat 11.30am-6.30pm, & Sun 11.30am-5.40pm

This cramped little shop, specialising in clothing from the 1930s to 1950s, has been trading for over twenty years. Downstairs in the basement a 50s cotton dress was £55, a fabulous prom dress £120 and a vintage Dior black velvet jacket £79. Besides all the wonderful clothes (a lot of which are imported from the United States), there is a good stock of shoes, handbags, necklaces made from exotically coloured plastics and chic, oversized sunglasses. This is a great place to look for special one-off items although the price tag is a little heftier to match.

Cornucopia

12 Upper Tachbrook Street, SW1V
Tel: 020 7828 5752
Tube: Victoria
Open Mon-Sat 11am-6pm - check?

The forerunner of vintage clothing shops in London, Cornucopia began as an antiques shop but evolved into a vintage and retro clothes emporium that has now been trading for over 40 years. A haven and source of inspiration for stylists – Kate Moss was spotted here recently- the shop is literally packed to the rafters with clothing from every era, Edwardian though to the present day. They have a tremendous amount of stock, so much so that rails of clothing hang from the ceiling and at times there can be piles of clothes littering the floor. The sheer volume of garments can seem a little intimidating but the staff know their stock so if you're looking for something in particular just ask them. On my visit, a 40s ladies' silk dress was £50 and a sensational 60s dusky-pink and heavily beaded floor-length satin dress worthy of a premiere was £95. For something a little more contemporary there were several 80s backless black sequined dresses for £20-£35.

Love Vintage
(map 1)

2nd Floor, Kingly Court, Carnaby St, W1
Tel: 020 3214 0044
Tube: Oxford Circus LU
Open: Mon-Wed 11am-7pm, Thurs-Sat 11am-8pm, Sun 12noon 6pm

If you scale the dizzy heights of Kingly Court – all 2 floors, you will find the little boutique Love Vintage. It sells similar stock to its sister shop, Marshmallow Mountain (downstairs), but leaning towards a younger market with smaller sizes and 'a bit more funky'! Shoes, boots, bags and accessories dominate. On my visit, a wonderful pair of blue Mary-Jane hand-made leather shoes in immacculate condition were £35 and a Joseph wool tanktop with a quirky Japanese landscape printed on the front was £30. Some original finds make the steps worthwhile!

Marshmallow Mountain

Unit G.5 Ground floor,
Kingly Court (off Carnaby St), W1
Tel: 020 7434 9498
Transport: Oxford Circus LU
Open: Mon-Sat 11am-7pm (until 8pm Thurs), Sun 12noon-6pm

(map 1)

Marshmallow Mountain has expanded what was primarily a vintage shoe shop into a wonderful little boutique with wooden floors, chandeliers and a large gilt mirror to admire yourself in your potentialy new purchase. The shop has everything a girl needs to dress head-to-toe in vintage attire, from hats and jewellery to fur coats, clutch bags and shoes – something this shop still has an eye for. There is a whole wall dedicated to fantastic footwear, from fantastic silver calf-length boots to patent 60s heels. Boots and shoes are organised in order of size with the owner making a point of sourcing the hard-to-find larger sizes. Boots start from £38, coats from £28 with a fabulous faux fur coat selling for only £45. Everything is hand-selected, inspected and cleaned with anything not up to the owners' high standard put in the bargain basket and sold for £10 or less, along with any garment not sold after a couple of weeks – giving the bargain hunter even more reason to drop in for some retro retail therapy.

Pop Boutique

6 Monmouth Street, WC2
Tel: 020 7497 5262
Webite: www.pop-boutique.com
Tube: Covent Garden
Open: Mon-Sat 11am-7pm, Sun 1pm-6pm

(map 1)

This great little shop in Covent Garden has been a magnet for those in search of good value retro clothing since 1983. The turnover of clothes is fast and furious and the garments are well chosen with many 60s or 70s originals – although they also have a small selection of clothes from the 1950s. Among the good deals were cords for men and women for £25, a great selection of ladies' leather boots for £25 and retro trackie tops from £25. Another bargain was the baskets of leather gloves from only £5. Pop Boutique are now selling their own range of clothing with recycled shifts made from vintage fabrics for only £15. As well as clothing the shop has a small selection of 70s nick-nacks including an orginal Fozzie Bear for £18 and an unusual desk lamp for £25. Pop is still the first port of call for anyone looking for good value vintage and retro in the Covent Garden area.

don't follow
fashion
buy
something
already out
of date!

London
Pop Boutique
6 Monmouth Street
Covent Garden
London WC2
020 7497 5262

Online
Pop Boutique
http://www.pop-boutique.com
Madaboutpop
http://www.madaboutpop.com

Dedicated to fashions of the past.
Bringing back to life clothes from the 60s, 70s
and 80s. Shops in London, Liverpool and Manchester.

Radio Days

87 Lower Marsh, SE1
Tel: 020 7928 0800
Website: www.radiodaysvintage.co.uk
Tube: Waterloo LU/Rail
Open: Mon-Sat 10am-6pm

This shop has bags of atmosphere, complete with big band swing in the air, and a mannequin that looks like Humphrey Bogart decked out in a Hawaian shirt complete with flower garland. There are racks of vintage magazines, postcards and advertising as well as a case full of cigarette boxes, pipes, cuflinks and lighters. The store is a treasure trove of kitsch furniture and paraphernalia from the 20s to the 60s; vintage radios, Bake-lite phones, ceramics, pill box hats, feather boas, corsets and hosiery in its original packaging. In the back room are clothes from every era but with emphasis on the 50s and 60s. A blue ladies' 2-piece suit from the 60s was £55 and there is a rail of faux and real fur coats from £30. Vintage men's suits could be found here for £65, which is great value considering their quality and condition. A great retro store and one of the few to have a good stock of pre-60s items.

Retromania

6 Upper Tachbrook Street, SW1V
Tel: 020 7630 7406
Website: www.faracharityshops.org
Tube: Victoria
Open: Mon–Sat 10am-6pm, Sun 11am-5pm

Named by the Evening Standard as one of the top five second-hand shops in London, Retromania sits next to Cornucopia and both are just a 5 minute stroll from Victoria Station. The accolade is well deserved, as this bright, organised little shop stocks a great selection of retro/vintage clothing and accessories with some retro furniture and household goodies at the back. They have a good choice of classic British labels with a Liberty's floral dress for £50 and Jaeger jackets from £10. For the men, lots of military and 60s suits from £27-£50, a new Dior jacket was £35, and Hermes men's ties for £35-£45. They also have a wonderful selection of 60s and 70s shoes starting from £15. All proceeds go to FARA's children's programmes in Romania.

Rokit

42 Shelton Street,
Covent Garden, WC2H 9HZ
Tel: 020 7836 6547
Website: www.rokit.co.uk
Tube: Covent Garden
Open: Mon-Sat 10am-7pm, Sun 11am-6pm

(map 1)

The growing popularity of vintage clothing is reflected in the opening of this huge vintage store in the centre of Covent Garden, just off Neal St. Wide, wooden steps lead down to this large modern store with rail upon rail of retro threads. Rokit specialises in more 70s and 80s gear with a sprinkling of 60s and has 3 deliveries a week to replenish the rails. The amount of stock makes this place a little bewildering - so take your time. Racks of shoes, arranged according to size and starting fron £15, are worth a look and among the mens' wear was a knitted cardy (featuring 'horses') that Starsky would be proud of for £45. The choice of clothes is even greater for women with retro tops from the 70s and 80s starting from £15. A bit more pricey because of the central location, but a great retro shop.

Sam Greenberg

1st Floor, Kingly Court
(off Carnaby St), W1
Tel: 020 7287 8474
Website: www.samgreenbergrnwl.co.uk
Transport: Oxford Circus LU
Open: Mon-Fri 11am-7pm (thurs till 8pm),
Sat 10am-7pm, Sun 12noon-6pm

(map 1)

Sam Greenberg is situated in the vintage enclave of Kingly Court with several other shops dedicated to the world of retro clothing. This smart, organised branch is the recipient of the hand-picked (better nick) clothing with the other items and unsold goods going to their other outlets. An old table in the centre is adorned with accessories and neatly stacked piles of cashmere cardigans and jumpers in his 'n' hers piles for £45. Men are well looked after with more than half the stock dedicated to the male of the species. Men's T's and shirts start at £15 and jackets go up to a modest £80. Ladies' clothing is carefully arranged into rails of coats, skirts, blouses and dresses. A fantastic pink pussy bow 70s blouse was among the bargains recently unearthed here for only £18. Sam Greenberg offer a further 10% discount for students.

Branches at: Topman, Oxford Street (concession)

Twinkled

First Floor 1.5 Kingly Court
(off Carnaby St), W1B
Tel: 020 7734 1978
Transport: Oxford Circus LU
Open: Mon-Wed and Sat 11am-7pm,
Thurs-Fri 11am-8pm, Sun 12noon-6pm

(map 1)

This fantastic retro emporium just off Carnaby Street started life as a humble stall in Greenwich market in 1994. Regarding itself as a 'retro-politan lifetyle concept store', Twinkled is more concerned with vintage 'St Michael' than vintage Ossie Clarke, celebrating domestic post-war British design at prices to suit everyone. Illuminated by a variety of retro lamps, this large well organised shop, has everything and anything to kit yourself, your home and probably your cat in a retro stylee. Stock is mainly from the 70s and 80s with a few items from earlier decades. There is also a stand of old vintage patterns for those keen to get the sewing machine out and a large range of vintage curtains (one with a Noddy print caught my eye), rolls of authentic 70s wallpaper and the classic 'Spanish lady' portrait prints. The stock is well priced and clearly labelled and the staff are helpful and friendly, making Twinkled close to vintage heaven.

What The Butler Wore

131 Lower Marsh, SE1
Tel: 020 7261 1353
Tube: Waterloo
Open: Mon-Sat 11am-6pm

This shop may not look like much from the outside with its faded sign but don't be fooled, inside is a wonderful stock of carefully selected and reasonably priced clothes, shoes and accessories. Unlike most of the bigger retro clothing shops that buy in bulk from the States, this store sources its goods mainly from Britain and hand-picks everything, which is reflected in the carefully arranged displays. The stock covers 60s and 70s with a few 50s items, all clearly labelled with ladies' jackets from £20, men's shirts from £20 and jackets for as little as £25. Womens' dresses average at about £40 and on my visit a wonderful Jaegar 70s A-line canary yellow skirt was £20. The shop has a great choice of accessories with boots and bags starting from a very reasonable £20. What The Butler Wore has the advantage of being located in Lower Marsh which has lots of interesting shops and cafés including another retro store – Radio Days (see page 39).

Berty & Gerty

Twinkled

Episode

Rokit

Old Hat

Lost & Found

WOW Retro

14-16 Mercer Street, WC2
Tel: 020 7379 5334
Website: www.wowretro.co.uk
Tube: Covent Garden
Open: Mon-Fri 11.30am-6.30pm, Sat 11am-7pm, Sun 12noon-5pm

Split between two shops on one of Covent Garden's deserted back alleys, Worn Out West on Mercer Street dedicates one shop to each sex. In the ladies' shop there are high street labels from the 90s to the 00s with names such as Topshop, Whistles and Oasis to be found here and prices starting from only £5. Female retro addicts will not be disappointed with garments like a 70s smock dress for only £15 and a rare 40s shirt dress for £40. Next door the men will have plenty to entertain them with hundreds of pairs of jeans to choose from including classic Levi's and plenty of designer labels such as Diesel and Armani with prices starting from £25. There is also a vast selection of leather jackets in all kinds of styles with prices starting from £50. A well organised store with helpful staff ready to help when asked.

WOW Retro

179 Drury Lane, WC2
Tel: 020 7831 1699
Website: www.wowretro.co.uk
Tube: Covent Garden
Open: Mon-Sat 11am-7pm

This second very large branch has been open since the summer of 2006 and is only 5 minutes walk from Mercer Street. The new store has over 1000 sq ft of retailing space for both men and women. The shop is great for extravagant party outfits with geometric print 70s shirts for £20 and some groovy flares from £25. Those wanting to make a more refined impression will find bow ties for £5, cravats for £10 and tail coats for £50. The Drury Lane store is also a great place to hunt down retro accessories such as 50s round suit cases for £75 and 60s floral cases from £35 – an ideal size for carrying a laptop. Wow is one of the few places in London where you can find an authentic Japanese kimono with prices starting from £40. A welcome addition to the West End retro clothing scene.

North

Camden

When you think of Camden, Marilyn Manson inspired teenagers donning black rubber spikey bags spring to mind, but beyond the sea of black PVC and rubber, there are plenty of good vintage and retro clothing shops to be found. For those in the know Camden is best visited on Friday, to bag the new stock before the weekend hordes arrive. A lot of retro stores sell similar imported 70s and 80s American clothing but there a few great shops stocking genuine vintage collectables that make the trek worth while. The part of Camden Market known as Stables Market has recently been redeveloped but fortunately many of the retro shops have continued trading from new units and these have been review below.

The Stables:

Berty & Gerty

69 The West Yard,
Camden Lock, NW1
Website: www.bertyandgerty.co.uk
Open: Mon-Fri 9am-6pm, Sat-Sun 9am-6pm

map 2

In the cobbled yard next to the lock, this colourful and organised little shop sells a wonderful selection of both old and new accessories for men and women. Their stock is chosen with an emphasis on quality as well as style with shoes, boots, bags, hats and jewellery from the 50s through to the present day. The stock is sourced from Europe with new stock put out every Friday. Everything is inspected, cleaned and reheeled (where necessary) and arranged by item. Footwear ranges from £10 up to £50 for a pair of Chanel evening shoes with boots from £25-£70. An 80s Mulberry saddle bag was £30 and boxed Chanel sunglasses could be found for £70. In the centre, a table is adorned with dead stock 80s jewellery (a specialty of B&G), silver snake bangles galore and new 50s-inspired jewellery. A great little shop with a really nice combination of old and new items.

What Goes Around Comes Around...

Unit 36, The Stables Market, Camden, NW1
Tel: 020 7424 9621
Open: Mon-Fri 12noon-6pm
Sat & Sun 10.30-6.30pm

This vintage outlet was trading for over 6 years from one of the arches in the Stables before the site was recently redeveloped. The store has managed to survive the upheaval by consolidating its operation into this second store at unit 36. The store has a fashionable warehouse feel with exposed brickwork and wooden floors. It's a good place for trainer fetishists seeking rare first issue and limited editions with plenty of rare trainers sold at equally rare prices. For something more affordable, dead stock trainers start from a reasonable £35. The bulk of the clothing is 70s and 80s American imports with things like men's Lacoste V-necked jumpers for £20, ladies' dresses from £10-£30 and printed 70s & 80s skirts from £5-£14. A cabinet displays a large selection of deadstock boxed vintage sunglasses with Diors selling for £120-£145. This store also has a special room dedicated to the more collectable items which can be viewed by appointment. Serious bargain hunters should look out for the shops end-of-season sales when many items are reduced to clear.

Lost and Found

Unit 25a, The Stables Market, Camden, NW1
Open: Mon-Fri 11am-6pm, Sat & Sun 10am-7pm
Tel: 020 7482 2848

One of best vintage/retro shops in the Stables, not just for the wonderful range of clothing, boots and accessories from the 40s to the present day, but also because of the strange and wonderful paraphernalia hung from the ceiling and sitting on shelves which make this a fun place to shop. New men and women's stock arrives weekly sourced from both Europe and America with ladies' summer dresses from £15-£45 and underwear and corsetry from £5-£30. Accessories are upstairs with recent finds including a 60s mustard leather and brown-fur bucket bag for £45 and 80s leather slouch boots for £25. To keep up the Americana theme, they have a large selection of men's brown-leather 60s US flight jackets from £85 and a vintage 50s Letterman Cardigan for £55. A great shop to peruse, you may find just what you're looking for behind the Micky Mouse wrapped in the fox-fur stole...

Funky Town

(map 2)

Unit 22, The Stables Market,
Camden, NW1
Tel: 020 7267 2499
Open: Mon-Fri 10.30am-6.30pm, Sat-Sun 10am-6.30pm

Funky Town offers cheap second-hand clothing from the 70s and 80s with enough polyester to power a small home on the static. Dresses start from £10, fur coats from £20 and shoes for as little as £5. If you're needing a little rest and recuperation make your way upstairs were you can find a little bohemian café.

Thea

(map 2)

Units 16, 1d and 8b ,
The Stables Market, Camden, NW1
Mon-Fri 11am-7pm, Sat & Sun 9.30am-7pm
Tel: 020 7267 6927

Thea has three outlets within the Stables offering a colourful array of reasonably cheap 70s and 80s clothing and accessories sourced mainly from Europe for both men and women but with more for the fairer sex. Stock is replenished 2-3 times weekly with £5 and £10 rails and a good choice of £1 clearance items for the more determined bargain hunters. Ladies shoes range from £10-£45, depending on age and condition. For something a little more contemporary they have a range of inhouse customised garments.

Berty & Gerty

Other shops in Camden:

Episode

26 Chalk Farm Road, NW1
Tel: 020 7485 9927
Website: www.episode.nu
Tube: Chalk Farm
Open: Daily 11am-7pm

This bright and well stocked reto clothing store is just across the road from the Stables Market. Despite its isolation from the main market Episode has an established following among the young retro shoppers visiting Camden. It is the only London branch of a Dutch clothing wholesaler with lots of vintage and second–hand clothing imported every week to keep the three floors well stocked. The prices are very competitive with ladies leather jackets for £40, 70s nylon dresses for £22 and men's dress trousers for around £18. There are usually a few discounted items making this one of the best places to bag a retro bargain in Camden.

Rokit

225 Camden High Street, NW1
Tel: 020 7267 3046
Website: www.rokit.co.uk
Tube: Camden Town
Open: Mon-Sun 10am-7pm

This Camden institution is the founding Rokit store in what has now become a successful chain. The shop is deceptively large with a sizeable ground floor and a smaller first floor, both well stocked with retro and second–hand clothing. Upstairs is more vintage 40s and 50s with 60s and 70s taking the ground floor. Every month the staff mark down items that haven't sold and these are mixed up with the normal price goods, so it's a matter of having a good rummage to get your hands on a bargain.

Also at:
42 Shelton Street, WC2 Tel: 020 7836 6547
101-107 Brick Lane, E1 Tel: 020 7375 3864

Modern Age Vintage Clothing

65 Chalk Farm Road, NW1

Tel: 020 7482 3787

Website: www.modern-age.co.uk

Tube: Chalk Farm

Open: Daily 10.30am-6pm

map 2

This established vintage clothing store is often missed by the hoards that fill Camden High Street at the weekend, but with the revamp of the Roundhouse opposite, Modern Age is getting a bit more of the attention it deserves. The shop has a bygone feel, with jazz playing and more of an emphasis on the 50s and 60s than subsequent periods. The prices are competitive with classic men's suits for £65, vintage bags for £6 and fake furs and leather jackets from £39. Unlike some small businesses, Modern Age Vintage has a good website which will give an idea of their stock and prices and also details about their hire service for those looking for vintage chic for parties or events.

North

Casino

136 Stoke Newington Church Street, N16
Tel: 020 7923 2225
Website: www.casinovintage.com
Rail: Stoke Newington
Open: Mon-Sat 11am-6pm, Sun 12noon-6pm

This compact vintage store is a recent arrival to Church Street, offering vintage from the 50s to the 80s and a selection of new clothes with retro style. Casino has limited space and handpicks its stock depending on the fashion with vintage dresses for £10-40 figuring strongly on a recent visit as were men's Western shirts and American vintage T-shirts for £5-25. The new clothes all have a classic feel to them including new dresses made from vintage material and a selection of babies' vests and kids' T-shirts recycled and reconstructed from adult vintage T-Shirts. Casino also stocks a selection of new kids' clothes from the label Nippaz with Attitude and Rock Your Baby. A welcome arrival to Stokie and just opposite the excellent Ocean Books (see page 231).

CHA CHA CHA

20-22 Avenue Mews, Muswell Hill, N10
Tel: 020 8815 9990
Website: www.cha-cha-cha.co.uk
Open: Thurs-Sat 10.30am-5pm

This retro clothing and furniture store is hidden away in a small mews behind the main Muswell Hill Broadway. It's a shop worth tracking down with a good selection of vintage clothing from the 20s to the 80s and a mix of retro furniture also on display from names like G-Plan and Ercol. The place is well organised but there is enough disorder to make it interesting and there are usually a few bargains to be found if you're prepared to have a rummage.

The Girl Can't Help It

Alfies Antique Market, 13-25 Church Street, NW8
Tel: 020 7724 8984
Website: www.sparklemoore.com
Tube: Marylebone, Edgware Road or Baker Street
Open: Tues-Sat 10am-6pm

This vintage specialist offers a well chosen selection of garments and accessories from a large unit within Alfies Antiques Market. The emphasis is definitely on vintage style and glamour rather than the imported second-hand street fashion that sometimes passes for vintage. This is a particularly good place to find rare vintage lingerie, but also has unusual 50s dresses and immaculate DJ's. A great place to visit for a more sophisticated approach to vintage fashion and style.

Ribbons & Taylor

157 Stoke Newington Church Street, N16
Tel: 020 7254 4735
Website: www.ribbonsandtaylor.co.uk
Rail: Stoke Newington
Open: Tues-Sun 11am-6pm

This Stoke Newington institution has been selling a well chosen stock of men's and women's clothing to the fashionable residents of the area for over 20 years. The stock here is always well organised, clean, clearly labelled and sold at a competitive price. On a recent visit women's shoes could be found for as little as £15 and the selection of boots ranged from £20-£38. The faux fur leopard skin coat was a real eye-catcher for only £36 and there was a good choice of 50s full skirted dresses for £45-55. Among the men's bargains there were jeans for £16 and leather jackets from £20. Ribbons & Taylor is one of Stokie's little treasures and well worth making the effort to visit. Take a look at the website to see a selection of their clothes – usually modelled by their customers.

21st Century Retro (Formerly 162)

162 Holloway Road, N7
Tel: 020 7700 2354
Tube: Holloway Road
Open: Mon-Sat 10am-6pm, Sun 12noon-5pm

This deceptively large shop has recently changed its name, but is still popular with the students of the nearby Metropolitan University who are drawn by the great selection of discounted retro clothing. The clothes are imported from thrift stores in the US and are therefore not always washed and ironed as in other fancy retro stores, but they are very cheap. Among the bargains are jeans for £7, denim jackets for £10, full-length dresses for £10-25, suit jackets for £20 and leather jackets for £15-£25. As well as being generally very good value they also have lots of discounted rails with many items reduced to half price, and other items on rails and in boxes outside for £1. A great bargain shop.

West

The 1920s-1970s Crazy Clothes Connection

$\overset{map}{6}$

134 Lancaster Road, W11
Tel: 020 7221 3989
Website: www.crazy-clothes.co.uk
Tube: Ladbroke Grove
Open: Tues-Sat 11am-7pm

This retro clothing outlet has been in the family for several generations and has a good reputation for its stock of vintage clothes for both men and women. Genuine vintage clothing is never cheap, but Crazy Clothes attempts to keep its prices competitive and has regular sales throughout the year when old stock is reduced to clear. For those looking for something vintage for a one-off event, the shop also has a hire service.

Crazy Clothes Connection

Old Hat

66 & 62 Fulham High Street, SW6 (map 9)
Tel: 020 7610 6558
Tube: Putney Bridge
Open: Mon-Sat 11am-7pm, Sun 1.30pm-7pm

David Saxby has been selling gentlemen's vintage clothing on Fulham High Street for 15 years, although the vintage nature of his stock and the old style decor of the shop makes the place seem a good deal older. The philosophy of the shop is one of gentlemanly decorum, where braces are favoured rather than belts and the jodphur is still regarded as a serious item of clothing. If you are in search of vintage men's style at a reasonable price then this should be a first port of call with suits starting from £30 for an off-the-peg two-piece and going up to around £100 for a fine three-piece suit with a Savile Row label. Shoes are vitally important to the properly attired gentleman and Old Hat has an excellent selection for £15-60. A unique shop and excellent value for those men seeking to cut a dash.

Rellik

8 Golborne Road, (map 6)
Ladbroke Grove, W10 5NW
Tel: 020 8962 0089
Website: www.relliklondon.co.uk
Tube: Westbourne Park
Open: Tues- Sat 10am-6pm

Rellik was established at the foot of the iconic Trellick Tower in 1999 by three market traders and has in the proceeding years established itself as among the best retro/vintage clothing stores in London. The bright white exterior with enormous plate glass windows displaying designer labels make this store stand out amid the more mundane shops of Golborne Road. Inside the large space is packed with designer labels with names like Vivienne Westwood, Thea Porter, Pucci and Ossie Clarke all to be found here along with accessories and a range of vintage garment, some dating from the 1920s. This is far too stylish and upmarket a place to be described as 'bargain', but there are enough good value items to please the shrewd shopper and there is a 20% discount on all stock during their sale in the first two trading weeks of January each year.

Retro Man
32 & 34 Pembridge Road, W11
Tel: 020 7598 2233 / 020 7792 1715

Retro Woman
20 Pembridge Road, W11
Tel: 020 7221 2055
Retro Clothing
28 Pembridge Road, W11

Retro Clothing
56 Notting Hill Gate, W11
Tel: 020 7792 8100
Tube: Notting Hill Gate
Open: Daily 10am-8pm

Part of the chain started by the Record and Tape Exchange on Notting Hill Gate, these shops stock second-hand and new clothing and accessories. The men's shops are at 32 & 34 Pembridge Road and offer some good deals and unusual garments. Retro Woman has a good selection of dresses, skirts and jackets at reasonable prices as well as garments to clear for £5. The largest and most interesting shop is at 56 Notting Hill Gate, offering a vast choice of clothing and accessories extending over two floors. The shops are not known for smart decor but with very competitive prices and a fast turnover of stock they are one of the best things about shopping in Notting Hill.

295
295 Portobello Road, W11
Tube: Ladbroke Grove
Open: Fri-Sat 8.30am-5pm

This shop has been going for many years and is always busy with regular customers stopping for a chat or on the hunt for a retro bargain. The shop is charmingly old-fashioned but stocks an excellent range of retro clothing at prices well below any of the rival retro stores in the area. Recent bargains included a wide choice of cotton dresses for £8.50 and a stylish 60s ladies two-piece for only £25. There is a good stock of men's clothing with dressing gowns for £6 and classic suit jackets for £30. The shop also keeps a few discount boxes stocked with clearance items for just £1.

South

Cenci

4 Nettlefold Place, SE27
Tel: 020 8766 8564
Website: www.cenci.co.uk
West Norwood Rail
Mon-Sat 11am-6pm (first Sunday of the month)

This shop has moved from its Covent Garden location to a large warehouse covering two floors in Norwood – just a few minutes' walk from the local station. The warehouse stocks an incredible variety of retro clothing, shoes and accessories for the whole family. Everything is organised into colour-coded rails with lots of retro bargains to tempt the bargain hunter out to this distant suburb. Among the good deals quality Knitwear was £26-£40 and stylish 80s dresses started from £20.

Chi Chi Ra Ra

Junction of Uplands Road & Hindmands Road, SE22
Rail: East Dulwich
Tel: 07714 961027
Open: Tues, Thurs & fri 10am-5pm, Sat 10am-5.30pm, Sun 11am-4pm

Dulwich's best kept secret, this unasuming little shop, just a few minutes walk from Northcross Market, is crammed with clothes, boots, bags and accessories. It is the variety and quality of the stock that makes this shop special with a vintage crushed velvet fur-trimed jacket for £85 and a 60s ladies two-piece suits for £35. Those after something more contemporary can find things like a Paul Smith coat for £80. A real treasure trove and well worth visiting.

The Emporium

330-332 Creek Road, Greenwich, SE10
Tel: 020 8305 1670
Website: www.emporiumoriginals.com
Rail: Cutty Sark   Tube: Island Gardens
Open: Wed-Sun 10.30am-6pm

This shop displays its collection of largely European vintage clothing and accessories from the 50s to the 80s with well justified care. All the stock is dry-cleaned, clearly priced and well organised with a greater emphasis on men's fashion, but plenty of garments for women in search of retro chic. The wooden cabinets full of accessories, chandeliers and varied decor make this a great place to shop but the attention to detail is not reflected in the prices with classic mens' suits for £75-85, Italian women's winter coats for around £68 and casual clothing such as jeans for just £18.

The Observatory

20 Greenwich Church Street, SE10
Tel: 020 8305 1998
Website: www.theobservatory.co.uk
Rail: Cutty Sark
Open: Daily 11am-6.30pm

The Observatory stocks four decades of fashion over two floors with thoughtfully provided giant posters defining the 20th century's major trends from 20s flappers to psychedelics. The shop is simply decorated and the clothes well organised and dry-cleaned to perfection. The ground floor is dedicated to retro fashion while upstairs has more formal wear like classic men's suits for around £55 and 50s evening dresses for only £45. The prices are competitive and anything that doesn't sell quickly is marked down, so it's possible to find bargains such as a funky 70s shirt reduced to £12 and summer skirts for just £8. Committed bargain hunters should look out for their January and July sales.

East

Absolute Vintage

15 Hanbury St, E1
Tel: 020 7247 3883
Website: www.absolutevintage.co.uk
Open: Mon-Sat 12noon-7pm, Sun 11am-7pm

map 12

Absolute Vintage offers a staggering array of second-hand and vintage footwear sourced from Canada and Europe as well as a small selection of dresses, coats and accessories. On a recent visit a pair of black Carvela sling backs were only £20 and a pair of 80s court shoes £15. There are plenty of bargains to be found here and prices to suit even the most hard-up fashionista. Absolute Vintage has a sister shop just around the corner (see entry below).

Blondie

Unit 2,
114 -118 Commercial Street, E1 6NF
Tel: 0207 247 0050
Open: Daily 10am-7pm

map 12

Blondie is the sister shop of Absolute Vintage, stocking high-end vintage and collectables with items such as Louis Vuitton trunks, Dior dresses and Hermes bags to name a few. For those on a budget it might be better to stick to Absolute Vintage, but if you have the money for something a little bit more upmarket this new shop is well worth a visit.

Beyond Retro

112 Cheshire Street, E2
Tel: 020 7613 3636
Website: www.beyondretro.com
Tube: Liverpool Street, Bethnal Green or Shoreditch
Open: Daily 10am-6pm

(map 12)

Beyond Retro's founding store occupies a vast warehouse just off Brick Lane. From the outside the building is not very prepossessing, but inside is an Aladdin's cave of classic and retro clothing with over 15,000 garments at any one time – some dating back to the 1920s. For everyday street wear Beyond Retro has hundreds of jeans for around £15, blouses from the 60s to the 90s for £15 and trackie tops for £10-15. For those wanting to make a more distinctive fashion statement there was a virgin wool 50s men's jacket for £20, a vast selection of trilbys for £16 and a beautiful 60s emerald green silk dress for only £28. The place is so vast that it's possible to spend several hours in here, particularly as the music played is as eclectic as the clothing – Pulp, Ginger Rodgers, Kate Bush and the Clash all providing a nostalgic background to the shopping on a recent trip. This is the largest retro store in London with enough room to stock all kinds of obscure things like a selection of authentic Japanese kimonos for as little as £48 and going up to £195. The store also has an unrivalled selection of accessories with a wall dedicated to shoes and more bags than you can wave a stick at. Determined bargain hunters should head to the back of the store where clothes are sold for half the original price with jeans for £8 and some great men's summer shirts for £7. Beyond Retro has rightly established itself as one of the most important fashion outlets in London and is a great place to visit on a Sunday when Cheshire Street becomes part of Brick Lane Market (see page 352).

Burt & Mary

5 Cheshire Street, E1
Tube: Aldgate East/Liverpool Street
Open: Mon-Fri 12noon-6pm, Sat 11am-7pm, Sun 10am-7pm

(map 12)

This well organised retro store is well stocked with great value retro street gear like jeans for £25-45, leather jackets for £50-80 and some great 70s men's shirts for £15. Women are well catered for here with lots of 60s style dresses for around £28 and a vast collection of bags and accessories to sift through. On a recent visit the store had a fabulous kaftan for £45 which brought back memories of my mother's more extravagant fashion experiments.

Sam Greenberg

Rellik

Torpedo Blue

Rokit Camden

Rokit

101 & 107 Brick Lane, E1
Tel: 020 7375 3864
Website: www.rokit.co.uk
Tube: Aldgate East/Liverpool Street
Open: Mon-Fri 10.30am-6.30pm, Sat-Sun 10am-7pm

These two large Rokit outlets on Brick Lane are at the heart of one of the most fashionable and fashion conscious parts of town. The stores are done out in a smart industrial style with stone floors, steel counters and scaffolding railing and offer a great selection of retro clothing. Number 101 offers a mixed selection for both men and women while number 107 is dedicated to women and has more of an emphasis on vintage garments. For basic street fashion the store at 101 is the best place to look with Hawaiian shirts for £20-£25, leather belts £6-£8 and jeans for about £20. They recently had a great selection of quality corderoy jackets for only £20 – allowing you to get a bit of student chic on the cheap.

The Shop

3A Cheshire Street, E1
Tel: 020 7739 5631
Tube: Aldgate East/Liverpool Street
Open: Thurs 12noon-6pm, Sun 9am-3pm

The non-committal name and limited opening hours make this a store that is difficult to visit or identify. These problems aside, it does stock a well chosen selection of retro clothing, accessories and household items and is worth visiting when wandering in the area during the fabulous Sunday market (see page 352). The Shop has a second store just a few doors down at number 7.

Torpedo Blue

226 Brick Lane, E1
Tel: 07932 018 965
Tube: Aldgate East/Liverpool Street
Open: Daily 11am-7pm (times may vary)

This little retro store has some very fine retro clothing – all of it imported from Italy. A stylish men's jacket can be found here for as little as £22 and a beautifully made 60s dress was only £35. There are lots of accessories with women's bags starting from £18 and going up to £70 for a classic 50s red leather handbag that takes pride of place in the window. A shop well worth visiting if you're visiting Brick Lane and just opposite the famous Beigel Bake.

Vintage Fashion Fairs

Vintage fairs are a great way to meet lots of different vintage traders under one roof, giving you a chance to compare and contrast the things on offer and hopefully barter yourself a few bargains in the process. Like the designer sales, the vintage fairs are quite lively affairs with great displays and plenty of fashion conscious beautiful people enjoying the experience. There are several vintage fairs held in London throughout the year the most established of which are featured below:

Battersea Vintage Fashion, Accessories and Textiles Fair

Battersea Arts Centre, Lavender Hill, London, SW11
020 8325 5789,
Website: www.vintagefashionfairs.com
Open: bimonthly on a Sunday 9.30am-4.30pm

Vintage dealers from all over the country come to this bimonthly fair. There are about 65 stands at this Battersea event with anything from an 18th century naval costume to 60s street fashion to be found on display.

Frock Me!

Chelsea Town Hall, King's Road, Chelsea, SW3
Website: www.frockmevintagefashion.com
Tel: 020 7254 4054
Tube: Sloane Square or South Kensington
Open: 2-3 times per year

Frock Me! offers around 50 specialists selling a varied collection of vintage clothing and accessories including hats, shoes, gloves and jewellery alongside modern designer wear. The event attracts a fashionable crowd in the search for vintage style with prices to suit all pockets and some great displays to marvel at even if you can't afford to buy.

The London Vintage Fashion, Textiles, and Accessories Fair

Hammersmith Town Hall, King St, W6
& Dulwich College, Dulwich Common, London SE21.
Tel: 020 8543-5075
Website: www.pa-antiques.co.uk
Open: Every 4 or 5 weeks in Hammersmith, biannually in Dulwich

This event has established itself as one of the largest and most popular vintage fairs in the country with over a hundred traders displaying their wares. The variety of vintage accessories from hats to jewellery and cigerette cases make this an Aladdin's cave worth making the effort to visit.

Designer Sale Shops

There are plenty of permanent designer discount outlets to be found in London that sell seconds, overstocks and samples for a fraction of their original price. The shops featured below are all well established, but keep a look out for temporary discount outlets which sometimes occupy a short lease to clear designer labels. These shops trade for as little as a few months and so are not featured here, but will be listed on our website (bargainhunterslondon.com). For more opportunities to find discounted designer labels refer to Dress Agencies (page 76) and Designer Warehouse Sales (page 67).

Central

Browns Labels for Less

50 South Molton Street, W1K
Tel: 020 7514 0052
Tube: Bond Street
Open: Mon-Sat 10am-6.30pm, Thurs 10am-7pm

Browns is an exclusive retailer offering fashionable labels such as D & G, Mission, Gill Sander and Paul Smith at equally exclusive prices. Bargain hunters should head to their central London discount outlet where last season's stock, slight seconds and samples are sold at between 30-90% discount. The store has made an effort with the decor and displays so that you can bargain hunt and still get some of the glamour of a full price Browns shop.

Paul Smith Sale Shop

23 Avery Row, W1
Tel: 020 7493 1287

Open: Mon-Sat 10.30am-6.30pm (Thurs until 7pm), Sun 1pm-5.30pm

Behind the rather tatty exterior this shop offers two floors of discounted menswear from Britain's most popular designer. The discounts are usually 30-75% off the retail price for clothes that are either old stock, overstock, seconds or samples. The seconds usually have only minor defects but its a good idea to check these garments before parting with your cash. Unlike some less imaginative discount stores, this outlet has some of the Paul Smith style with the top floor decorated with vintage 80s vinyl on the walls to inspire nostalgia in those old enough to remember the decade.

TK Maxx
www.tkmaxx.co.uk
Stateside clothing outlet TK Maxx prides itself on selling famous label womenswear, menswear and homewares at up to 60% off the usual price. The store has a no-frills approach to retailing with low overheads and piles of cheap gear. The cash-strapped but cunning shopper can pick up items from Diesel, Calvin Klein or even Jasper Conran for a fraction of the usual price. For a more detailed review of TK Maxx see the review in Street Fashion (page 32).

West

LK Bennett Clearance Store
239 Kings Road, SW3
Tel: 020 7376 4108
Open: Mon-Sat 10am-6.30pm, Sun 12noon-6pm
The L.K. Bennett Clearance Shop sells last year´s range of stylish ladies´ shoes, clothes, handbags and accessories at discounts of up to 70%. On a recent visit calf-length leather boots were a great deal for only £39 (reduced from £189). Alongside the LK Bennentt range they occasionally stock designer brands such as DKNY and Moschino with offers such as a smart DKNY coat reduced from £729 to a very reasonable £399.
Branch at:
38b High Street, Wimbledon Village, SW19
Tel: 020 8947 4507 (see Shoes section on p.94).

Caroline Charles
18 Hill Rise, Richmond, TW10 6UA
Tel: 020 8948 7777
Website: www.carolinecharles.co.uk
Tube/Rail: Richmond
Open: Mon-Sat 10am-5.30pm, Sun 11am-4pm
Caroline Charles offers her exclusive range of ladies fashion from this Richmond store with about half the stock dedicated to discounted samples and old stock. Among the bargains on a recent visit were fully lined tweed trousers that originally sold for £295, reduced to only £25, and last year's skirts being sold for the same discount. For those with a little more money to spend they also had a stylish ladies evening jacket reduced to £1,000, which was half the original price. Take a look at the website to find out more about the label.

Joseph Clearance Shop
53 King's Road, SW3
Tel: 020 7730 7562
Tube: Sloane Square
Open: Mon-Sat 10am-6.30pm (wed till 7pm), Sun 12noon-5pm

Joseph is an established designer label specialising in tailored suits and other beautiful clothes that are priced accordingly. The Joseph Clearance Shop offers last season's stock of samples, handbags, shoes and accessories at up to 80% discount all year round. As well as their own labels they also offer 7 Jeans at up to 60% discount and a limited selection of discounted designer garments from names such as Prada, Gucci and D&G.

East

The Carhartt Clearance Store
18 Ellingfort Road, E8
Tel: 020 8986 8875
Train: London Fields
Open: Mon-Sat 11am-5pm, Sun 11am-4pm

Carhartt make practical workware in the States, but in Europe the label has become popular as fashionable men's streetwear. This modest warehouse space in East London is both the distribution centre for the brand and also a clearance shop offering a great selection of last season's stock, seconds and samples at considerable discounts. Among the bargains on a recent visit was a chunky camouflage jacket for £85 (reduced from £130) and heavy duty cotton slacks for £25 (reduced from £55). Items are usually discounted by 25-30% and then discounted further if they don't sell with some trousers reduced to only £10. A great discount outlet and one well worth making your way to Hackney to explore.

The Laden Showroom
103 Brick Lane, E1
Tel: 020 7247 2431
Website: www.laden.co.uk
Tube: Aldgate East/Liverpool Street
Open: Mon-Sat 12noon-6pm, Sun 10.30am-6pm

(map 12)

This outlet acts as a showcase for young designers who pay for a concession within the store. The labels may not be ones you are familiar with but the quality and originality of the clothing makes this place popular with the fashionistas of Brick Lane. There are always a few bargains to be found such as the fabulous Jovonna dresses for only £30-59. Committed bargain hunters should look out for their January sales.

Designer Warehouse Sales

Designer Warehouse Sales are temporary events that take place to sell designer labels that are either surplus stock, samples, last season or slight seconds at a considerable discount. The first sales started around 25 years ago and with their success many more have sprung up, making London one of the best places to hunt down designer bargains. On any weekend in the Capital there will usually be desiger sales taking place, but the busiest times of the year are at the end of each fashion season when there are sales all over the city. Those featured here vary from modest single room events such as the Duffer of St George Sale to the big fashion sales such as DWS which occupy a vast space and have thousands of visitors. In most cases, you must sign up to a mailing list to find out about the sales. There is usually a charge for admission, but this is a small price to pay to get your hands on great fashion at a fraction of the original price.

Central

Designer Showroom Sale

5 Bywell Place, London, W1
Tel: 020 7580 5075
email: info@bld.co.uk
Tube: Oxford Circus
Women's Fashion

Importer and wholesaler BLD run end-of-season and sample sales from their showroom twice a year. At the sales you can find Italian labels such as Shirt Passion and Liu Jo catering for the smart mature woman at prices reduced by 50-70%. The sales are something that BLD host to clear surplus stock and samples and are not well publicised or regularly held. Join their mailing list to be kept informed of their future events.

Jasper Conran End of Season Sales

36 Sackville Street, W1
Tel: 020 7292 9080
email: info@jasperconran.com
Men's fashion

Jasper Conran hosts two end of season sample sales in August and January. The sales are not well publicised and initial entrance is restricted to established customers. Members of the public can get their hands on Conran's discounted samples by giving the store on Sackville Street a call or sending an e-mail asking about their next sale

Louis Féraud
4 New Burlington Place, W1
Tel: 020 7734 2039
Women's Fashion

De Keyser Fashion is the sole distributor for Louis Féraud ladies fashion and holds end-of-season/sample sales for the label once or twice a year- with discounts of between 20 and 70%. Phone the office to find out about their next sale and put your name on the mailing list.

North

David Charles
1 Thane Works,
Thane Villas, N7
Tel: 020 7609 4797
email: davidcharles19@btconnect.com
Childrenswear

David Charles holds spring and winter sales of their childrenswear at their showroom in Holloway. The clothes cater for children from 2-16 years old and the prices are well below those found in the high street. Phone or e-mail to be put on their mailing list.

The Designer Warehouse Sales

The Worx, 45 Balfe Street, N1
Tel: 020 7837 3322
Website: www.designerwarehousesales.com
Tube: King's Cross
Entrance fee: £2
Open: 12 times a year for three-day sessions,
e-mail or sign up on the website for advance information
Women's and Men's Fashion

This monthly designer sale is held in a smart photographer's studio over three days and is the largest and most established of London's designer sales. Be ready to paw through racks and racks of high-fashion clothing from makers like Nicole Farhi, Vivienne Westwood and Prada with lots of London Fashion Week designers also featuring on the rails. DWS events are always busy with fashionable punters sifting through the rails for bargains, great music discreetly playing in the background and plenty of staff on hand to make sure things run smoothly. There are plenty of garments and accessories to be found here to suit every pocket with lots of smaller items for a tenner or less, so no one need leave empty handed. Turn up with enthusiasm, energy and cash to pick up this season's designer labels at about 60% less than retail.

Junior Style

Alphaville 2, 14 Shepherdess Walk, N1
Tel: 020 7689 3925
Website: www.juniorstylesales.co.uk
Kids designer and brand-name clothing for 0-12yrs
Open: 4 sales per year

Junior Style sources baby and children's clothes from many different designers and manufacturers and sells them at considerable discounts to the public at their regular sales. The location for the sale is small but there are lots of rails crammed into the space and plenty of staff on hand to help. A recent sale included labels such as D & G Junior, Joseph Baby, Replay, Evisu and Nolita Pocket with most clothes being sold at about half the usual retail price. Bargains included a Milky Silki dress for a 7-8 year old for £19 (originally £49). Junior Style also have a good selection of discounted gifts for new-borns including accessories, shoes and UV protective swimwear. A great sale for kid's designer clothing and one well worth going out of your way to visit.

West

Ghost Ltd

263 Kensal Road, W10
Tel: 020 8960 3121
Website: www.ghost.co.uk
Women's Fashion

Elegant and ethereal fashion is the forte of this local design house. Usually out of reach for bargain hunters, Ghost's floaty dresses, baggy pants and loose tops are put on sale at their regular designer sales. The events offer slight seconds, samples and end-of-season stock all at a discount and are held at various London venues. Contact them by phone or via their website to put your name on the mailing list.

London Fashion Weekend

www.londonfashionweek.co.uk
e-mail: lfw-end@single-market.co.uk
Tel: 020 8948 5522
Entrance fee: £12-15
Men's and Women's Fashion

After the exclusive London Fashion Week, the fashion élite throw open their doors to the public for a weekend of shopping. Find designer clothing and accessories aplenty at seriously reduced prices. Most London designers are here from Jasper Conran to Philip Treacy with plenty of smaller labels represented too. Besides the fashion, there's also the lifestyle – with delicious food, pampering beauty treatments and other little luxuries on offer to help you part with your money. If you've got the energy and the dedication, you can find some unique pieces for lower than usual prices here.

Designer Sales UK

Designer Sales UK

Designer Sales

On the QT

On the QT

20th Century Theatre
291 Westbourne Grove, W11
Tel: 0797 090 8786
Website: www.ontheqtfashion.com
Admission: £1
Open: 4 sales per year

$$\text{map } 6$$

On the QT started business in 2003 and has quickly established itself as one of the best value designer sales in the Capital. The events takes place at the 20th Century Theatre, just off Portobello Road, four times a year, extending over four days – allowing visitors to combine their search for fashion with a visit to Portobello Market. On offer are seconds and end of season stock from new designers and established labels such as Stella McCartney, Alexander McQueen and Vivienne Westwood. There are plenty of bargains to be found among the rails of men's and women's fashion with some garments reduced by as much as 70%. The event is friendly and relaxed, making this a great place to look for fashion bargains. Take a look at their website to find out about their next event.

South

The British Designers Sale

42 York Mansions, Prince of Wales Drive, SW11
Tel: 020 7627 2777
Open: Five times a year for women; twice a year for men
Men's and Women's Fashion

Chelsea Old Town Hall is the venue for this fashion club – the first of its kind in the UK. You will find wonderful bargains from top designers including Shirin Guild, Allegra Hicks, Jenny Packham, Lotus, 120% Linen and many more. All garments are discounted by at least 50% and some are as much as 80% off the retail price. Despite the name, this long established designer sale offers labels from all over Europe. There are two men's sales in May and November, which are open to all, and five women's sales requiring membership, which costs £35 per year or £5 for entry just on the Saturday.

East

Designer Sales UK

Tel: 01273 470 880
Website: www.designersales.co.uk
Open: Five to seven seasonal sample sales per year in or around Feb/March
for Winter, April/May for Spring, June/July for Summer, Sept/October for
Autumn and Nov/Dec for Christmas. Each sale usually lasts four days from
Thursday to Sunday with Thursday reserved for mailing list customers.
Contact name: Ellain Foster-Gandey
Entrance fee: £2
Men and Women's Fashion

Designer Sales UK is one of the longest running sample sales having been established in 1989. It has since become a regular event in venues such as The Old Truman Brewery and The New Connaught Rooms in Covent Garden. The space used for the sale is always large enough to display 100's of rails holding clothing from over 60 designer labels and all at substantial discounts of 40-90%. The atmosphere of the sales is great with lots of attractive, fashionable people, milling between the rails and often emerging with a mountain of clothing in their arms. Featured labels include Jean-Paul Gaultier, Gucci and Vivienne Westwood. For those on a limited budget there are always cheaper items such as fashionable T-shirts reduced from £39 to only £10. Phone the office or check out their website to get on the mailing list.

The Duffer of St George Sample Sale

St George's House
140 Shoreditch High Street, E1
Tel: 020 7920 7700

This sample sale takes place regularly at the offices of Duffer of St George. The sale is almost exclusively of samples and end of lines of Duffer menswear, although one or two other labels occasionally show up here. There are plenty of bargains to be found with great quality hooded tops for £30 (reduced from £75), heavy Duffer denim jeans for £40 (reduced from £120) and stylish cotton shirts for only £15 (reduced form £70). These regular sales are a definite must for men on the hunt for fashionable bargains – give them a call to find out about the next sale and join their mailing list to keep informed about future sales.

Fashion East

The Old Truman Brewery Complex, (map 12)
Brick Lane, E1
Tel: 020 7770 6150
Website: www.fashioneast.co.uk
Open: Three times a year (spring, summer and winter)
Men and Women's Fashion

Fashion East offer a great selection of young London designers at their regular warehouse sales held at the Truman Brewery. Featured labels include Zakee Shariff, PPQ, Backhand and many other contemporary designers. Among the rails there are always plenty of bargains to be found including at a recent sale a Jonathan Saunders dress for £45 and Jens Laugensen cashmere for only £35 with some items reduced by as much as 85%. For details of future events give them a call to put your name on their mailing list or take a look at their website.

Fashion Made Fair

The Old Truman Brewery Complex, (map 12)
Brick Lane, E1
Tel: 020 7739 9659
Website: www.peopletree.co.uk
Open: Two times a year, usually May and November

This event is dedicated to the sale of samples and end-of-season stock from the growing number of companies that specialise in ethically produced fashion and accessories. This is a unique event and the only sample sale where you can walk away with a bag full of discounted fashion and have the added satisfaction of knowing that your goodies have been produced in an ethically and environmentally responsible way. Have a look at the website to find out more about the organisers, People Tree.

Lezley George

49 Columbia Road, E2
Tel: 020 7729 9905
Website: www.lezleygeorge.co.uk
Open: Sunday 10am-3pm

Lezley George designs a spectacular range of woman's clothes with the emphasis upon style and glamour. Her website shows all the current designs and gives you some idea of her style. Lezley has recently opened her workshop to the public on Sundays where women can get their hands on a bit of glamour at 50-70% less than the usual retail price. The Columbia Road Flower Market is just outside her workshop.

The Secret Sample Sale

The Old Truman Brewery Complex,
Brick Lane, E1
Tel: 020 3132 2878
Website: www.secretsamplesales.co.uk / www.girlsnightin-uk.co.uk
Open: Six sales per year
Men and Women's Fashion

The Secret Sample Sale offers a great selection of designer labels from Gucci and Prada to contemporary London labels like Billy Bags and Michael Keller. There is a £1 admission fee but this is easily rewarded with bargains in both men and women's fashion to suit every pocket. Among the bargains on a recent visit was an original Prada Bag for £379 (originally £579), a stylish Billy Bags wallet for £15 (reduced from £55) and a beautiful 50s-style ladies jacket by Chan Chan for £45 (originally £68). These sample sales are held in conjunction with Girls Night In, who are responsible for the excellent range of accessories. Log on to their website or give them a call to find out the dates and venue of their next sale.

Also at: 20th Century Cinema Theatre, 291 Westbourne Grove, W11

Two Agent See

The Old Truman Brewery Complex,
Brick Lane, E1
Tel: 020 7739 4355
email: leighcolgate@twoagentsee.com
Open: Four to five sales per year
Men and Women's Fashion

Two Agent See are distributors and agents who source contemporary fashion from a wide variety of labels and also have their own in-house labels. The company holds regular sales at the Truman Brewery where vast quantities of seconds and surplus stock is sold at discounts of 50% or more. The sales are great fun with lots to sift through and plenty of bargains to be found amongst the fashionable labels like Sesson, Laura Lees and Dexter Wong. To find out about the next sale send an e-mail or give them a call.

Dress Agencies

Dress agencies are brilliant places to find second-hand designer clothing as well as big name bags, shoes and accessories. They are also an excellent way of recouping money for garments that you no longer wear, with agencies usually splitting the sale price 50/50 with sellers. Many agencies only cater for women, but there are a few who carry clothing for men and children, enabling the skilful bargain hunter to pick up stylish deals for the whole family under one roof. Although the stock consists largely of other people's cast-offs this is no indication of their quality as most agencies will not even consider clothes that are more than two years old and the smarter ones will only accept top names. Other agencies are more laid-back and will take high street labels like Jigsaw, Kookai and Gap. Reviewed within this chapter are over 30 of the Capital's best dress agencies from long established shops like Designs on Her (see page 80) to relative newcomers such as Bang Bang (below). The savings you can make are considerable and most dress agencies hold winter and summer sales when garments that have failed to sell are reduced to clear.

Central

Bang Bang
(Women's Clothing Exchange)
21 Goodge Street, W1
Tel: 020 7631 4191
Tube: Goodge Street
Open: Mon-Fri 10am-6.30pm, Sat 11am-6pm

This funky little shop with its furry sofa and scarlet decor is different from most dress agencies, catering as it does for the young and young at heart and offering a good selection of clothing from cheap street fashion to exclusive designer labels. On a recent visit a 1930s vintage wedding dress was £300, a bargain considering this item could be considered an antique. Cheaper items are also in store including skirts from £10 and shoes from £90. The glass counters at the front of the shop display lots of interesting jewellery with rings starting at £5 and brooches from £6. You will also find funky sunglasses and even a vintage telephone for your home. The exchange policy here is simple and original with cash paid for clothes, or clients allowed to spend double the cash amount in the shop.

Bang Bang

9 Berwick Street, W1
Tel: 020 7494 2042
Tube: Leicester Square or Tottenham Court Road
Open: Mon–Sat 11.30am-7pm

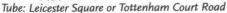
(map 1)

This second branch of Bang Bang sells vintage household goods, women's fashion and has now become the sole store for menswear with the entire basement dedicated to men's fashion and accessories.

Catwalk

52 Blandford Street, W1
Tel: 020 7935 1052
Tube: Baker Street
Open: Mon 12.30pm-6pm, Tues-Fri 11.15am-6pm, Sat 11.30am-5pm

This small boutique is packed full of funky gear from the top end of the high street like Whistles to carefully selected designer labels, such as Alexander McQueen, Mami and Dior. The latest styles of jeans and Chanel and Dior sunglasses are a prominent feature. Catwalk stands out from other dress agencies thanks to its selection of Louis Vuitton accessories. L'Homme Designer Exchange for men is next door.

Dress for Less

391 St. John Street, EC1
Tel: 020 7713 5591
Website: www.dressforless.uk.com
Tube: Angel
Open: Mon 12noon-7.30pm, Tues-Wed 12noon-8pm,
Thurs (irregular hours - phone), Fri 12noon-7.30pm,
Sat 12noon-7pm, Sun 12noon-5pm (irregular hours - phone)

(map 3)

Dress for Less is a friendly agency that is always busy with its clientele of loyal customers. It's a great place to shop for designer and high street labels at very competitive prices including anything from a Jigsaw dress to a Gucci handbag. The stock is carefully laid out with the selection of handbags taking pride of place on the top shelf and smart glass cabinets containing jewellery, designer sunglasses and accessories. The agency also has a decent selection of men's fashion and always has items that are reduced to clear for the determined bargain hunter.

L'Homme Designer Exchange

50 Blandford Street, W1
Tel: 020 7224 3266
Tube: Baker Street
Open: Mon-Sat: 1130am-5pm

A small, well-established boutique with big names in designerwear exclusively for men. Prada, Gucci and Versace mingle on hangers alongside Paul Smith, Jean-Paul Gaultier and Armani. While you can pick up trousers and shirts for £15 and jackets from £40, you could also pay £350 for a Galliano suit which would have set you back £1,500 when new. Most of the clothes come off the catwalk, from photo shoots, film and television sets, or from celebrities who get 50% of the sale price. We found Visou jeans for £40 and an outrageous Alexander McQueen sheepskin coat for £500 (was £2,000). All clothes are less than three years old and are only held for six months, guaranteeing that the garments are in good condition.

The Loft

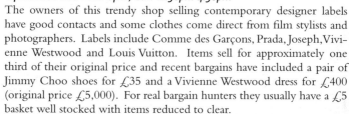

35 Monmouth Street,
Covent Garden, WC2H
Tel: 020 7240 3807
Website: www.the-loft.co.uk
Tube: Covent Garden/Leicester Square
Open: Mon-Sat 11am-6pm, Sun 12:30pm-4.30pm

The owners of this trendy shop selling contemporary designer labels have good contacts and some clothes come direct from film stylists and photographers. Labels include Comme des Garçons, Prada, Joseph, Vivienne Westwood and Louis Vuitton. Items sell for approximately one third of their original price and recent bargains have included a pair of Jimmy Choo shoes for £35 and a Vivienne Westwood dress for £400 (original price £5,000). For real bargain hunters they usually have a £5 basket well stocked with items reduced to clear.

North

Change of Heart

The Old School,
59c Park Road, N8
Tel: 020 8341 1575
Tube: Finsbury Park/Highgate
Open: Mon-Sat 10am-6pm, Sun 10am-5pm

Spacious, stylish showroom offering hardly worn, top quality women's designer clothing. Children have their own play area, and weary shoppers or their patient partners are offered a glass of wine and the papers. They no longer have established designer labels such as Armani and Dolce and Gabbana, and prefer the likes of Mark Jacobs, Chloé, Ghost and Paul & Joe sold at very reasonable prices. We recently found Birkinstocks and Chloé bags at half price.

Designs on Her

60 Rosslyn Hill, NW3
Tel: 020 7435 0100
Tube: Hampstead
Open: Mon-Sat 10am-5.45pm

Long-established agency specialising in contemporary designerwear in top condition. They have a good selection of accessories from current Prada bags to Jimmy Choo shoes. Labels include Gucci, Armani, Missoni and Marc Jacobs. On offer as we went to press was an Armani floral dress for £129 and an Alexander McQueen skirt for £75.

Deuxieme

Bang Bang

Deuxieme

SALE
NOW ON

Dress For Less

Exclusivo

24 High Street, NW3
Tel: 020 7431 8618
Tube: Hampstead
Open: Daily 11.30am-6pm

Set among the boutiques and coffee shops of Hampstead Village, this dimly-lit, cramped shop is stuffed with designer labels, bags, boots and accessories. Lots of men's suits (from £60) with Prada, Gucci, Chanel being the names to look for here. Other bargains include Chanel bags for £1,000 (original price £4,000) and Prada jackets from £150. Clothes stay for ten weeks and sellers decide for themselves what price they want – the shop then adds its own mark-up. The stock also includes samples of new ranges.

Laurel Herman

18a Lambolle Place, NW3
Tel: 020 7586 7925
Tube: Belsize Park/Swiss Cottage
Open: By appointment only

A discreet business run from a private showroom in a quiet mews offering a large collection of hardly worn labels like MaxMara and Donna Karan. including evening wear and accessories. A recent bargain was an Armani trouser suit for £450 (original cost over £900). Also available is a free image consultation from the MD whose paying clients include large banks and businesses.

Resurrection Recycle Boutique

3a Archway Close, Archway Island, N19
Tel: 020 7263 2600
Tube: Archway   Rail: Upper Holloway
Open: Mon-Sat 10am-6pm

Spacious shop selling designer and vintage clothes as well as samples and graduate designs from the London College of Fashion. We found a Clarke Kennedy dress and Michelle Ambert skirt for under £30 each and Prada shoes from £60. They have a considerable stock of brand new clothes – anything from a Jigsaw dress for £15 to an Armani suit for £150. The choice of bags and accessories is also impressive and they offer a fittings and alterations service if your chosen garment needs a bit of adjustment.

Seconda Mano

(map 3)

114 Upper Street, N1
Tel: 020 7359 5284
Tube: Angel/Highbury & Islington
Rail: Highbury & Islington or Angel
Open: Mon-Tues & Sat 10am-6pm, Wed-Fri 10am-8pm, Sun 12noon-4pm

This dress agency has moved in recent years to the basement of Giovanni hairdressers, but still manages to cram a great selection of fashion and accessiories into a small space. The shop sources its clothes from the wealthy residents of Islington, so there are plenty of top labels going for a fraction of the original price. Recent bargains included a very fine leather box jacket by 'Sixty 6' for only £70 and a beautiful Francesco Bianca hand-bag for £38. This shop does a good trade in designer bags and accessories and is also one of the few shops to hold a good range of men's fashion.

Wellingtons

1 Wellington Place, NW8
Tel: 020 7483 0688
Tube: St. John's Wood
Open: Mon-Sat 11am-5pm

Mother-and-daughter-run agency, just off St. John's Wood High Street, has a fast turnover of clothes and accessories at reasonable prices. The range of stock is impressive with leather and suede jackets from £20 and Prada and Armani suits for around £400. They also stock high street labels like M&S and Whistles and a good selection of shoes, bags and jewellery. The bargain rail is kept well stocked with items reduced to clear for £20 or less.

West

Deuxieme

299 New King's Road, SW6
Tel: 020 7736 3696
Tube: Parson's Green
Open: Mon-Sat 10am-6pm, Sun 11am-5pm

Friendly, good value agency on two floors with lots of bargains. Labels include Jimmy Choo, Prada, Gucci, and Marc Jacobs with prices from £5-£300. We found Prada handbags from £90. They also hire out evening wear and hats for special occasions and stock accessories and jewellery. Deuxieme are always getting new stock from contemporary designer labels to more unusual items such as a vintage 70s Gucci dress recently on display in the window. A great dress agency.

The Dress Box

8 Cheval Place, SW7
Tel: 020 7589 2240
Tube: Knightsbridge/South Kensington
Open: Mon-Fri 10am-6pm, Sat-Sun 10.30am-6pm

One of the oldest dress agencies in town offering the top end of the designer range as well as couture clothes. A Valentino evening dress that retails for around £4,600 was a snip at £1,200, and an Andrew GN white beaded evening jacket was £3,000 which was originally £7,500. The Dress Box also has a vast selection of designer shoes and now stocks a limited number of fine vintage items at prices that reflect the quality and rarity of the clothes. Next door at No.10, Stelios (same owner), specialises exclusively in Hermes and Chanel as well as leather goods. They have a waiting list for Hermes bags, so get in line and you might just get lucky and snap up a large crocodile Kelly bag for £6,400 (retails at £12,500). A bargain outlet but only for those with very deep pockets.

The Dresser

10 Porchester Place, Connaught Village
Marble Arch, W2 2BS
Tel: 020 7724 7212
Website: dresseronline.co.uk
Email: thedresser@mac.com
Tube: Marble Arch
Open: Mon-Fri 11am-5.30pm, Sat 11am-5pm

Contemporary designerwear and couture for women and men (although there's less choice for the latter). A Chloe two piece suit was being snapped up when we visited for £250 (retails for £2,000 plus) and a Helmut Lang jacket was £160. Other top notch labels included Prada, Paul Smith and Dolce & Gabbana. Also bags and shoes, think Gucci, Prada and the divine Manolo Blahnik.

Dynasty (almost new) Designer Wear

12A Turnham Green Terrace, W4
Tel: 020 8995 3846
Tube: Turnham Green
Open: Mon-Sat 10.30am-5pm

This designer shop that caters for all budgets and is run by a helpful staff that will lead you to the best bargains. Classic labels include Gucci, Galliano, Burberry, and Fendi. Bargains included Escada suits from £199 (£700 new) and Prada suits from £275 (£1,000 new). Stock includes high street names like Kookai and Karen Millen and also jewellery, shoes and scarves. The choice of brand new designer bags is impressive with such as a Chanel handbag for £100 (original price £800). Their collection of eveningwear makes this a good agency if you're looking for something for a special occasion. The men's wear is next door (see below).

Dynasty (almost new) Menswear

12 Turnham Green Terrace, W4
Tel: 020 8994 4450
Tube: Turnham Green
Open: Mon-Sat 10.30am-5pm

Rich pickings for the well-dressed bargain hunter. Expect Armani and Versace suits from £150, Blazer suits from £79 and natty Thomas Pink and Dolce & Gabbana shirts for under £20. There are also lots of casual shirts for the dressed-down gent. With prices so low, it's possible to leave this shop looking like a million dollars for less than £100.

Felt

13 Cale Street, SW3
Tel: 020 7349 8829
Website: www.felt-london.com
Tube: Sloane Square/South Kensington
Open: Mon: 1pm-6pm, Tues-Sat: 11am-6pm

A unique boutique and sassy owner who claims this is one of the "best shops in London". Felt does fur in the winter and "groovy" clothes in the summer as well as a selection of contemporary jewellery.

Insight

201 Munster Road, SW6
Tel: 020 7385 5501
Tube: Fulham Broadway, Parsons Green
Open: Times vary – phone in advance

Dress agency in a two-storey house, selling designer labels for men and women (Prada, Gucci, Dolce & Gabbana), shoes and an excellent selection of handbags. Also vintage clothes, antique linen, decorative textiles and costume jewellery at very competitive prices. In addition they offer a hire service.

Pandora

16-22 Cheval Place, SW7
Tel: 020 7589 5289
Tube: Knightsbridge/South Kensington
Open: Mon-Sat 10am-7pm, Sun 12pm-6pm

Established in Sloane Square in 1947, Pandora is the doyenne of dress agencies and, with some 7,000 items in stock, offers a huge choice. Chanel suits sell from £300–£900 (over £3,000 new) but you might also find a Gaultier or Yves St. Laurent T-shirt from £35. If it's accessories you're after, they have Fendi and Gucci bags for £165 (original cost £400) and designer shoes from £47.

Salou

6 Cheval Place, SW7
Tel: 020 7581 2380
Tube: Knightsbridge/South Kensington
Open: Mon-Sat 10am-5pm

One of a row of dress agencies in Cheval Place (across the road from Harrods), Salou offers second-hand designer clothes. You will find classics like Prada, Chanel, Yves Saint Laurent, Gucci (bags from £99), alongside Joseph and Bluemarine. They also stock a good choice of accessories such as shoes and jewellery.

La Scala

39 Elystan Street, SW3
Tel: 020 7589 2784
Tube: South Kensington
Open: Mon-Sat 10am-5.30pm

This charming and very smart dress agency has a vast selection of Italian labels for women and men including Gucci, Prada and Marni. The agency is a good place to find top labels at reasonable prices and features lots of suede and cashmere on its rails. La Scala is particularly good for accessories, bags and shoes and often stocks both this season and last season's fashion items.

Sign of the Times

17 Elystan Street, SW3
Tel: 020 7589 4774
Tube: South Kensington
Open: Mon-Fri 10am-6pm; Sat 10am-5.30pm

Well-established (30 years) dress agency with a loyal clientele and a quick turnover. We found a bright blue Dolce & Gabbana coat, made famous by Carrie of 'Sex in the City' in her falling over on the catwalk scene for £295. All the major labels are here including Marc Jacobs, Docle & Gabbana, Armani, Prada and Miu Miu. They have an excellent selection of brand new Chloe and Louis Vuitton handbags as well as shoes, hats and scarves.

Stelios

10 Cheval Place, SW7
Tel: 020 7584 4424
See The Dress Box (page 84).

South

The Anerley Frock Exchange

122 Anerley Road, SE20
Tel: 020 8778 2030
Tube: Crystal Palace
Rail: Anerley
Open: Mon-Sat 9am-5pm, Wed 9am-1pm

A large shop in its ninth year, located down the road from Crystal Palace. The stock caters for women and children, with clothes ranging from Next and Gap to Armani and Versace. There are plenty of bargains, with prices starting from a few pounds and going up to several hundred.

Frock Market

50 Lower Richmond Road, SW15
Tel: 020 8788 7748
Tube: Putney Bridge
Open: Mon-Sat 10.30am-6pm

(map 8)

An Aladdin's cave of designer bargains, owned by a painter who chooses clothes as much for their colour and originality as for their designer labels. Unusual, offbeat and even wacky items are in store alongside classic labels. On a recent visit we found a Prada jacket for £60, an Armani suit for £150, and new beaded pashmina and cashmere shawls for £30. Also Manolo Blahnik and Jimmy Choo shoes.

The Second Look

236 Upper Richmond Road West, SW14
Tel: 020 8878 7233
Rail: Mortlake
Open: Mon-Sat 10am-6pm, Wed 11am-5pm

This shop has recently expanded and is newly decorated, giving it a different flair. The large shop space is well-stocked with designer and high street clothes for women from labels such as DKNY and Morgan to Paul Smith and Prada. They only take clothes up to a year old and also have a good selection of shoes, bags and jewellery. Prices range from £10-£200.

Twice as Nice

228 Battersea Park Road, SW11
Tel: 020 7720 2234
Rail: Battersea Park
Open: Mon-Wed 10.30-6pm, Thurs 10am-8pm, Fri 10.30am-7pm,
Sat 10am-5.30pm, Sun 12noon-5pm

A small shop that buys 'anything up-to-date in good condition', with labels from Joseph and Jimmy Choo as well as exclusive names like Prada. You will find both evening and day wear from top labels at reasonable prices. They have a waiting list for some accessories and clothing.

East

Revive

3 High Street, Wanstead, E11
Tel: 020 8989 8030
Tube: Snaresbrook
Open: Mon-Sat 10am-5.30pm

This dress agency has a loyal following and a reputation for being tidy and well organised with clear labelling on all garments. Among the bargains on offer are high street labels for men and women and pricier designer labels from names such as DKNY and Moschino. Fake Jeans were £60, a Prada coat £600 and men's suits from £60. They also have a good selection of bags and shoes.

Sequel

Website: www.sequelfashion.co.uk

This website offers mint condition labels such as Missoni, Karl Lagerfeld, Dior, Gucci and Marc Jacobs at a fraction of the original price as well as high quality vintage items. Recent great offers included a Louis Vuitton bag by Robert Wilson for £145 and an unworn chevron knit jacket from Missoni for £175. The website is easy to use with a great search facility which allows you to find what you're looking for among Sequel's extensive stock. The website is an offshoot of the highly successful Harrogate boutique of the same name, so you can be sure that the quality and service are high.

Vintage

10 High Street, Wanstead, E11
Tel: 020 8989 7530
Tube: Wanstead, Snaresbrook
Open: Mon-Sat 9.30am-5.30pm

A well-established agency choc-a-bloc with a loyal clientele. Vintage has a large variety of evening and day wear and clothes from high street and designer labels. There are lots of bargains among the cocktail dresses, bags, shoes and jewellery and the agency also has a good selection of stock for larger sizes.

Children

There are many dress agencies dealing with kids' clothes the best of which are covered in the Kid's Clothes & Equipment section (page 207). In the designer warehouse section there is Junior Style which specializes in discounted designerware for kids up to 12 years old (page 69).

Shoes, Boots & Bags

There are many shops in London which offer great value shoes and bags, from basic discount outlets selling everyday footwear to smart designer shops which have occasional sales when their exclusive ranges are discounted by about 50%. In this section all kinds of London's shoe outlets are featured with Shoreditch getting special attention because of the number of shoe wholesalers in the area selling to the public at considerable discounts. As well as the shops featured below there are numerous clothing retailers that also sell good value shoes – see the Street Fashion (page 22). The designer warehouse sales are good places to look for designer footwear on the cheap (see page 67) and if you're prepared to buy second-hand then dress agencies (page 76), charity shops (page 287) and classic and retro clothing stores (page 36) are all worth exploring.

Central

Discount Shoe Sales

31 Strutton Ground, SW1
Tel: 020 7222 5223
Tube: St. James's Park
Open: Mon-Fri 9.30am-5pm

This shop has been trading for over 25 years and offers 'traditional shoes for everyone'. While you can find cheap (both in quality and price) shoes here, this men's shoe retailer also stocks some high-quality, upmarket leather shoes worth seeking out. Leather-soled Oxfords cost about £60 and would normally retail at about £100. Cheaper deals are also to be found with prices starting from £20. They carry a few work and leisure shoes, but excel in business and dress shoes.

Office

Unit 2a, 135-155
Charing Cross Road, WC2H
Tel: 020 7287 9935
Open: Mon-Tues: 10am-7pm, Wed-Fri: 10am-8pm,
Sat: 10.30am-7pm, Sun: 12noon-6pm

(map 1)

Office shoes are strictly up-to-the-minute, trend-setting footwear. Although Office no longer has a discount sale shop you can still find some cheap deals at three of their branches (Charing Cross, Camden and Queensway). The discount shelves can include items that were being sold at retail price just a few weeks before and single pairs from previous sales. Ladies' shoes start at £15 and men's shoes at £25.

Branches at:
210 Camden High Street, Camden NW1 Tel: 020 7424 9255
107 Queensay, W2. Tel: 020 7792 4000

Shoe Express

72 Oxford Street, W1
Tel: 020 7436 8791
Tube: Oxford Circus
Open: Mon-Wed & Fri-Sat 10am-7pm, Thurs 10am-8pm, Sun 2pm-6pm
This chain of shoe shops keeps its stock cheap and cheerful. The expertly and cheaply imitated fashion footwear in leather and plastic is satisfactory for a few nights out. Sandals go for £15 and children's trainers for about £10.

Also at: 498 Harrow Road, W9; 437 North End Road, SW6; 103 High Street, SE9, 67 High Street, NW10; 19/21 North Mall, The Green, N9; 103 Eltham High Street, SE9

North

ALDO Sale Shop

231-233 Camden High Street, NW1
Tel: 020 7284 1982
Website: www.aldoshoes.com
Tube: Camden Town
Open: Mon-Wed, Sun 10am-6.15pm, Thurs-Sat 10am-6.50pm
ALDO is a fashionable chain of shoe and accessory retailers with 17 stores in the UK and two sale stores in London. The discount branches are just as smart as the usual stores but expect discounts of 30-50% with most men's and women's shoes for between £29.95 and £39.95. Among the recent bargains was a pair of stylish ladies sandals for £9.95 and a large black leather handbag reduced from £49.99 to £29.95.
Also at:
Unit 10, Wood Green Shopping Centre, N22 Tel: 020 8881 5321

Clarks Factory Shop

Unit 2, 67-83 Seven Sisters Road, N7
Tel: 020 7281 9364
Tube: Finsbury Park
Open: Mon-Sat 9.30am-5.30pm, Sun 11am-4.45pm
See the main review on page 95.

Shoe Centre For Men

88 Stamford Hill, N16
Tel: 020 8806 1602
Rail: Stoke Newington
Open: Mon-Fri 2pm-7pm, Sun 11.30am-4pm

Good, old-fashioned service is a feature at this unusual shop at the tail end of Stoke Newington. Men will find plenty of classic shoes such as Brogues, Oxfords and Loafers by decent shoemakers and reasonably priced Barkers and Dr Marten's boots. One of the best deals are the slightly imperfect shoes for £60 instead of the normal price of £150.

Shoe Zone

map 10

750 High Road Finchley, N12
Tel: 020 8446 4875
Website: www.shoezone.net
Tube: East Finchley
Open: Mon-Sat 9am-5.30pm, Sun 12pnoon-4pm

Offering dirt-cheap shoes for the whole family, the Shoe Zone is a chain of discount shoe shops all over the UK. If you have kids whose feet grow fast you might consider coming here for cheap shoes: trainers cost £2.99 and sandals £3.99. The shoes are not built to last but will do the job for a season's wear. You can also pick up all the accessories here such as shoe trees and polishes at slightly discounted prices. We have listed a few London branches below.

Also at:
1 Arndale Walk, SW18, Tel: 020 8877 1317
55-57 Mitcham Road, SW17, Tel: 0208 767 9849
19 St John's Road, SW11, Tel: 02072284747
124-126 Rushey Green, SE6, Tel: 020 8690 5244

Zaga

map 2

88 Camden High Street, NW1
Tel: 020 7383 5872
Tube: Camden Town
Open: Mon-Sat 10am-6.30pm, Sun 11am-6.30pm

This unassuming shop on Camden High Street offers great value fashion shoes for men and women and a selection of women's bags. On a recent visit they had many items on sale including a pair of trendy Gola suede shoes for £24.99, a pair of smart ladies high heels for £19.99 and a selection of kids' shoes for £9.99 a pair. A great value shoe shop that is always worth a visit if you're in the Camden area.

West

Manolo Blahnik International Ltd

49-51 Old Church Street, SW3
Tel: 020 7352 3863
Tube: South Kensington
Open: Mon-Fri 10am-5.30pm, Sat 10.30am-5pm

A designer shoe shop selling handmade shoes for around £300 a pair. Twice a year, however, usually around the second week of January and July, prices are reduced by at least 50% in one of the season's most anticipated sales. You may find older styles reduced by as much as 70%. Ladies' shoes range from flat and classic styles, to more flamboyant, high-heeled creations. Shoe-loving bargain hunters should make the effort to attend.

Jimmy Choo

27 New Bond Street, W1S
Tel: 020 7493 5858
Website: www.jimmychoo.com
Tube: Bond Street
Open: Mon-Tues, Thurs-Sat 10am-6pm, Wed 10am-7pm, Sun 12noon-5pm

Jimmy Choo are one of the most sought-after brands of ladies shoes which are usually beyond the budget of most women. Fashion conscious bargain hunters should not despair because in the first or second week of January and July the stores have a major sale where you can pick up sexy, high-heeled footwear for 50% below the normal retail price of between £200-£300.

Also at:
32, Sloane Street, SW1X Tel: 020 7823 1051
Selfridges, 400 Oxford Stret, W1A Tel: 020 7318 2326

I Mark

90 Fulham Palace Road, W6
Tel: 020 8748 3947
Tube: Hammersmith
Open: Mon-Sat 9am-6pm

This is a quaint, old-fashioned shop with a carefully prepared window display. Inside the shop specialises in shoes for older folk – rubber-soled corduroy slippers, canvas shoes and sheepskin booties. Those not in their dotage should look out for the plain black and brown men's shoes and no-name brand trainers for £20 and monkey boots and stylish stiletto boots for £15.

Shaukat Fabrics
168-172 Old Brompton Road, SW5
Tel: 020 7373 8956
Tube: Gloucester Road
Open: Mon-Sat 10am-6.30pm
A large fabric outlet with a small but good value range of bags and suitcases. Bargains on a recent visit included quality nylon rucksacks for £11.99 and good quality suitcases from £20. They also sell all sorts of fabric and specialise in cotton (see pages 149 and 186).

Sid's
70 Fulham Palace Road, W6
Tel: 020 8748 4697
Tube: Hammersmith
Open: Mon-Fri 8.30am-5.30pm, Sat 10am-2pm
This key cutting, shoe repair, dry cleaning, trophy and engraving shop also manages to keep a few styles of business/dress Loake men's shoes in stock. They stock seconds with slight defects and these upmarket shoes are sold for half the usual price making a pair of Oxfords just £59.

Travel Zone
128 Uxbridge Road, W12
Tel: 020 8740 9040
Tube: Shepherd's Bush
Open: Mon-Fri 10am-6.30pm, Sat 9.30am-6.30pm

(map 5)

This large store specialises in bags of all kinds at very reasonable prices with basic cloth ruck sacks for just £5 and small leather handbags for only £10. A great value shop just outside Shepherd's Bush tube station.

South

LK Bennett Clearance Store (shoes only)
38b High St, Wimbledon Village, SW19 5AB
Tel: 020 8947 4507
Tube: Wimbledon (then bus)
Open: Mon-Sat 9.30am-6pm, Sun 11am-5pm
Back where it all began, LK Bennett started their shoes and clothing business with a store in the village many years ago and this outlet continues to offer last season's stock of ladies shoes at considerable discounts. The shoes range from evening to casual with prices starting from £19 and going up to £199. Recent offers included kitten heel boots for £89 (originally £199) and satin sling-backs for £29 reduced from £129.

Clarks Factory Shop
61-63 Rye Lane Peckham, SE15
Tel: 020 7732 2530
Rail: Peckham Rye
Open: Mon-Sat 9.30am-5pm

Find end-of-line styles or slightly defective footwear here that can't be sold on the high street. Expect to pay half the usual price with offers such as two pairs of ladies shoes for £25 or three pairs of men's shoes for £40. You can also choose from single pairs of shoes that cost between £22 and £30. The factory shops stock the full range of Clarks' trainers, sandals and dress shoes for kids, women and men. They have some of the latest styles in stock, but the best deals are on discontinued shoes.

Branches at:
113-117 Powis Street, Woolwich, SE18 Tel: 020 8854 3163
Unit 2, 67-83 Seven Sisters Road, N7 Tel: 020 7281 9364
Unit 323-324 Elephant & Castle Shopping Centre, SE1 Tel: 020 7252 6673

East

Blackmans Shoes
22 Cheshire Street, E2
Tel: 07850 883 505
Tube: Liverpool Street
Open: Mon 12noon-5.30pm, Tues-Sat 11.30am-5.30pm, Sun 8am-2pm

Blackmans Shoes has been trading on Cheshire Street for donkeys years. The old couple that used to run the place have retired but the great value shoes and boots and the décor remain the same. The shop might be a little basic but the bargains keep people coming back to the store with Wrangler walking boots for only £24 and Dunlop wellies for just £5. An East End institution well worth seeking out for shoe bargains.

Dreamsport
8-14 Seven Sisters Road, N7
Tel: 020 7700 6999
Open: Mon-Sat 9.30am-6.30pm, Sun 10-5.30pm

Dreamsport is a citywide chain with quite a few bargains amongst the discontinued trainers. The stores stock brands such as Adidas, Nike, Puma and Reebok with prices starting from around £20 and going up to £70 for the latest trainer designs.

Branches at:
180-182 Queensway, W2, Tel: 020 7243 2333
Kings Mall, 25 King Street, W6, Tel: 020 8563 1197
58 Neal Street, WC2H, Tel: 020 7836 5860

Second Tread

261 Hackney Road, E2
Tel: 020 7033 9862
Tube: Liverpool Street or Old Street
Open: Monday to Saturday 9.30am - 5pm

This discount shoe business started trading on Bethnal Green Market over ten years ago but has since acquired a shop on Hackney Road. The stock consists of last season's designs as well as slight seconds and rejects. There are bargains to be found here for both men and women, but it's a good idea to check the shoes before buying as they offer no refunds or exchanges.

Shaw Leather Goods

21 Wentworth Street E1
Tel: 020 7247 4057
Website: www.shawleathergoods.co.uk
Tube: Aldgate/Aldgate East
Open: Daily 9.30am-6.30pm

This store sells a selection of handbags, travel goods and accessories with top-end suitcases from brands such as Samsonite, Delsey and Antler. These supersize suitcases retail from £25 and you can also find large suitcases for £10, lightweight compact umbrellas for £2 and Fiorelli handbags for just £20.

Sport Teck Ltd.

102-105 Whitechapel High Street, E1
Tel: 020 7247 5111
Tube: Aldgate/Aldgate East
Open: Mon-Fri 9.30am-6pm, Sat 10am-5.30pm, Sun 9am-5pm

Sport Teck and Dreamsport were once part of the same chain and still offer a similar range of good value casual footwear from top manufacturers. Prices here go as low as £25, but mostly hover around £55 for a fashionable pair of brand name trainers. During sales Adidas, Nikes and Pumas are among the brands reduced to around £35. They also have a limited range of kids' footwear and some men's and women's dress shoes.
Branches at:
45 Ealing Broadway, W5, Tel: 020 8567 9961.
12 Rye Lane, SE15, Tel: 020 7277 6611

Shoreditch

There are a number of wholesale outlets for good quality designer shoes on Shoreditch High Street. Many of them, such as Barbarella at no 128, Davina at no 133 and Mary Shoes at no 135 are happy to sell on a normal retail basis to individual customers.

Barbarella Shoes
128 Shoreditch High Street, E1
Tel: 020 7739 9283
Tube: Liverpool Street/Shoreditch
Open: Mon-Fri 10am-6pm, Sun 10am-4pm
Barbarella Shoes has been trading since 1978. Despite its name, this shop doesn't trade in futuristic footwear, but stocks a good range of smart shoes for men, women and children at reduced prices. The handmade Italian shoes are a real draw here. Though mainly wholesale, they do offer their knockdown prices to the general public. A pair of elegant high heel shoes goes for as little as £20.

Davina
133 Shoreditch High Street, E1
Tel: 020 7739 2811
Tube: Liverpool Street
Open: Mon-Fri 9.30am-5.30pm, Sun 10.30am-3pm
One of the best of the Shoreditch High Street lot, Davina is an airy, open shop with modern styles and helpful staff. They have got a good range of everyday wear with leather sandals for £14 and ladies knee-high leather boots for £40 (reduced from £60). There are also discount racks where shoes are sold for even greater discounts.
Also at: 45 Wentworth Street, E1. Tel: 020 7247 6629

Mary Shoes
137 Shoreditch High Street, E1
Tel: 020 7739 8537
Tube: Liverpool Street
Open: Mon-Fri 10am-6pm, Sun 10am-3pm
This Italian-run shop stocks a great selection of shoes, boots, bags and accessories from the mother country and displays several posters of Italian sporting and film stars just to make the staff feel at home. The shoes are of a very high standard and there are plenty of bargains to be found including smart men's and women's dress shoes for only £35, men's dress boots for the same price and some fantastic leather bags for £75-85. Probably the best shoe shop in the Shoreditch area.

Dalston

What Shoreditch has in terms of wholesale outlets can be matched by Dalston's range of retail shoe shops. There are easily a dozen on Kingsland Road alone, on the busy stretch near Ridley Road Market. Reviewed below are two of the cheapest:

Gemini Shoes

110 Kingsland High Street, E8
Tel: 020 7254 8264
Open: Mon-Sat 9.30am-6pm

Shoes, boots and sandals for ladies and gents are on offer here. Boots go for about £25 and sandals are as cheap as £10 for synthetic material and £20 for leather. In the summer months they offer a cheaper range of sandals, clogs and jellies for just £5 a pair. The sale rack offers good value with many shoes priced at less than £10. On a lucky day you may find items for £1.

Miss Cardini

122 Kingsland High Street, E8
Tel: 020 7254 1515
Open: Mon-Sat 11am-5pm

Miss Cardini's specialises in sandals and also has a good selection of shoes for men and women with a particularly good choice in larger sizes. The stock is basic and good value with prices starting at £5 and going up to £25 for their smarter footwear. Miss Cardini also do a budget range of handbags to match the shoes.

100...Computers
103...Computer Fairs & Auctions
105...Computer Games
107...Hifi, DVD & TV
112...Miscellaneous
115...Tottenham Court Road

Computers

Buying a computer can be a stressful experience with so many different things to consider and constantly changing technology. The complexity of the task is not helped by pushy sales people, usually very keen to sell you over-priced extended warranties. To avoid being misled it's a good idea to consult computer magazines and get a bit of background information before embarking on your quest. The main decision to make is whether to buy a personal computer (PC) which can be made by a wide range of manufacturers and will almost certainly use Microsoft system software, or to buy an Apple Mac which runs on its own software. The choice is a fundamental one and you should probably ask your computer literate friends about what they use and try out both systems before making your decision. Apple Macs are a little more user-friendly, but the new Microsoft software has progressed in recent years and the differences are now less marked. One advantage of going down the PC route is the availability of PC software and the fact that PCs tend to be significantly cheaper than the equivalent Mac. Below are reviewed some of the best outlets in London to find new and used computer equipment; the shops only deal in PCs unless otherwise stated.

Central

Morgan
64-72 New Oxford Street, WC1
Tel: 020 7255 2115; 0870 120 4930 (internet sales)
012 0145 65565 (mail order)
Website: www.morgancomputers.co.uk
Tube: Tottenham Court Road
Open: Mon-Fri 10am-6.30pm, Sat 10am-6pm, Sun 11am-5pm

Morgan sell surplus, end-of-line and reconditioned PCs at very low prices and often with a full manufacturer's warranty. Recently they had Acer laptops, with 1GB RAM, 120 GB hard disk, DVD writer, and WiFi networking for £446.49, with a 1 year warranty. A great place to get a budget PC, and they also now sell a limited range of digital cameras. Sign up for their monthly flyer with latest stock and prices.

Micro Anvika

245 Tottenham Court Road, W1
Tel: 020 7467 6000 (all Tottenham Court branches)
Website: www.microanvika.com
Tube: Goodge Street/Tottenham Court Road
Open: Mon-Fri 9.30am-7pm, Sat 9.30am-6pm, Sun 11am-5pm

This smart chain of computer stores sells largely Macs and accessories but also a limited range of PCs. They are probably not the cheapest outlet in town, but they are reasonably priced. They have an efficient delivery service and a 6 months interest free credit scheme. Prices for laptops start at £450 and go up to £2000. They usually have special offers; a recent bargain included an HP laptop with 1GB RAM and DVD burner for £500.

Also at:
6-17 Tottenham Court Road W1   Harrods, 87-135 Brompton Road,
53-54 Tottenham Court Road, W1   SW1X, Tel: 020 7893 8259
13 Chenies Street, WC1 (Macs only) Selfridges, 400 Oxford Street, W1A,
*   Tel: 020 7318 3955*

North

BJ Computers Ltd

259 Eversholt Street, NW1
Tel: 020 7383 3444
Website: www.bjcomputer.co.uk
Tube: Mornington Crescent
Open: Mon-Fri 9.30am-6.30pm, Sat 10am-6pm

This small business sells made-to-order PCs as well as upgrades, networking and a repairs service. On a recent visit they were offering an Intel Pentium IV with a 30 GB hard drive, DVD writer, modem, WiFi network and graphics card for £240. They also provide IT maintenance and solutions for small businesses.

Computer Precision Ltd

185 Upper Street, N1
Tel: 020 7359 9797
Tube: Highbury & Islington
Open: Mon-Fri 9.30am-6pm

This place is busy because they offer very competitive quotes for all kinds of computer accessories and hardware. Although they have a limited stock, they can order most items for next day delivery. They also construct their own brand of PCs starting at only £205 (exc VAT).

West

Personal Computer Solutions
52 Northfield Avenue, W13
Tel: 020 8567 3800
Website: www.fixmycomputer.co.uk
Tube: Northfields
Open: Mon-Fri 9am-6pm, Sat 10am-5pm

This small shop has been established for over 15 years, offering their own bespoke PCs, upgrades and repairs. All new goods come with a 1 year guarantee. A good value independent computer outlet. Their services also include office and home networking installation.

South

Modern Computers
171 Old Kent Road, SE1
Tel: 020 7231 1313
Website: www.moderncomputers.com
Tube: Elephant & Castle
Open: Mon-Sat 9am-6pm

This is a good value computer outlet offering brand-new, custom-built and second-hand computers at very competitive prices. Refurbished PCs start at £189, monitors at £25, and laptops for as little as £179. Used goods come with a 3 month warranty and new goods are sold with a full manufacturer's warranty. An excellent place to find PC bargains.

Outer London

Computer Warehouse (Macs only)
1 Amalgamated Drive, West Cross Centre,
Brentford, Middlesex, TW8
Tel: 020 8400 1234
Website: www.computerwarehouse.co.uk
Tube: Boston Manor/Osterley   Rail: Syon Lane
Open: Mon-Fri 9am-5.30pm, Sun 10am-4pm

This large warehouse specialises in Apple Macs and will attempt to match any quote. Brentford is quite a way to travel for most Londoners, but ordering via their order line or the web is relatively painless and they provide an efficient delivery service. An easy and trusted outlet for all the latest Apple hardware and accessories.

Computer Fairs and Auctions

You can buy absolutely anything computer-related at computer fairs. They are great places to pick up bargain parts, accessories and software once you've got your PC or Mac, although it is not advisable to purchase your first actual computer at a fair, simply because after-sales, warranty and repairs are impractical to set up.

British Computer Fairs

UCL Windeyer Building, Cleveland Street, WC2
Tel: 01943 817 300
Website: www.britishcomputerfairs.com
Tube: Goodge Street or Warren Street
Admission charge: £1.50 Adults, £1 Concessions
Open: Every Saturday 10am-5pm

British Computer Fairs is a great opportunity to buy from a wide variety of computer traders selling both new and used equipment. All the traders have power supplies which allows you to see the equipment working before buying. There were also many traders dealing in accessories for computers with bargains such as 20 Verbatum CDs for only £8. BCF aim to provide the same consumer rights as you would find on the high street. To find out about any of the fairs run by BCF, view their website which is regularly updated.

Schools Connect Auction

See full entry in the Auctions section (page 278).

Stratford Computer Fair (Three Gems Ltd)

Carpenters & Dockland Centre, 98 Gibbins Road, Stratford, E15
Tel: 0795 842 8447
Website: www.londoncomputerfairs.com
Tube: Stratford
Open: Sat 10.30am-5.30pm, Sun 10.30am-4pm
Entry: £2 Adults, £1 Children (accompanied children free)

Stratford Computer Fair is one of the largest in the UK and a great place to find computers and accessories at very competitive prices. Tottenham Court Road PC Market is managed by the same company (see p.104).

Tottenham Court Road PC Market (Three Gems Ltd)

Jury's Inn Hotel, 16-22 Great Russell Street, WC1B
Tel:0794 914 3042
Website: www.londoncomputerfairs.com
Tube: Tottenham Court Road, Covent Garden
Open: Sat 10.30am-5pm
Entry: £2 Adults, £1 Children (accompanied children free)

Established over ten years ago Tottenham Court Market is the largest indoor computer fair in Central London. They offer new and second-hand systems, hardware, software and peripherals.

Buying Online

There are several UK-based websites selling machines that have been refurbished and are re-sold at a significant discount with a full warranty.

Data Serve

Tel: 0870 772 2010
Website: www.lowcostcomputer.co.uk

Dell Outlet

Tel: 0870 907 5219
Website: www.euro.dell.com/content/default

Misco

Tel: 0800 038 8880
Website: www.misco.co.uk

RDC

Tel: 0870 774 4777
Website: www.rdc-shop.co.uk

Ink Cartridges and Refills

The Ink Factory

Tel: 0870 7500 710
Website: www.inkfactory.co.uk

This website has a good range of printer cartridges to fit most makes and models of printer. Check out their website for current offers.

Computer Games and Consoles

This is a new section for Bargain Hunters' London, but one that is destined to expand as the computer games market grows. As well as the stores featured below you could also take a look at pawnbrokers such as Cash Converters that usually sell used computer games and consoles (page 362). The community notice board www.gumtree.com is also a good place to find used consoles and games.

Gamestation

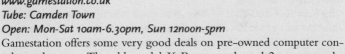

43 Camden High Street, NW1
Tel: 020 7380 0161
Mail Order: 0845 345 0335
www.gamestation.co.uk
Tube: Camden Town
Open: Mon-Sat 10am-6.30pm, Sun 12noon-5pm

Gamestation offers some very good deals on pre-owned computer consoles and games. The old model X-Box console and 2 games can be bought here for only £39.99, while a Playstation 2 console with 2 games was only £49.99. They also stock all the latest console gear, but if you fancy picking up one of the older consoles, there are some fantastic deals to be found.

Branches at:
111 High Street, East Ham, E6
Tel: 020 8472 9128
37 Church Street, EN2
Tel: 020 8363 7297
172-74 High Road, Ilford, IG1
Tel: 020 8514 4034
212 Lewisham High Street, SE13
Tel: 020 8318 6518
31 Chequers Square, Uxbridge, UB8
Tel: 01895 520 051
174 High Street, Walthamstow, E17
Tel: 020 8520 9319
458 High Road, Wembley, HA9
Tel: 020 8795 4737
83 High Street, Wood Green, N22
Tel: 020 8889 1521
112 Powis Street, Woolwich, SE18
Tel: 020 8317 6746

Games Planet

142 Uxbridge Road, W12
Tel: 020 8746 0285
Tube: Shepherd's Bush
Open: Mon–Sat 10am-9pm, Sun 11am-6pm

(map 5)

This small games store is well stocked with all kinds of used computer games for all the major consoles. There are plenty of good deals to be found – particularly if you are in the market for superseded games.

Computer Games Exchange

40 Notting Hill Gate, W11
Tel: 020 7792 9393
Tube: Notting Hill Gate
Open: Daily 10am-8pm

This branch of the Music & Video Exchange group specialises in second-hand computer games. All games formats are stocked with prices varying from £4-18 depending on the age and desirability of the game.

Hi-fi, DVD & TV

There are some great shops in London to find deals on hi-fi equipment, DVD players and TVs but the market is cut-throat and there are always changes in promotions and offers. Listed in this chapter are both new and second-hand outlets for you to choose from with a few high-end retailers included if they have discounted items. If you are buying new it's a good idea to find the best online price using a price comparison site such as moneysupermarket.com and then use that information to beat the price down in-store, particularly at places such as Richer Sounds which guarantee to beat any price. There are several other places to look for cheap electronic equipment including the outlets along Tottenham Court Road (page 115), pawnbrokers (page 361) and several of the Auctions (page 276).

Richer Sounds
Branches at:

258 Fulham Road, SW10
Tel: 020 7352 8496

87-90 Houndsditch, EC3
Tel: 020 7626 8006

29 Bloomsbury Way, WC1
Tel: 020 7831 2888

2 London Bridge Walk, SE1
Tel: 020 7403 1201

25 Northways Parade,
College Crescent, Swiss
Cottage, NW3
Tel: 020 7722 3359

48 East Street, Bromley, BR1
Tel: 020 8466 6565

105 West Ealing Broadway, W13
Tel: 020 8566 4422

Mail order: 087001 12345
www.richersounds.co.uk

The clever way to acquire a good hi-fi is to construct a system from separates as this allows you to choose the best value parts and to upgrade your system at a later date. The best place to buy new hi-fi separates is very likely to be Richer Sounds. It stocks recently discontinued lines at well below the original price, and buys new items direct from the factory. Richer Sounds guarantees to beat rivals' prices by at least £10 and by up to £100 for items over £1,000 (see website for details). Most of their goods are in the middle ground (between £80–£200), but they also have a reasonable selection of the top-notch equipment to keep the hi-fi buffs happy. The recent development in home cinema systems is now reflected in Richer Sounds' copious stock of cinema sound systems with plenty of bargains to be found in HD flat screen televisions. To find out about Richer Sounds latest deals view their website which also offers you the chance to download the most current sales catalogue or join the VIP Club for even better deals.

Musical Images

18 Monmouth Street, WC2
Tel: 020 7497 1346
Website: www.musicalimages.co.uk
Tube: Covent Garden or Leicester Square
Open: Mon-Sat 10am-6pm

(map 1)

This is another high-end hi-fi and television outlet that stocks a wide variety of manufacturers. The general stock is by no means cheap, but there are plenty of discounted ex-demo models that are listed on the website and sold at between 20-25% of the original price. A recent bargain was a set of Kef Q1 ex-demo speakers for £180 (reduced from £250). Well worth checking out if you are looking for top quality hi-fi deals.

Walrus

11 New Quebec Street, W1
Tel: 020 7724 7224
Website: www.walrus.co.uk
Tube: Marble Arch
Open: Mon–Sat 10.30am-5.30pm

This shop is definitely for the music buff with many rare makes and models and an emphasis on equipment such as turntables and traditional amplifiers containing valves. If you are looking for something cheap and cheerful then this is not the place to visit, but there are still plenty of upmarket bargains such as Deuvel Planet loudspeakers for £599 (reduced from £799). A wonderful shop.

North

Audio Gold
308-310 Park Road, N8
Tel: 020 8341 9007
Website: www.audiogold.co.uk
Tube: Finsbury Park then W7 bus
Open: Mon-Sat 10.30am-6.30pm

This shop has a fantastic selection of used and collectable hi-fi equipment all sold at reasonable prices. There are lots of very fine pieces of vintage hi-fi equipment but the shop also does a lot of business putting together second-hand systems for as little as £150. The website is great to look at and gives an idea of what the shop stocks at the higher price bracket, but it's a good idea to give them a call if you're looking for a bargain. They also serve cappuccino and have a large stock of vinyl.

Audio T
159a Chase Side, Enfield, Middx EN2
Tel: 020 8367 3132
Website: www.audio-t.co.uk
Rail: Enfield Chase
Open: Tues-Sat 9.30am-5.30pm

A store that stocks amplifiers for over £3,000 may not seem a good place to find bargains, but they offer to match any price on the same item and they also have a selection of ex-display items. The website is excellent and lists all the current offers.

Blue Audio Visual

(map 3)

44 Duncan Street, N1
Tel: 020 7713 6865
Website: www.blueaudiovisual.co.uk
Tube: Angel
Open: Mon-Sat 10am-7pm, Sun 12noon-6pm

This established outlet has moved in recent years from Upper Street to its present more discreet address on Duncan Street. It is still a good place to track down used hi-fi, camera, video, film and music equipment. The stock ranges from budget domestic to high-end professional equipment. A recent bargain was a hardly used Tivoli Model Two radio for only £100 which retails for £150 in other outlets. Blue is particularly strong on musical equipment with lots of synthesisers and studio mixers as well as traditional electric guitars. They are also one of the few outlets in London that sell 16mm and Super 8 film and equipment.

Satellite Electronics

104 Cricklewood Broadway, NW2
Tel: 020 8450 0272
Tube: Cricklewood
Open: Mon-Sat 9.30am-7pm

A well-ordered shop offering reconditioned TVs, DVDs and even some video machines. The prices are very low with a Hitachi 14" starting from £40 and going up to £200 for a 32" Philips widescreen. The DVD players are also great value with prices starting from only £20. Any item under £100 gets a 6 month guarantee, anything over that price a full year.

Shantel AV Ltd

11-13 Long Lane, Finchley, N3
Tel: 020 8371 6671
Website: www.shantelav.co.uk
Tube: Finchley Central
Open: Mon-Sat 10am-6pm

This local electrical outlet offers great value for a wide range of electronic goods such as hi-fis and TVs. Recently they were offering a 32" Sony LCD TV for only £550 (reduced from £800) and there are always similar good deals to be found here along with the excellent service and advice. Give them a call or visit their website to find out about the latest offers.

Superfi London

2 Camden High Street, NW1
Tel: 020 7388 1300
Website: www.superfi.co.uk
Tube: Mornington Crescent
Open: Mon-Sat 10am-6pm

This shop is the only London branch of a chain of 19 stores, and offers a great selection of new quality hi-fi separates. There are always discounts available for special promotions and clearance stock. Among the bargains on a recent visit was an Audio Lab 800 AV Pack (surround sound system) for £1,500 (reduced from £2,500) and a set of Kef KHT 1005 speakers for £299 (reduced from £500).

TV4U

115 Cricklewood Broadway, NW2

map 4

Tel: 020 8450 9598

Tube: Cricklewood

Open: Mon-Sat 9am-7pm

This small shop offers reconditioned televisions, videos, DVDs and a selection of new hi-fi systems. The demand for flat screen TVs has had an impact but they are still doing a reasonable business by offering bargains such as a reconditioned conventional 21" Sanyo TV for only £55, and a Sanyo 28" for £99. The shop also sells new DVD players with a Toshiba multi-region machine for only £65. Guarantees depend on the item you're buying, and go up to a full year on new items.

West

X Electrical

125 King Street, W6

map 5

Tel: 020 8563 7383

Website: www.xelectrical.com

Tube: Hammersmith

Open: Mon-Sat 10am-6pm

A second-hand music and home entertainment shop selling anything from studio equipment to digital cameras. X Electrical is a particularly good place for budding musicians to find second-hand things like synths, mics and mixers with plenty of unusual items showing up that would be difficult to find anywhere else. There is also enough here to appeal to less musical members of the public looking for good deals on domestic electronic equipment such as hi-fis and games consoles.

Branches at:

4 Station Buildings, Fife Road, Kingston KT1, Tel: 020 8546 1233

43 Church Street, Croydon CR0, Tel: 020 8680 0007

Open: Mon-Sat 10am-6pm, Sun 11am-4pm

Miscellaneous

The shops reviewed here are difficult to classify, but very useful for those looking for blank audio and video tapes, batteries and CDs. All the stores featured also sell smaller electronic items, with Maplin offering a particularly wide range of goods. KVJ Fairdeal is the cheapest and the best of the lot and now has a thriving online business which might be worth using if you can't make it all the way to Whitechapel.

KVJ Fairdeal
76 Whitechapel High Street, E1
Tel: 020 7247 6029
Website: www.totalblankmedia.com
Tube: Aldgate East
Open: Mon-Fri 9.30am-6pm, Sat 9.30am-1.30pm

map 12

KVJ is the best place in town to buy cheap CDs, DVDs, batteries, memory cards, ink cartridges and even sticky tape. Although a small shop, it sells vast quantities via mail order and this allows it to keep prices lower than anywhere in town. Among the recent bargains were 1GB Fuji Film compact flash cards for only £8.74, 50 Datawrite DVD-R disks for only £7.50 and a pack of 100 sheets of matt photo paper for only £3.50. The only disadvantage is that they do not accept credit or debit cards, so you will need to bring cash or cheque book and card. This problem is solved when you shop from their easy to use website which does accept cards and contains all the stock to be found at the Whitechapel shop. Ordering online does incur a £7.50 delivery charge, but with so many discounted goods this cost is easily covered by the savings you will make.

Maplin Electronics

186 Edgware Road, Marble Arch, W2
Tel: 020 7723 6641 / 0870 264 6000 (national order line)
Website: www.maplin.co.uk
Tube: Marble Arch
Open: Mon-Fri 9am-8pm, Sat 9am-6pm, Sun 11am-5pm (times vary from store to store)

This chain of electronics stores sells all kinds of electronic goods from satellite navigation systems to computer accessories with prices considerably below most high street rivals and regular promotions. Recent bargains included computer tool kits for £9.99 (half-price), printer cartridge refill kits for £14.99 (reduced by £8), high spec GPS with MP3 for only £99.99 and 50 Verbatim CDs for only £14.99 (half-price). There are Maplin stores all over London from where you can pick up their latest sales catalogue and the website is also a good place to shop or view their product range.

Branches at:
120-124 King Street, Hammersmith W6; 52-54 High Holborn WC1; 15-23 Parkway, Camden NW1; 166-168 Queensway W2; 218-219 Tottenham Court Road W1; 6-10 Great Portland Street W1; 1-3 Camomile Street, Bishopsgate EC3 (View website for other stores).

Stanley Productions

147 Wardour Street, W1
Tel: 020 7494 4545 / 7439 0311
Website: www.stanleyproductions.co.uk
Tube: Piccadilly Circus/Tottenham Court Road
Open: Mon-Fri 9am-5.30pm
Catalogue available

This company is based in the heart of Soho and caters to the needs of the film and media industry whose offices are also located in the area. They offer lots of good deals on video and audio tapes, CDs and other forms of data storage. They also sell a wide range of TVs, video recorders and video cameras as well as providing a data transfer service for those wanting to copy CDs or VHS tapes. View their website to download one of their extensive catalogues.

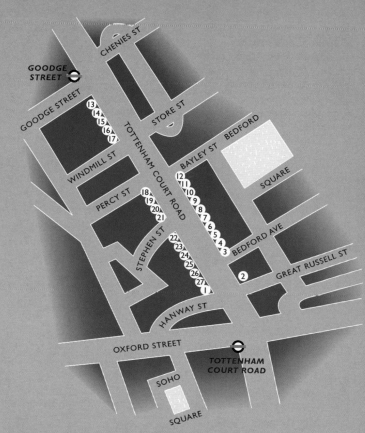

1) Micro Anvika
2) Hi-Fi Surplus Store
3) MBA
4) Microworld 2000
5) Kamla
6) ask
7) Shyamtronics
8) Micro Anvika
9) MBA
10) Shasonic
11) n-genious
12) Harp Electronics
13) Micro Anvika
14) Gultronics
15) Epsilon Computers
16) Sunrise Digital
17) GHS Technology
18) The Digital Centre
19) C&A Electronics
20) Spatial Audio & Video
21) PNR Audiovision
22) Samuel King
23) Microworld
24) Sony Centre
25) Musical Vision
26) Brains
27) Arena Electronics

Tottenham Court Road

Tube: Tottenham Court Road & Goodge Street
Open: Mon-Sat 9am-6pm, (some stores open Sunday)

This busy West End street has more electronics stores than anywhere else in London and it is therefore an excellent place to visit to find electronic bargains. Many of the shops house not one business but several trading under one roof from different counters, so you will find one company selling hi-fi equipment and another digital cameras. All this is not particularly relevant for the casual visitor to TCR, but it does explain the restless nature of the place with businesses frequently changing hands in a very competitive environment. The best way to find a good deal is by visiting each store in turn and bartering the price down; it usually takes about an hour of wandering from store to store before you get a price that makes retailers blanche and refuse to go any lower. In the course of your travels you will probably find a number of superseded models which are on special offer and these are often a great deal.

Main Stores on Tottenham Court Road

Hi-Fi Surplus Store

260 Tottenham Court Road, W1
Tel: 020 7323 6712

Micro Anvika

245 Tottenham Court Road, W1
Tel: 020 7467 6000
6-17 Tottenham Court Road, W1
53-54 Tottenham Court Road, W1
245 Tottenham Court Road, W1
13 Chenies Street, W1 (Mac dedicated)

MBA

243 Tottenham Court Road, W1
Tel: 020 7636 7685
Branch at: 257-258 Tottenham Court Road, W1

Microworld 2000

254-6 Tottenham Court Road, W1
Tel: 020 7580 6460
Branches at:
26 Tottenham Court Road, W1
Tel: 020 7636 5234

Kamla

251 Tottenham Court Road, W1
Tel: 020 7323 2747
Website: www.askdirect.co.uk

ask

248 Tottenham Court Road, W1
Tel: 020 7637 0353 / 0590
Website: www.askdirect.co.uk

Shyamtronics

246 Tottenham Court Road, W1
Tel: 020 7637 1961/ 1990

Shasonic Megastore
241-2 Tottenham Court Road, W1
Tel: 0845 634 0333

n-genious
239-240 Tottenham Court Road, W1
Tel: 020 7631 2020

Harp
237-38 Tottenham Court Road, W1
Tel: 020 7636 4611
Website: www.askdirect.co.uk

Arena Electronics
18 Tottenham Court Road, W1
Tel: 020 7580 5380

Brains Hi-Fi & Video
19 Tottenham Court Road, W1
Tel: 020 7631 1109

Musical Vision
20-21 Tottenham Court Road, W1
Tel: 0845 634 0320

Sony Centre Galleria
22-24 Tottenham Court Road, W1
Tel: 0845 634 0350

Samuel King
27 Tottenham Court Road, W1
Tel: 020 7580 2727

PNR
28 Tottenham Court Road, W1
Tel: 0845 634 0310

Spatial Audio & Video
29 tottenham Court Road, W1
Tel: 020 7637 8702

C & A Electronics
37 Tottenham Court Road, W1
Tel: 020 7436 2628

The Digital Centre
38 Tottenham Court Road, W1
Tel: 020 7323 5441

GHS Technology
47 Tottenham Court Road, W1
Tel: 020 7436 8200

Sunrise Digital
48 Tottenham Court Road, W1
Tel: 020 7323 5510

Epsilon Computers
49A Tottenham Court Road, W1
Tel: 020 7436 8393

Gultronics
52 Tottenham Court Road, W1
Tel: 020 7580 2931

118…Contact Lenses & Glasses
125…Haircare & Cosmetics
128…Hairdressing

Health & Beauty

Contact Lenses & Glasses

Central

20/20 Optical Store

216-217 Tottenham Court Road, W1
Tel: 020 7596 2020
Website: www.20-20.co.uk
Tube: Goodge Street
Open: Mon-Fri 9am-8pm, Sat 9am-7pm, Sun 11.30am-6pm

This modern and busy West End optician stocks a great range of frames and lenses. Besides offering interest-free credit, they also have great offers on frames from brand names such as Donna Karan and Hugo Boss. Contact lens wearers get one-year's aftercare service when paying by direct debit. They always have special deals and were recently offering a second pair of glasses for 50% discount or a second pair of glasses free with purchases over £150.

Spex in the City

1 Short Gardens, WC2H
Tel: 020 7240 0243
Website: www.spexinthecity.com
Tube: Covent Garden
Open: Mon-Fri 11am-6.30pm, Sat 11am-6pm, Sun 1-5pm

map
1

This small but stylish shop offers great value designer specs and even has its own range of designs that are unique to the shop. A pair of designer frames and lenses start from as little as £150 and there is always a tray of designer frames reduced to clear. Prescription designer sunglasses start from only £150 a pair and if you mention the website an eye test is only £20.

Specsavers Opticians

6-17 Tottenham Court Road, W1
Tel: 020 7580 5115
Website: www.specsavers.co.uk
Tube: Goodge Street
Open: Mon-Fri 10am-8pm, Sat 10am-7pm, Sun 10am-6pm

Plenty of attractive frames for £75 as well as Specsavers' cheapest range of £39 frames and some designer styles that go for about £125. They often offer deals like two pairs for the price of one so it's worth checking what's on offer. The downside is you will probably have to spend more than £75 to be entitled to their promotions. Check their website for the locations of the 23 other London branches.

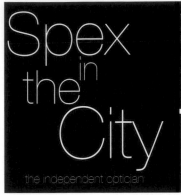

University Vision

University of London Union Building, Malet Street, WC1
Tel: 020 7636 8925
Tube: Euston Square
Open: Mon-Fri 9am-5.30pm

The stock here runs the gamut from cheap and cheerful to expensive designer frames. They usually offer some sort of deal involving frames and lenses for less than £50.

Vision Express

263-265 Oxford Street, W1
Tel: 020 7409 7880
Website: www.visionexpress.co.uk
Tube: Oxford Circus
Open: Mon-Sat 9.30am-8pm, Sun 12noon-6pm

Obviously, the emphasis here is on quick service. They stock a large variety of designer frames and often offer two for one specials when spending over £79. Prices for frames start from £39, with designer frames from £150. If you want a reasonably priced frame with good lenses you'll pay about £190 for the package. They also do speciality eyewear like swimming goggles and offer 15% discount for students.

Also at:
Whiteley Centre, Queens Way, Bayswater W2, Tel: 020 7727 1888
Brent Cross Shopping Centre NW4, Tel: 020 8202 6715
Canada Square, Canary Wharf E14, Tel: 020 7513 2408
324 High Road, Chiswick W4, Tel: 020 8994 6534
82 The Broadway Centre, Ealing W5, Tel: 020 8840 1880
37-39 High Holborn WC1, Tel: 020 7831 2670

Camden Contact Lens Centre

North

Camden Contact Lens Centre

(map 2)

32-36 Camden High Street, NW1
Tel: 020 7383 3838
Website: www.camdenopticians.co.uk
Tube: Camden Town
Open: Mon to Fri 9.30am-6.30pm, Sat 9am-5pm, Sun 11am-4pm

This shop offers great value contact lenses plus quick and efficient service. Good deals include 3 months' supply of Bausch & Lomb daily contact lenses for only £65. The shop also has a good range of prescription spectacles and sunglasses with offers like free lenses with every pair of designer frames and 25% off all designer sunglasses including top names such as Gucci, Prada and Ray-Ban.

The Eye Warehouse

104 Regents Park Road, N3
Website: www.theeyewarehouse.co.uk
Tel: 020 8346 1999
Tube Finchley Central or Golders Green and Bus
Open: Mon-Fri 9.30am-6pm, Sun 10am-4pm

This company offers fantastic value designer frames with single vision prescription lenses from only £39. They stock hundreds of frames from names such as DKNY, Armani, Hugo Boss and Moschino and if you don't care about the name they offer budget frames and lenses for only £20. The contact lenses are also great value with a years supply of Bausch & Lomb daily lenses for only £235. A great value opticians – view their website or give them a call to find out about their latest offers.

West

Optical World

166 Uxbridge Road, W12
Tel: 020 8740 7100
Tube: Shepherd's Bush
Open: Mon-Fri 9am-5.30pm, Sat 9am-3pm

Optical World is a small shop offering a reasonable range of spectacles. The most keenly priced plastic frames sell for around £35-£40. They also have competitively priced contact lenses and offer discounts for the over 60s. The owner claims any customer visiting his store with a copy of Bargain Hunters' London will be entitled to a 25% discount.

East

Bleetman Opticians
347 Bethnal Green Road, E2
Tel: 020 7739 2356
Tube: Bethnal Green
Open: Mon-Sat 9.15am-5.15pm

This friendly opticians stocks the full spectrum from cheap to more expensive designer frames. Chunky plastic frames will set you back at least £15 while more delicate metal frames start from £20 with designer frames starting at £89. They offer a computer imaging system that allows customers to see their faces with a variety of different frame styles.

New Era Optical
114 High Street, E17
Tel: 020 8509 1935
Tube: Walthamstow Central
Open: Thu-Sat 9.30am-5pm

54 Leather Lane, EC1
Tel: 020 7405 0618
Tube: Chancery Lane
Open: Mon-Fri 9.30am-5.30pm

This family business has many loyal customers acquired over years of good service, competitive prices and a good range of stylish frames. Plastic frames start at £29.50 and the cheapest metal frames are £39.50. Some of the better metal frames go for as little as £49-£59. The Leather Lane branch is much bigger and has better opening hours than the Walthamstow store.

Outer London

Mr Scher's Spectacle Shop
278 High Road, Loughton, IG10
Tel: 020 8508 5852
Tube: Loughton
& 4 Jubilee Parade, Snakes Lane East, Woodford Green, IG8
Tel: 020 8504 9243
Tube: Woodford
Open Mon-Sat 9.30am-5pm, closed 1pm-2pm (both branches)
This family-run business supplies excellent frames at low prices. Plastic
frames start at £20, lighter metal frames cost from £59 a pair, while
designer frames start at £100 and go up to £300. Daily wear contact
lenses run from £85 for a three-month supply. The opticians do both
NHS and private care.

Online shopping

The following grocery retailers offer excellent deals and will save you up to 30% on high street prices. Ordering is simple and can be done online or over the telephone, but best deals are found on their websites. Procedures for ordering are similar at all stores. Before placing an order you will need a prescription from your optician. Once you have registered you will need to send a copy of your prescription by fax, post or email. All deliveries are free of charge and will take from five to ten days. The downsides include the minimum purchase of a three months' supply and the devastating impact supermarkets will have on local opticians.

ASDA

Website: www.asda-contactlenses.co.uk
Tel: 0845 366 6998
Email: customerservices@asda-contactlenses.co.uk
ASDA offer a selection of brands, such as Bausch & Lomb, CIBA Vision and Johnson & Johnson. The cheapest deal is a three-month supply of ASDA's brand name lenses for £52.50. They also have designer sunglasses and swimming goggles.

Sainsbury's

Website: www.sainsburyscontactlenses.co.uk
Tel: 0845 7078 332
Email: customerservices@sainsburycontactlenses.co.uk
Sainsbury's offer all the major brands of contact lenses.
Prices start at £54.90 for a three months' supply of Focus Dailies. Ordering is best done online, as there is an additional £5 charge on purchases made over telephone. Once you have registered and ordered Sainsbury's also offer a 20% discount on contact lens aftercare at D & A opticians.

Tesco

Website: www.tescoopticians.com
239/241 High Street, Watford, Herts WD1 2BD
Tel: 0845 601 3479
Email: help@tescoopticians.com
Tesco offer a three-month supply of Bausch & Lomb daily lenses for £54 and CIBA Vision dailies for £63. Tesco also have in-store opticians where you can have an eye test done and order lenses. However, you will save 5% by ordering online.

Haircare & Cosmetics

Below are featured many of the best value cosmetic and haircare outlets in London, but remember to check out the high street stores such as Superdrug and Boots for temporary seasonal knock-down prices and two-for-the-price-of-one offers. Body Shop's £1 sale in the new year is particularly good for bargain cosmetics. London's street markets are also good places to find cheap cosmetics and hair products – Shepherd's Bush, North End Road and Whitechapel markets are particularly good for these types of bargains.

Central

Beauty Base

Unit C3 – Ground floor, Whiteley's Centre, 151 Queensway, W2
Tel: 0207 229 5600
Tube: Queensway, Bayswater
Website: www.beautybase.com
Open: Mon-Sat 10am-8pm, Sun 12pm-6pm

The Beauty Base has four branches in the London area and is a good place to look for discounted designer fragrances with names such as Prada, Christian Dior and Burberry among their stock. Discounts vary depending on the season, but great deals on perfume and cosmetic kits are available all year round.

Also at:
Unit 1 42/A The Broadway Centre, Ealing Broadway, W5.
Tel: 020 8579 8223
17 Treaty Centre, Hounslow, TW3. Tel: 020 8572 1206
Unit 18, Elmsleigh Centre, Staines, TW 18. Tel: 017 84445 9769.

Sally Hair and Beauty Supplies

(map 1)

81 Shaftesbury Avenue, W1
Tel: 020 7434 0064
Website: www.sallybeauty.co.uk
Tube: Leicester Square
Open: Mon-Sat 8am-8pm, Sun 11am-5pm

This shop serves the salon industry, but is open to the public for most purchases. Find all kinds of beauty products from lipsticks to manicure kits at very competitive prices. Hairdressers are well catered for with an outstanding range of permanent hair colours, extensions and accessories. There are ten branches in London, see their website for details.

North

Top Value Drug Store
23 Temple Fortune Parade,
Finchley Road, NW11
Tel: 020 8905 5448
Tube: Golders Green
Open: Mon-Sat 8.30am-6pm, Sun 9.30am-1.30pm

Small family-run business just north of Golders Green, which regularly undercuts neighbouring supermarkets and chemists on some, but not all, brands of toiletries and household goods. Their stock includes sunscreens, haircare products, film, cleaning materials, picture frames and even bakeware. The store always has special offers making it one of the best places to hunt down toiletry bargains.

East

Beauty Collection
85 Whitechapel High Street, E1
Tel: 020 7375 2612
Tube: Aldgate East
Open: Mon-Fri 10am-6.30pm, Sat-Sun 10am-4pm

This dinky little shop is mainly a wholesale outfit but welcomes retail trade. Beauty Collection stocks cosmetics and offers a large selection of fragrances for both men and women. A 100ml bottle of Iceberg perfume goes for £9.99 (original price £48) and a 100 ml bottle of Calvin Klein's Provocation can be found for £29.99. The store also has regular clearance sales when prices are cut even further. We recently found designer sunglasses on sale at half price including a trendy pair of Dolce & Gabanna sunglasses.

East End Cosmetics

131 Middlesex Street, E1
Tel: 020 7626 4015
Tube: Liverpool Street
Open: Mon-Fri 9.30am-5.30pm, Sun 9am-4pm

Bustling on Sundays when the market is open, East End Cosmetics draws the ladies in with booming speakers on the pavement advertising the amazing bargains. An excellent selection of ethnic hair accessories lines one wall, and others are filled with brand name perfume at half-price, make-up displays and hair colouring kits. Find a selection of perfume from £1 and designer names such as Elizabeth Arden 5th Avenue for £14.99. Revlon and Max Factor nail polish go for £1 and L'Oreal body cream was marked down from £30.99 to £6.99. This place has by far the biggest selection and best prices in the area.

Silverfields Chemist

141 Homerton High Street, E9
Tel: 020 8985 2030
Rail: Homerton
Open: Mon-Wed, Fri 9am-7pm, Thurs & Sat 9am-6pm

This dispensing chemist is a great place to come for discounted brand name perfumes and aftershaves. Most perfumes are sold at a 50% discount. Men can find a 30ml bottle of Calvin Klein's CK1 eau de toilette for £14.99 and a 50ml bottle of Christian Dior eau de toilette for £24.99. Women are well catered for as well with bargains such as a 30ml bottle of Estée Lauder eau de toilette for £14.99 and Moschino for £9.99. Iceberg perfume was marked down from £48 to £7.99.

South Molton Drug Store

53 Roman Road, E2
Tel: 020 8981 5040
Tube: Bethnal Green
Website: www.southmoltondrugstore.co.uk
Open: Tues, Thurs 9.30am-5.30pm, Mon, Wed,
Fri 10am-5.30pm, Sat 9.30am-6pm

Don't expect a load of help or young women attacking you with brushes and powder. This unassuming shop specialises in discounts on end-of-lines from major cosmetic houses like Christian Dior, Estée Lauder and Max Factor. The best discounts are on Revlon cosmetics and Elizabeth Arden products. We found Revlon lipstick for £1, polish for £1.50 and Elizabeth Arden foundation for £5.99 and cream for £8.99. Their selection of hair brushes and blusher brushes are also very popular with customers.

Hairdressing

This chapter reviews many of the places in London where you can get a cheap or free haircut by having the job done by a student hairdresser. This is not as risky as it sounds as the students tend to be very careful and there is a qualified hairdresser to help out if problems arise. The opening hours listed are specifically for model/trainee haircuts only. Models should also bear in mind that cuts or colouring can take up to three hours at the hairdressing schools since students tend be slower and more meticulous.

Central

Nicky Clarke

130 Mount Street, W1
Tel: 020 7499 9023
Website: www.nickyclarke.com
Tube: Bond Street/Green Park
Open: Tues, Wed (5pm for colour; 6pm for cuts)

Trainee hairdressers, supervised by a stylist (sometimes even Nicky Clarke himself), can cut and colour your hair during one of the training sessions at this sleek salon. Book your appointment at least three weeks in advance. Colour costs £20 and a cut is £10.

John Frieda

75 New Cavendish Street, W1
Tel: 020 7436 3979/ 02076361401
Tube: Great Portland Street/Oxford Circus
Website:www.johnfieda.co.uk
Open: Wed-Thurs from 6pm

John Frieda is famous as a celebrity stylist and even worked on Halle Berry's Oscar night coiffure. To take advantage of the style expertise at this salon, you need to book in advance for their model evenings. Occasionally, it's possible to get same day service. A basic cut costs £10, colouring starts at £20.

Also at:
4 Aldford Street, W1. Tel: 020 7491 0840

Daniel Galvin

42-44 George Street, W1
Tel: 020 7486 9661 / 02070343096
Website: www.danielgalvin.com
Tube: Baker Street/Bond Street
Open: Tues-Wed 6pm-9pm by appointment

This salon is the place to get your hair coloured on the cheap during one of its model evenings. Daniel Galvin is renowned for his colouring techniques and his trainees (supervised by a teacher) can give a basic cut for £10, half a head of highlights for £35, a tint for £20 or vegetable colour for £25. You will need to book three weeks in advance.

Andrew Jose

1 Charlotte Street, W1T
Tel: 0207 323 4679
Tube: Goodge Street/Tottenham Court Road
Website: www.andrewjose.com
Open: Mon-Tues, 9.30am-7pm

Clients are not restricted to odd hours at this very busy salon, but you do need to ring a couple of days in advance to make an appointment. There are discounts of 50% on Mondays and Tuesdays when recently qualified stylists are working on speed practice with models. A basic cut will cost around £10, full head colouring £20.

Macmillan

33 Endell Street, WC2
Tel: 020 7240 4973
Website: www.macmillan-london.co.uk
Tube: Covent Garden
Open: Mon-Fri from 7pm

This trendy salon is home to Kene Franklin's 'invisible layers' technique that makes your hair look one length whilst adding volume and texture. Popular with celebrities for its full-price cuts, bargain hunters can book in for a trainee session for free at Factory, the academy here. More complicated cuts may require you to pay £10 and colouring by trainees can be done for about £30. A free cut is subject to the styles trainees are working on at the moment of booking. On a recent visit a short layer cut was the only option. You can also have your hair done by a junior stylist for £35. In this case you will need to drop in for a consultation before booking an appointment.

Health & Beauty • Hairdressing

129

Mr Toppers

148 Charing Cross Road, WC2
Tel: 020 7240 4744
Tube: Tottenham Court Road/Leicester Square
Open: Daily 10am-8.30pm

The flagship salon of this cut-rate hairdresser has the longest opening hours and the most chairs. Most of the stylists have trained at London's best salons and some have completed training academy courses elsewhere. A minimum of five years experience is required of all stylists. A simple cut (no washing) will cost £6, but be aware you may have to pay the standard price of £10 for a wash and cut if your hair is "difficult" (i.e. curly, long or big). Prices are low because the turnover is high. No appointments are necessary, but don't expect a cutting-edge style.

Also at:
14 Moor Street, (off Cambridge Circus) WC2, Tel: 020 7434 4088
13a Great Russell Street WC1, Tel: 020 7631 3233
61 Tottenham Court Road, W1, Tel: 020 7636 9966
160 Tottenham Court Road, W1, Tel: 020 7388 2601
80 Camden High Street NW1, Tel: 020 738
48 Goodge Street W1, Tel: 020 7436 1380

Toni & Guy

28, Kensington Church Street, W8
Tel: 020 7937 0030
Website: www.toniandguy.co.uk
Tube: High Street Kensington
Open: Appointments Tues 9.30am, 1.30-5.30pm

Toni & Guy hairdressing salons are famous worldwide for their trend-setting styles. Save money by going to one of their training sessions where beginner students practice on cutting and colouring under the supervision of a professional stylist. Before booking an appointment you will have to drop in for a consultation. A deposit of £10 is required, which is the cost of the cut. Colouring is done once a month and costs £25-£35. There are several branches in London, check their website to see where your local salon is.

Toni & Guy Advanced Academy

75 New Oxford Street, WC1
Tel: 020 7836 0606
Website: www.toniandguy.co.uk
Tube: Tottenham Court Road
Open: Appointments Mon-Fri 9.30am or 1.45pm

This is the advanced academy with the focus on trend setting and innovation so expect a complete change of style. The cost of a cut is £5, colouring is £20, but can occasionally be free if the funky cut requires colour to emphasize it. Don't expect to have any input into your new style, but do expect something trendy, original and head turning. Book a week in advance.

Trevor Sorbie

27 Floral Street, WC2
0870 920 1103
Website: www.trevorsorbie.com
Tube: Covent Garden/Leicester Square
Open: Mon-Tues 9am-7pm, Wed 9am-8pm,
Thurs- Fri 9am-8.30pm

A practically unbeatable price, the colouring and cuts are free. Assistants supervised by teachers will style your hair for you, but the whole procedure costs an investment of time. Basically, you put your name on a waiting list and, depending on the style wanted and the students' availability, you will be booked for an appointment. The wait could be from one week to six months.

Vidal Sassoon Advanced Academy

20 Grosvenor Street, W1
Tel: 020 7491 0030
Website: www.vidalsassoon.co.uk
Tube: Bond Street
Open: Appointments Mon-Fri 9.30am or 1.30pm

Vidal Sassoon has three schools just off Bond Street. Each one specialises in a different look. The advanced academy is the most innovative of the salons and is looking for models that are between 15–35 years old. Be prepared for a very high fashion, cutting-edge look. Cuts and colour are complimentary, but subject to availability and you must book in advance. Cutting is by fully trained staff as opposed to trainees and will cost around £11.

Health & Beauty ● Hairdressing

Vidal Sassoon Master Academy
48 Brooke Street, W1
Tel: 020 7399 6903
Tube: Bond Street
Open: Appointments Mon-Fri 9.30am or 1.30pm
This salon works on the same principle as the Advanced Academy meaning that you should be in the market for an avant-garde restyle. However, this school does less daring cuts than the Advanced Academy and you are welcome to have an input in your final style and bring along a photo of what you want.

Vidal Sassoon School
56-58 Davies Mews, W1
Tel: 020 7399 6901
Tube: Bond Street
Open: Appointments Mon-Fri 9.30am or 1.30pm
Students from around the globe come here to learn the secrets of Vidal Sassoon. Occasionally, you can find a voucher in Metro or The Evening Standard. Otherwise, prices are as follows: £11 for a cut, students £4.50, OAPs and unemployed £6.50. Colouring costs £17.50 for basic colour; a half-head of highlights will set you back £35; and a perm is only £5.50. This is the most traditional of the schools, a good salon if you want a simple trim or bob. Like the Academy, you are welcome to have an input in your final style and bring along a photo of what you want. Book two weeks in advance.

North

Cutting Bar
27b Islington High Street (on White Lion Street), N1
Tel: 020 7278 8720
Tube: Angel
Open: Mon-Sat 10am-7pm, Sun 11am-5
Drop into this wee salon to get a quick cut for £5. If you want a shampoo or styling with a blow-dry, the price skyrockets to £10 or £25 depending on hair length. In an innovative move, you provide the colouring product (you can have someone take you to nearby Boots or Superdrug to pick one out) and they do the colouring for £10. Highlights cost £30-£45 and they provide the chemicals. No appointment needed.
Also at:
23-25 Queensway W2, Tel: 020 7727 9594

Supreme Hair Design

10-12 West Green Road, N15
Tel: 020 8800 7459
Tube/Rail: Seven Sisters
Open: Mon-Thurs 9.30am-5.30pm, Fri 9.30am-7.30pm,
Sat 8.30am-5.30pm

This salon specialises in Afro hair, but also works on European hair. Hair relaxing costs from £32 and a trim is a paltry £7. Colouring a whole head or highlights is from £18 and tinting roots is £35. These bargain prices are for the salon and if you have more time and less money, prices are about 30% cheaper if you book in with one of the six students who train here. There is also a discount of 10% for students and 20% for senior citizens.

West

L'Oréal Technical Centre

255 Hammersmith Road, W6
Tel: 020 8762 4292
Tube: Hammersmith
Open: Appointments Mon-Fri 9.30am, 1.30pm-4.30pm

L'Oréal Technical Centre is a large training school and is always looking for different types of models. You need to drop in to register and let them know what you want done. They will book you into a class that is working on the particular style you are after. The first appointment is free. From then on the basic haircut costs £8-10, colouring (plain tint) £10-13. Trainees are not novices but do have more experience in cutting than in colouring.

136...Bathrooms
143...Beds & Bedding
151...Carpets, Rugs & Tiles
160...Curtains
167...DIY & Equipment
175...Domestic Appliances
181...Fabrics & Haberdashery
191...Furniture
200...Kitchenware
205...Picture Frames & Mirrors

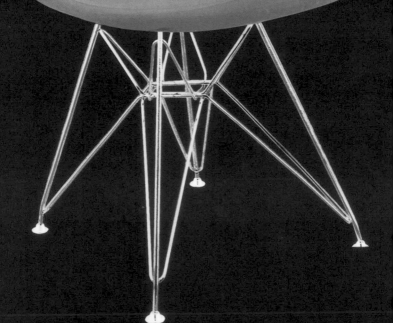

Bathrooms

This chapter reviews many of the good value specialist bathroom outlets in London. It's a good idea to phone a few of these places – with many of the shops offering to match any price you may be able to get a further discount. Builders' merchants (see page 167) are also worth checking out as many of them have a competitively-priced bathroom department.

North

British Bathroom Centre
Oxgate House Oxgate Lane, NW2
Tel: 020 8453 7000
Website: www.britishbathroomcentre.com
Tube: Brent Cross / Neasden
Open: Mon-Fri 9am-6pm, Sat-Sun 10am-4pm
This massive warehouse offers a wide variety of bathroom suites extending over three floors. British Bathroom Centre may seem expensive but they offer a wide range of styles and complete suites start from £290 (inc VAT). There is a delivery charge of between £15 and £30 in the London area.
Also at:
Islington Showroom, 537-541 Holloway Road, N19, 020 7561 1791

Chris Stephens Ltd
545-561 Holloway Road N19
Tel: 020 7272 1228
Tube: Holloway
Open: Mon-Fri 7am-6pm, Sat 8am-6pm
This huge shop has four departments specialising in bathrooms, tiles, plumbing and paint and wallpaper. The shop is not fancy but provides excellent value across the board and is probably the cheapest place in London for bathroom furniture and fittings. On a recent visit a standard size steel bath (1700x700) was only £55 (inc VAT) and white tiles were as little as £3.99 per square metre. They offer further discounts when you spend £50 or more. One of the busiest and certainly the best bathroom showroom in London.

Colourwash

165 Chamberlayne Road, NW10
Tel: 020 8459 8918
Website: www.colourwash.co.uk
Tube: Kensal Green
Rail: Kensal Rise
Open: Mon-Fri 9am-5.30pm, Sat 10am-5pm

This is a well-known outlet for competitively priced designer bathroom suites and accessories offering both contract and luxury ranges. They concentrate on style and service rather than price, but offer good value at the quality end of the market with bathroom suites starting from £500 (inc VAT). Colourwash produce a regular brochure with details of all their core products and prices.

Also at:
150-152 Forits Green Road Muswell Hill N10, Tel: 020 8365 3222
71-73 Gloucester Avenue Primrose Hill, NW1, Tel: 020 7586 1441
223-225 Westbourne Park Road, Notting Hill W11, Tel: 020 7243 3300
1-3 Chiswick Terrace Acton Lane, W4, Tel: 020 8742 7787
63-65 Fulham High Street Fulham SW6, Tel: 020 7371 0911
18 Weir Road Wimbledon SW19, Tel: 020 8947 5578

N & C Tile Style

Unit 1a-b Alexander Place, Lower Park Road N11,
Tel: 020 8361 6050
Website: www.nichollsandclarke.com
Tube: Arnos Grove
Open: Mon-Fri 7.30am-5pm, Sat 8.30am-12.30pm

Nicholls & Clarke have been trading for over a hundred years, expanding to become a large building materials manufacturer as well as a retailer. Since the closure of their Shoreditch branch the company now only has outlets in the outskirts of London but these are well worth visiting for good value tiles and bathroom suits. Recently they were offering an entire bathroom suite (including taps, toilet mechanism and a steel bath) for only £172.50 (inc VAT), which is cheap enough to justify the journey.

Also at:
Unit 14 Meridian Trading Estate, Bugsby's Way, Charlton SE7
Tel: 020 8269 5960

West

Bathroom Discount Centre

297 Munster Road, Fulham, SW6
Tel: 020 7381 4222
Website: www.bathroomdiscount.co.uk
Tube: Parsons Green
Open: Mon-Fri 8am-6pm, Sat-Sun 9am-5pm

This large and impressively stocked bathroom showroom has been providing great value and service since 1978. The staff are very helpful, and they produce regular price lists and send out manufacturer's catalogues free of charge. Recent special offers included a standard steel bath for only £92 and a complete bathroom suite for only £179 (exc VAT). All major brands are stocked and they guarantee to offer the lowest price on any item.

Bathstore

(map 9)

50 Sulivan Road, Fulham, SW6
Tel: 020 7736 1503
Brochure Line: 0800 023 2323
Website: www.bathstore.com
Tube: Parson's Green
Open: Mon-Fri 9,30am-6pm, Sat 9am-6pm, Sun 11am-5pm

This chain of bathroom outlets has a reasonable range of bathroom suites and fittings. The emphasis is on quality rather than the budget end of the market, but they are good value and guarantee to beat any written quote for the same item. They also have regular sales. Check their website for your local branch.

M & S Supplies Bathroom Centre

140 Horn Lane, Acton, W3
Tel: 020 8992 9653
Website: www.mssupplies.co.uk
Rail: Acton Central
Open: Mon-Fri 8am-5pm, Sat 9am-4pm

This is a very long established company, trading for over 50 years, but which moved to its present site in the last 10 years. They offer sound advice, excellent service and give the general public the same discounts as trade customers. They concentrate on recognised manufacturers, with suites starting from £350 (exc VAT).

Waterforce

103-7 Windmill Road, South Ealing, W5
Tel: 020 8568 7672
Rail: Brentford
Open: Mon-Fri 8am-6pm, Sat 9am-5pm

This shop offers some cracking bathroom deals with suites including taps and fittings starting from £199 (exc VAT). They don't have a catalogue, but will try to match any price if you find the same product cheaper elsewhere. There are promotions and special deals all year round have regular clearance sales with discounts of up to 50%.

South

Burge and Gunson

13-27 and 38 High Street, Colliers Wood, SW19
Tel: 020 8543 5166
Website: www.burgeandgunson.co.uk
Tube: Colliers Wood
Open: Mon-Fri 8am-5.30pm, Sat 8am-4pm

This large store offers a complete bathroom suite with a steel bath for £208 (inc VAT) and will match all quotes. The staff are generally helpful and on a recent price check this shop offered the lowest prices on a range of bathroom products. They produce a regular catalogue showing all their major lines and will offer free delivery in the London area for larger purchases.

Also at:
165 Garth Road, Morden, Surrey, SM4 4LH, Tel: 020 8330 0101

Diamond Merchants

43-45 Acre Lane, SW2
Tel: 020 7274 6624/5
Website: www.diamond-merchants.co.uk
Tube/Rail: Brixton
Open: Mon-Fri 8am-5.30pm, Sat 9am-1pm / 2pm-5pm

This no-nonsense outlet offers good value with a standard sink starting from £50 and steel baths from £77. They hold a small selection, but can order anything from their manufacturers' catalogues within two days. They also act as a plumbing suppliers with all the copper pipe, fittings and equipment you need to do the job yourself. Check out their special offers – on a recent visit we found a WC suite for £95.

Plumbcraft Ltd

Unit 2, Ellerslie Square,
Lyham Road, SW2
Tel: 020 7274 0174
Website: www.plumbcraft.co.uk / www.plumcraftshop.co.uk
Tube: Clapham North
Open: Mon-Fri 8am-5.30pm, Sat 8.30am-12.30pm

Plumbcraft is an established business offering helpful service, free delivery in the London area and some very good deals. A large steel bath (1.8m x 0.8m) was only £275 (inc VAT) while an electronic shower (85kW) starts from £125. They have regular promotions on specific items and on a recent visit offered complete bathroom suites for £301 (inc VAT). An excellent outlet for bathroom bargains.

Reflections

54-58 Wandsworth High Street, SW18
Tel: 020 8874 6608
www.reflectionsworld.co.uk
Train: Wandsworth Town
Open: Mon-Sat 9am-6pm, Sun 11am-5pm

(map 8)

This established Wandsworth retailer sells good value bathroom suites, as well as tiles and a more limited selection of domestic appliances such as washing machines and cookers. They recently had on offer a budget bathroom suite (with chrome fittings) for only £299 (inc VAT). Their selection of tiles is also good value with prices starting from as little as £5 per square metre. Take a look at their website or give them a call to find out about their latest deals.

East

A D Jones Ltd

857/861 Forest Road, Walthamstow, E17
Tel: 020 8527 7189
Website: www.adjonesbathrooms.co.uk
Rail: Wood Street
Open: Mon-Sat 9am-5pm, Thurs till 1pm

This shop extends over three units on Forest Road and holds a reasonable range in stock as well as being able to source anything unusual. The shop offers advice and free delivery in the London area and complete bathroom suites start from a very reasonable £300 (inc VAT).

Bargain Tile Centre
150 Plashet Road, E13
Tel: 020 8472 5780
Website: www.bargain-tiles.co.uk
Tube: Upton Park
Open: Mon-Sat 9am-6pm

This family-run business offers reliable service and a helpful staff that will point out the best bargain. Check out their special offers including sinks from £80, a thermostatic bath for £199 and a whirlpool bath marked down from £545 to £300. They also have vanity units, accessories and a wide selection of tiles (see page 159).

London Plumbing & Heating Supplies
322 Hackney Road, E9
Tel: 020 7739 8883 / 7729 0060
Tube: Liverpool Street or Bethnal Green
Open: Mon-Fri 7am-5pm, Sat 8am-1pm

This shop is popular with professional plumbers and offers great deals on kitchen and bathroom taps, bathroom fittings and boilers. They were recently offering a complete bathroom suite (with taps and fittings) for only £235 (inc VAT) and were discounting ex-display taps for around £50. A great local shop for bathroom bargains.

Outer London

Discount Bathroom Warehouse
Unit 4 Brooklands Approach,
North Street, Romford, RM1
Tel: 01708 725 513
Website: www.discountbathroomcentre.co.uk
Rail: Romford
Open: Mon-Sat 10am-5.30pm (closed Wed)

This large warehouse is a long journey for many Londoners, but worth the effort with a wide choice of bathroom fixtures and fittings all at competitive prices. Bargains included a steel bath for only £67, basins from only £30 and toilets for £100. As well as basic bathroom suites they also have more unusual items such as large steel baths (1.8m x 0.8m) for only £178 (exc VAT). They can send out catalogues on request and will attempt to match any price.

Half Price Bathrooms

Hydrex House, Garden Road, Richmond, TW9
Tel: 020 8878 2824
Website: www.bath1959.com
Tube/Rail: Richmond, Kew Gardens

Half Price Bathrooms occupies a large warehouse in Richmond and does most of its business online. They welcome visitors to the warehouse where you can check out the goods before purchasing. Some of the recent deals included a bathroom suite (WC and sink) for £214 (retail price £427) and a classic freestanding bath for £399 – a bargain considering the retail price of £599. Delivery costs vary depending on your purchase and where you live.

Beds

If you are looking for a second-hand bed frame or headboard it might be worth trawling around a few junk shops (page 339) or visiting one of the many auctions reviewed in this book (page 276). In the furniture section (page 191) you will find futon retailers which sell good value beds as well as futons and Unto This Last (page 198), which makes great value beds among its range of unique furniture. If you are looking for something unique Daniel Spring (page 333) makes bespoke metal beds for a very reasonable price.

North

Bargain Bedstores

24 Baron Street, N1
Tel: 020 7713 7047/0800 3897
Tube: Angel
Open: Mon-Sat 9.30am-5.30pm, Sun 11am-3pm
Website: futons2you.co.uk

Bargain Bedstores specialises in beds and futons. It deals mostly with the trade but welcomes retail enquiries. They stock a large selection of futons in a choice of fabrics, the cheapest starting from £390. Pine head-boards cost as little as £15 while metal and draylon go for £20. There are special offers and deals available throughout the year with a solid pine double bed and mattress recently on offer for only £169 and single mattresses for only £39.

Also at:
155-157 Hornsey Road, N7, Tel 020 7609 6320.

Big Bed & Pine Co

125 Essex Road, N1
Tel: 020 7359 9614
Tube: Angel or Highbury & Islington
Open: Mon-Sat 9am-5pm

This shop sells beds and quality pine and oak furniture. A 4"6 pine bed frame with a quality mattress was excellent value for only £199, while a single pine frame is £99 with a mattress for £49. All the chests are very well made with solid wood backs and drawers and are competitively priced with a medium chest of drawers for £229 and a large one for £259. As well as having competitive prices the shop will also stain the furniture to your liking, deliver in the London area, and when necessary assemble the furniture – all without charge. A great value shop.

Taurus Beds
167 Finchley Road, NW6
Tel: 020 7372 1166
Website: www.taurusbeds.co.uk
Tube: Finchley Road
Open: Mon-Sat 10am-6pm, Sun 11am-4pm

Taurus have a reputation for great value solid wooden beds, which they have been manufacturing now for over 25 years. A single bed and mattress costs from £218, a double with orthopaedic mattress from £308. Most beds are guaranteed for 5 years and come in a range of finishes including mahogany, lacquer and painted. Taurus also make a range of matching bedroom furniture which is reasonably priced and matches the design and finish of the bed. View their website or give them a call to request a free colour brochure.

West

Bedtime Superstore
1-5 Westway, W12
Tel: 020 8746 1990
Tube: East Acton
Open: Mon-Sat 9,30-5,30, Sun 10am-4pm
Website: www.bedtimesuperstores.co.uk

Bedtime Superstore is a family run business in west London with a small and friendly staff. A wide range of beds in both wood and metal are in stock with a stylish brass double bed for £99 and a double divan for £149. They have plenty of leather and suede beds for those with a larger budget. The store also offers a variety of sofa beds in both modern and classic styles – prices start from £250 for a two-seater. Check out their January and July sales when there are discounts of up to 40%.
Also at:
691, London Road, TW7, Tel:0208568 2574
153-155 High Street, TW18, Tel: 01784 463 449

Beds Ltd

220 North End Road, W14
Tel: 0207 385 7711
Website: www.beds.ltd.uk
Tube: West Kensington/West Brompton
Open: Mon-Sat 10am-6pm, Sun 11am-4pm
Website: www.beds.ltd.uk

One of the largest showrooms in London, Beds Ltd stocks a wide range of discontinued beds, mattresses and divans at reasonable prices. The shop is located in a converted church which provides an unusual atmosphere for bed hunting. Brands include Silent Night, Sleepy, Staples, Sleep Easy and Miles. They have regular special offers and promotions which are worth looking out for with recent deals including a single bed for £120 and a metal double bed frame with elegant floral designs for £150.

Big Table Furniture Co-op Ltd

56 Great Western Road, W9
Tel: 020 7221 5058
www.bigtable.co.uk
Tube: Westbourne Park
Open: Mon-Sat 10am-6pm, Thurs 10am-8pm, Sun 12noon-5pm

Although they started off making tables about 18 years ago, the Big Table Furniture Co-op soon found bed frames and mattresses more profitable. They manufacture everything themselves on the premises using Swedish pine with a range of finishes and natural fillings for the mattresses. Prices for single beds start from around £240 (including mattress) with doubles from £430. They can offer lengths of up to 7ft and widths of 6ft. They also make under bed storage units. Brochure available.

West End Beds

313 North End Road, W14
Tel: 0207 385 2000
Tube: West Brompton
Open: Mon-Sat 10am-6pm, Sun 11am-4pm

West End Beds is just down the road from Beds Ltd and is part of the same company. You will find lower prices at this store as they do not have as many top name brands in stock. If you are after fast delivery and practicality, West End Beds is the best bet with a single bed with storage starting from only £109. They have a good selection of divans with bargains including a single divan for £99 and a double for £139. They also offer up to 50% discount on discontinued lines.

South

Just Beds

Elephant & Castle Shopping Centre
233 Elephant & Castle, SE1
Tel: 020 7701 7788
Tube: Elephant & Castle
Open: Mon-Sat 10am-6pm

A budget of £100 will get you a good-quality bed and mattress at Just Beds. Prices start at £60 for a single pine bed, £90 for a double bed. They also offer wood and metal headboards and a pine double bed frame goes for £80. Find special deals such as bunk beds (mattresses included) for £180. The staff are keen to point out the quality of their inexpensive mattresses with prices starting from £35 for a double mattress.

Also at:
Unit 2, Elephant Road, SE17, Tel 020 7708 8880

East

Citybeds Ltd

17-39 Gibbins Road, Stratford, E15
Tel: 020 8534 9000 or 0800 026 3414
Website: www.citybeds.co.uk
Tube/Rail: Stratford
Open: Mon-Sat 9am-5.30pm, Sun 11am-4pm

In business for more than two decades, this bed warehouse specialises in Silentnight , Myers, Staples, Sealy and Airsprung at discount prices. They deliver throughout the Greater London and Essex areas. Find futon and sofa beds for £169, pine or metal beds for only £75, beds with storage for £99, sturdy bunk beds for £139 and mattresses for only £38. A company well worth visiting if you're looking for a cheap bed.

Also at:
20-22 Fowler Rd, Hainault Industrial Estate, Essex IG6, Tel: 020 8501 2426
Unit 2C, Claydons Lane, Rayleigh Weir, Essex SS6, Tel: 01268 772 422

Litvinoff and Fawcett

281 Hackney Road, E2
Tel: 020 7739 3480
Website: www.landf.co.uk
Tube: Liverpool Street or Old Street
Rail: Cambridge Heath
Free off road parking Monday - Saturday
Open: Mon-Fri 10am-6pm, Sat 10am-5pm, Sun 10:30am-4.30pm

Litvinoff and Fawcett make high quality beds in various woods, and handmade mattresses with natural fillings. The bed frames have a lifetime guarantee and both are sold at workshop prices from their Shoreditch showrooms. A simple pine bed starts from £160, and they cater for a wide variety of tastes and pockets. They have also sourced a range of stylish, good value furniture from around the world to complement their own furniture.

Bedding

Below are some of the best outlets for quality bedding in London. If you are looking for top quality pre-war linen (which is beautifully made and much sought after) try The Cloth Shop (see page 186). If you don't mind the idea of buying hotel linen, there are several outlets on Sclater Street (part of Brick Lane Market) that sell these good condition 100% cotton sheets for just a few pounds.

Central

The Linen Cupboard
21 Great Castle Street, W1G
Tel: 020 7629 4062
Tube: Oxford Circus
Open: Mon-Sat 9.30am-7pm, Sun 11am-5pm

Just off Regent Street stands this modest shop offering bedding at discount prices. There is a wide selection of materials including fine Egyptian cotton, pure linen, polyester and union cotton (50% polyester). Recent bargains included an Egyptian cotton double duvet for £29 (original price £70) and a matching set of sheets for £15.99 (original price £35).

North

Austrian Bedding Co
205 Belsize Road, NW6
Tel: 020 7372 3121
Tube: Kilburn Park
Open: Mon-Fri: 10am-5.30pm, Sat 10am-5pm

Austrian Bedding is a small shop offering top quality duvets, pillows and bed linen at affordable prices. If you have a larger budget this shop offers personal service and a wide range of internationally sourced bedding. Silk and goose-down-filled duvets in both British and Continental sizes can be found, prices starting at £80. There is a good selection of high-end Egyptian cotton linen in the latest Italian styles and look out for their 'genuine sale' in January – when all prices are reduced. A specialist cleaning service is also offered for those who are interested in recycling their old duvet.

Bradleys Curtain and Linen Centre

184 Kentish Town Road, NW5
Tel: 020 7485 0029
Tube: Kentish Town Road
Open: Mon-Sat 9am-5.30pm
Website: www.bradleyscurtains.co.uk

In business for over 30 years, Bradleys is a neighbourhood institution. The family-run shop is a good place to find quality sheets at fair prices. Luxurious Egyptian cotton double sheets were only £19.99 and a good quality feather duvet £60, while a cover sheet with pillowcases was £19.99. They also stock every other household linen from towels to curtains. Their summer sales are also well worth a visit.

West

The Linen Mill

Unit 8, Sullivan Enterprise Centre,
Sullivan Road, SW6
Tel: 020 7731 3262
Website: www.thelinenmill.com
Tube: Parsons Green / Fulham Broadway
Open: Mon-Sat 10am-6pm

(map 1)

The Linen Mill is a family run business that caters for those with a particular liking for all that is linen, including the design and manufacture of their own range of linens. As well as clothing, they also sell 100% linen bed sheets, duvet covers and pillowcases in unique styles and natural colours. Find a top-quality set of double sheets for £45 or a bed spread for £80. As some items might seem pricey make sure to check when their end of line sale takes place (usually in July). This is the time to find real bargains with prices being reduced by up to 90%.

Shaukat Fabrics

168-172 Old Brompton Road, SW5
Tel: 020 7373 8956
Tube: Gloucester Road
Bus: 49, 70, 74, C1
Open: Mon-Sat 10am-6.30pm

As well as fabrics and bags, Shaukat also sell a great value selection of bedding from their basement. The good deals include a double cotton sheet for £19.99 and a king size nylon sheet for £10.99. You can negotiate with staff to get the best deal. For more details about Shaukat's fabric and bags see page 186.

East

Autumn Down
Unit 3, 26-42 Plumstead High Street, SE18
Tel: 020 8331 0888
Website: www.autumndown.co.uk
Rail: Plumstead
Open: Mon–Fri 8am-6pm

Specialists in duvets and pillows, Autumn Down has been trading for over 15 years. This is the shop to visit if you are looking for top quality duvets, but also stocks quilts and sheets. A wide selection of duvets and pillows in different styles are in stock. Most items are marked down by at least 20% with goose feather double duvets for £28 (usual price £38). Their website often has more sale items than does the shop.

Dreamland Linen
342 Bethnal Green Road, E2
Tel: 020 7739 0051
Tube: Bethnal Green
Open: Mon-Sat 9am-6pm

Dreamland offer exceptional deals on bedding, including single 100% cotton sheets for £4.99 and double sheets for only £5.99. They also have great value duvet covers with a king size 100 % cotton duvet cover including pillowcases for only £12.99. Dreamland also offer a range of curtains and accessories such as curtain rails at very competitive prices.

Out of Town

King of Cotton
Unit 5, The Sandycombe Centre, 1-9 Sandycombe Road
Richmond on Thames, Surrey, TW9
Tel: 020 8332 7999
Website: www.kingofcotton.co.uk
Tube/Rail: Kew Gardens, Richmond
Open: Mon-Sat 10am-4pm

Located between the leafy villages of Richmond and Kew, King of Cotton is an outlet offering a wide selection of bed linen. Although they usually sell to wholesalers, there are sales and special deals for the public all year round. As they usually deal with hotels, all types and sizes of duvets, Egyptian cotton bed linen, bedding protection and bedspreads are available. Visitors should look out for discontinued lines and overstock from previous seasons.

Carpets, Rugs & Tiles

Central

West End Carpets

1 Baker Street, W1
Tel: 020 7224 6635
Website: www.westendcarpets.co.uk
Sales Line: 0800 146 447
Tube: Baker Street
Open: Mon-Fri 9am-5.30pm

& 928 High Road,
North Finchley, N12
Tel: 020 8446 5331
Tube: Woodside Park
Open: Mon-Fri 9am-5.30pm,
Sun 10am-4pm

Dealing in high-quality carpets, West End Carpets is one of the smarter carpet shops in the city. Bargains can be found in their stock of room-size remnants and quality mixed fibre carpeting starts at £10 per square metre. In general, prices here are good considering the quality of carpets on offer.

North

Battens Carpets & Wood Floors

413 Holloway Road, N7
Tel: 020 7609 4268
Tube: Holloway Road
Open: Mon-Sat 9am-5.30pm, Sun 10.30am-4.30pm

Battens is a long established carpet store that always has a good range of remnants at a 50% discount. The shop also offers good value among its main stock items with 80% wool mix carpet starting from as little as £9.99 a square yard. As well as carpets Battens also sells a range of very competitively priced laminate floorings.

Carpet Tile Centre

map
10

227 Woodhouse Road, N12
Tel: 020 8361 1261
Tube: Arnos Grove
Open: Mon-Sat 9am-5pm, Sat 9am-1pm

A wide range of perfect tiles at reasonable prices can be found here, but the real bargains are among their range of seconds. You can pick up discounted Huega tiles from £1.95 each, which is about half the original price.

Leebanks Carpet Centre
71-75 Essex Road, N1
Tel: 020 7359 6482
Tube: Angel
Open: Mon-Fri 8am-5pm, Sat 9am-4.30pm
This local carpet shop sells some very cheap economy carpets for £3 per square metre, but also stocks good quality 80% wool carpets for a very reasonable £12.99 per square metre. The shop also offers laminates, vinyl and solid wood flooring with the wood flooring starting at only £12 per square metre.

S & M Myers
100-106 Mackenzie Road, N7
Tel: 020 7609 0091
Website: www.myerscarpets.co.uk
Tube: Caledonian Road
Open: Mon, Wed, Fri 8am-5.30pm, Tues & Thurs 8am-5pm,
Sat 9.30am-2pm
This family business started in 1819 and still offers good quality new carpets and a wide range of remnants at very keen prices. Among the bargains was an 80% wool mix carpet for only £12.99 a square metre, seagrass for as little as £8.99 a square metre and sisal for £14.95 a square metre. The remnants are displayed on a board and labelled with the dimensions and price, making it easy to choose what you want. The East End Road branch has a wide range of rugs, but all remnants can be cut and the edges sewn at very little cost to make a bespoke rug. Probably the best budget carpet outlet in the capital.
Also at:
81-85 East End Road N2, Tel: 020 8444 3457
Open: Mon-Fri 8am-5.30pm, Sat 9.30am-5pm

Plush Floorings Ltd
20 Palace Gates Road, N22
Tel: 020 8881 2538
Rail: Alexandra Palace
Open: Mon-Sat 9.15am-5.30pm
This small shop has been trading for over 25 years and offers a good range of carpets and vinyls as well as an expert fitting service. Hard-wearing, synthetic carpets cost as little as £3.99 per square metre, while 100% wool carpets start from a very reasonable £9.99 per square metre. They also have a limited range of remnants at even greater discounts.

Soviet Carpet and Art Galleries

303-305 Cricklewood Broadway, NW2
Tel: 020 8452 2445
Website: www.russian-art.co.uk
e-mail: rr@soviet-world.fsnet.co.uk
Tube: Cricklewood Broadway
Open: Mon-Fri and Sun 10.30am-5.30pm (by appointment)

This former trade warehouse has been opening its doors to the public since 1992, offering large discounts on paintings from the former Soviet Union and rugs from Eastern Europe as well as Afghanistan, Iran, China and Turkey. There are thousands of hand-made rugs to choose from and all are sold at roughly half the usual retail price. The quality is high and the range of art and rugs is unrivalled in London. The company's lease is soon to expire and they are currently seeking a new more central location – visit their website or e-mail them to confirm the new address details.

West End Carpets

922-928 High Road, North Finchley, N12
See main entry in Central page 151.

Home • Carpets, Rugs & Tiles

West

The Carpetstore
167 King Street, W6
Tel: 020 8563 2221
Tube: Hammersmith

& 156 Goldhawk Road, W12
Tel: 020 8749 9340
Tube: Goldhawk Road
Open: Mon-Fri 8am-5pm, Sat 8.30-5pm

The Goldhawk Road branch is where a wide range of remnants are sold. There are lots of bargains to be found with a 16ft x 13ft, 80% wool, remnant for only £201. The rest of their carpets, linos and laminates offer a good selection of flooring options, but are not generally discounted. They also offer a free fitting service.

Gray and Lowe
91 Uxbridge Road, W12
Tel: 020 8743 5854
Tube: Shepherd's Bush
Open: Mon-Wed, Fri 7am-5.30pm, Sat 8am-5.30pm
This family business has been trading for over 50 years. Bargain hunters should start with a search through the room-size remnants before moving on to the decently priced natural and synthetic carpets that go as low as £3.35 per square metre. Top quality wool carpet weighs in at a hefty £65 per square metre.

Hani Wells Carpets
450-2 Edgware Road, W2
Tel: 020 7723 5522
Tube: Edgware Road
Open: Daily 9am-6pm
Serious bargains await you at this retailer offering carpets, vinyls, laminates and wood flooring at a minimum 30% discount. Carpet prices start at the unbelievably low price of £5-6 per square metre. Extra-wide carpet rolls are also on offer. Dedicated bargain hunters might like to take advantage of their price-matching guarantee.

South

Carpetman

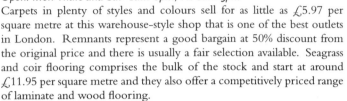

7A Putney Bridge Road, SW18
Tel: 020 8875 0232
Website: www.carpetman.co.uk
Rail: Wandsworth Town
Open: Mon-Thurs and Sat 8am-6pm, Fri 8am-5pm

Carpets in plenty of styles and colours sell for as little as £5.97 per square metre at this warehouse–style shop that is one of the best outlets in London. Remnants represent a good bargain at 50% discount from the original price and there is usually a fair selection available. Seagrass and coir flooring comprises the bulk of the stock and start at around £11.95 per square metre and they also offer a competitively priced range of laminate and wood flooring.

L.W. Carpet Warehouse

239-241 Balham High Road, SW17
Tel: 020 8672 1902
Tube: Tooting Bec
Open: Mon-Fri 9am-5.30pm

In business for more than three decades, this Balham shop offers good value flooring and beds and the helpful staff provide a fitting service and express delivery within the city. Find carpets, vinyls and wood laminates at a discount.

Discount Carpets

382 Streatham High Road, SW16
Tel: 020 8677 7010
Rail: Streatham
Open: Mon-Fri 9am-6pm, Sat 9am-5pm

This south London shop stocks over 100 room–size remnants to choose from as well as about forty end–of–line carpet rolls with varying colours and designs. Prices start from as low as £2.80 per square metre.

H Dourof & Sons Ltd

70-72 Rushey Green, Catford, SE6
Tel: 020 8690 3938
Rail: Catford/Catford Bridge
Open: Mon-Wed, Fri-Sat 9am-5pm, Thurs 9am-1pm

A popular local shop, this family-run business has been trading for over 45 years. Prices for synthetic carpet start at a reasonable £2.99 per square metre with 80% wool mix carpets for only £8.95. The best value is represented in the discounted end of rolls and a good range of end of line carpet designs which are sold at a considerable discount.

East

Abbott's

470-480 Roman Road, E3
Tel: 0800 716 783
Website: www.abbottscarpets.co.uk
Tube: Mile End/Bethnal Green
Open: Mon-Fri 8.30am-5.30pm, Sat 8.30am-5pm

Cheap rugs (for as little as £14), trendy Dalsouple rubber flooring for £39 per square metre and heavily discounted room-size remnants, are some of the reasons customers keep coming back to this shop that has been trading for over a century. The selection of carpets, lino and laminates are all competitively priced, making Abbott's a great place to hunt for top-value flooring solutions.

Carpet Warehouse

40-41 Valentine Road, E9
Tel: 020 8985 0878
Tube: Bethnal Green
Open: Mon-Sat 9am-5pm

This business has been supplying good value carpets, lino and laminates to the citizens of Hackney for over 25 years and deserves wider recognition. The warehouse is a little difficult to find but well worth the effort with low prices and lots of large remnants at even greater discounts.

Tiles

North

Topps Tiles
Unit 2, 92-94 Stamford Hill, N16
Tel: 020 8806 4688
Website: www.toppstiles.co.uk
Rail: Stoke Newington
Open: Mon-Fri 8am-6pm, Sat 9am-5.30pm, Sun 10am-4pm
Covering over 7,500 square feet, this warehouse tile outlet will beat any price by 5%. If you're not into price-matching schemes, you can still come away with a bargain such as simple white tiles for £3.52 per square metre. Topps Tiles usually has a selection of special offer tiles which are discounted by 40–50%.

Also at:
Rookery Way, The Hyde, Collindale NW9, Tel: 020 8200 8100
78-79 Goding Street, Vauxhall SE11, Tel: 020 7820 8882
Station Road, New Southgate N11, Tel: 020 8368 2400
596-598 Old Kent Road SE15, Tel: 020 7732 7272
Unit 1 Meridian Trade Estate Lombard Wall,
Charlton SE7, Tel: 020 82931233
2-6 Rushey Green, Catford SE6, Tel: 020 8690 2917
124 Oakfield Road, Penge SE20, Tel: 020 8778 6447
Unit 25, Carnwath Industrial Estate,
Carnwath Rd SW6, Tel: 020 7384 1300
Unit 3 Beckton Retail Park (off Alpine Way),
Beckton E6, Tel: 020 7511 2663

West

Criterion #2 Tiles

178 Wandsworth Bridge Road, SW6
Tel: 020 7731 6098
Website: www.criterion-tiles.co.uk
Tube: Parson's Green
Open: Mon-Fri 9.30am-5.30pm, Sat 9.30am-5pm

This store is part of the larger Criterion group, but specialises in discounted tiles that are largely end-of-lines with a few slight seconds also among the stock. There are all kinds of stylish tiles to be found here with end-of-line Italian tiles selling here for £37.50 per square metre – a considerable saving considering they usually retail for over £100 per square metre.

Stone Zone

157-159 Goldhawk Road, W12
Tel: 020 8749 1115
Tube: Goldhawk Road

Unit 6 Sergeants Industrial Estate (map 8)
102 Garratt Lane, SW18
Tel: 020 8877 3919
Tube: Wandsworth Town
Open: Mon-Fri 8am-5pm, Sat 9am-1pm

Stone Zone offer good value quality tiles imported direct from the manufacturer and sold for as little as £9 per square metre. The stock is of a much high quality than you will find in DIY superstores and they usually have some end-of-line clearance stock which is sold at a discount.

South

Stone Zone

102 Garratt Lane, SW18
See main entry in West London (above) for full details.

Topps Tiles

See main entry in North London (page 157) for full details.

East

Bargain Tile Centre

150 Plashet Road, E13
Tel: 020 8472 5780
Website: www.bargain-tiles.co.uk
Tube: Upton Park
Open: Mon-Sat 9am-6pm

Prices are very competitive at this large tile retailers which holds a considerable stock of all items at their nearby warehouse. Ceramic tiles of varying quality are all discounted with basic white tiles going for £2 per square metre. Designer tile prices rise to about £40 per square metre. The Bargain Tile Centre is true to its name and now offers excellent value in bathroom fittings and suites (see Bathrooms page 141).

N & C Tile Style

Unit 14 Meridian Trading Estate,
Bugsby Way, Charlton, SE7
Tel: 020 8269 5960

Units 1A/B Alexander Place,
Lower Park Road, New Southgate, N11
Tel: 020 8361 6050
Website: www.nichollsandclarke.com or www.ncdirect.co.uk
Open: Mon-Fri 7.30am-5pm, Sat 8.30am-12.30pm

Part of a huge building materials distribution company, these large shops stock a wide range of wall and floor tiles. Prices are very competitive with plain white bathroom tiles starting from only £3.51 per square metre and there are even greater bargains among the special offers on the end-of-line tiles. N & C also offer very good value bathroom suites – view their website for further details.

Topps Tiles

See main entry in North London (page 157) for full details.

Curtains

Curtains can cost a small fortune if you don't know where to shop. London has many outlets selling cut-price fabrics both from UK designers and imported from abroad, all of which offer a curtain-making service. Also reviewed below are the shops that sell second-hand curtains – usually supplied by local people moving home or from big hotels. In addition to the outlets listed below some of the most reasonably priced curtain materials and ready-made curtains can be found at John Lewis branches, Ikea, Habitat, M&S, British Home Stores, Homebase or Laura Ashley. Otherwise sale time at department stores like Harrods and Selfridges can produce bargains.

Central

Alexander Furnishings
51-61 Wigmore Street, W1
Tel: 020 7935 2624
Tube: Bond Street
Open: Mon-Sat 9am-6pm, Thurs 9am-7pm

The largest independent curtain retailer in London, offering an assortment of soft furnishings, upholstery, wallpaper and blinds and curtain fabrics at prices discounted by up to 60%. Housed in a warren of six connecting shops just behind Oxford Street, discontinued fabrics and clearance lines that were originally £18 a metre can be found here for £4.95-£5.95. Alexander Furnishings also offer a making-up and installation service, make cushions and upholster furniture.

North

Changing Curtains
186 Archway Road, Highgate, N6
Tel: 020 8340 9801
website: www.changingcurtains.co.uk
Tube: Highgate
Open: Tues-Sat 10am-4pm

This second-hand curtain agency gets most of its quality stock supplied by local people moving home as well as the odd hotel. The second-hand stock varies in price from £85 up to as much as £1,500 and they also offer made-to-measure new curtains and blinds with some designer fabrics. Planter's shutters are a popular addition to the shop's services.

The Curtain Factory Outlet

269 Ballards Lane,
North Finchley, N12
Tel: 020 8492 0093
Tube: West Finchley
Open: Mon-Sat 9am-6pm, Sun 10am-4pm

A curtain wholesalers and exporters with over half a million metres of top designer names on offer in a large complex of six buildings - including two large warehouses. The wholesale and export nature of the business means there is a fast turnover of stock with new material arriving daily. They have all the top designer names in curtaining and upholstery fabrics with no fabric sold for over £6.99 per metre (exc VAT). The stock originates directly from printers, dryers, weavers and finishers of Designer Guild, Harlequin, Sandersons and other well known leading designer names. The fabrics arrive unlabeled so if you are looking for a particular fabric you will need to visit the outlet, e-mail a photo or send a sample. At the back is the trade warehouse which the public are allowed into when there are no trade clients. They also sell curtain lining at approximately half the usual retail price, sell ready-made curtains and have a made-to-measure service for both curtains and blinds.

161

CSN Curtains & Blinds Ltd

61-63 Watford Way, Hendon, NW4
Tel: 020 8201 5945
Tube: Hendon Central
Open: Mon-Sat 9am-5.30pm, Sun 10am-4pm

This shop is part of the Curtain Mill company based in Watford. The shop has a select range of fabrics in stock, but also has over 1,000 samples which can be quickly ordered. The prices are very competitive with fabric starting from £2 a metre and going up to £70 a metre for designer fabrics. They also stock ready-made curtains and offer a wide range of materials including weaves, prints, velvets and linings plus all the trimmings, poles and tie-backs. In addition, CSN offer a making-up service.

Martin's Fabric

24-26 South Mall, Edmonton Green Shopping Centre, N9
Tel: 020 8807 4222
Rail: Edmonton Green
Open: Mon-Wed, Fri-Sat 10am-5pm, Thurs 10am-2pm

This outlet sells a great range of curtain fabrics at very competitive prices. If you don't fancy getting the sewing machine out they also sell a selection of ready-made curtains, net curtains and blinds.

Peter Jude

644 Finchley Road, NW11
Tel: 020 8458 1222
Website: www.peterjude.com
Tube: Golders Green
Open: Mon-Fri 9am-6pm

This small workshop offers a curtain-making service, sells fabrics at very competitive prices and also repairs and re-upholsters furniture as well as making bespoke furniture at a very reasonable price. Give them a call or visit their website to find out more about their services and items for sale.

West

The Cloth Shop
290 Portobello Road, W10
Tel: 020 8968 6001
Website: www.clothshop.net
Tube: Ladbroke Grove
Open: Mon-Sat 10am-6pm
See review in Fabrics and Haberdashers (page 186).

The Curtain Exchange
129-131 Stephendale Road, SW6
Tel: 020 7731 8316
Website: www.thecurtainexchange.co.uk
Tube: Fulham Broadway/Parson's Green
Open: Mon-Sat 10am-5pm

The Curtain Exchange will only take high quality fabrics (usually in-terlined) in tip-top condition and offer them for about a third of their original price. A warren of eight rooms is lined floor to ceiling with rich velvets, patterned textiles and other sumptuous fabrics. Prices start at around £80 to over £1,000 a pair and provided you leave a cheque for the full amount you can take curtains home on approval for 24 hours to see how they look. Take detailed measurements of your rail rather than the window, plus the drop, before you visit. In addition the shop has lots of swags, cushions and other accessories. Sellers get 60% of the sale price for curtains priced at over £500, 50% for those less than £500. There is a made-to-measure service, home fitting service and easy parking.
Also at: 80 Park Hall Road, Dulwich SE21, Tel: 020 8670 5570

The Curtain Fabric Factory
236a North End Road, W14
Tel: 020 7381 1777
Tube: Brompton Road or West Kensington
Open: Mon-Sat 9.30am-5.30pm

Large importers of furnishing fabrics with a massive warehouse behind a busy shop near the market. There are as many as 1,500 rolls of fabric to choose from supplied direct from manufacturers and offered at discounts of up to 40%. There are some seconds and samples but most of the material is regular stock supplied in bulk and on sale from £3.99 to £20 a metre. They do their own printing and if they don't have what you want they can order it. The company also offers a made-to-measure service for curtains and blinds, plus tracks and fitting.

East

Epra Fabrics
52/56 Brick Lane, E1
Tel: 020 7247 1248
Tube: Aldgate East/Shoreditch
Open: Mon-Fri 9am-5.30pm, Sun 9am-2pm
They have a room dedicated to curtain fabrics. For more details see their review in Fabrics and Haberdashers (page 189).

Fancy Curtains
65 Queens Market, Green Street, E13
Tel: 020 8470 1331
Website: www.fancycurtains.co.uk
Tube: Upton Park
Open: Tues-Fri 10am-5.30pm, Sat 9.30am-6pm
Over 700 fabrics and swatches of all descriptions crammed into a little shop opposite West Ham football ground. The fabrics start from 50p a metre and go up to £95 a metre for curtain designer fabrics. Everything you could possibly need from nets and trimmings to made-to-measure blinds and curtains, they have a particularly good stock of metal tracks for bay windows.

Mermaid Fabrics
364 Mare Street, E8
Tel: 020 8985 3694
Rail: Hackney Central
Open: Mon-Sat 9.30am-5.30pm
This is a large fabric outlet with an established reputation and loyal customer base. There are many thousands of reams to choose from and on fine days reduced items are placed on the pavement to attract trade. Felts, cords and velvets are all £3.95 per metre and there are lots of remnant reams for just £1. The shop is even bigger than it looks from the pavement with two large rooms at the back for furnishing and curtain material. Mermaid also offer a curtain-making and fitting service.

Outer London

Corcoran & May

31-35 Blagdon Road, New Malden, Surrey, KT3
Tel: 020 8949 0234
Rail: New Malden
Open: Mon-Sat 9.30am-5.30pm, Sun and Bank Holidays 10am-4pm

A vast store filled with overstocks from well-known curtain fabric designers (Osborne & Little, Crowson, G.P. & J. Baker, Monkwell, Malabar Cotton Company) as well as fabric from some of the brightest newcomers. Corcoran and May offer material for all budgets with prices starting from £1.99 and going up to £19.99 per metre. A reputable make-up service is available and they now have a large area of the store dedicated to blinds of all kinds at very competitive prices.

Curtain Mill Ltd

19 Grey Caine Road, Grey Caine Industrial Estate,
off Bushey Mill Lane, Watford, WD24
Tel: 01923 220 339
Rail: Watford
Open: Mon-Sat 9am-5.30pm, Sun 10am-4pm

This large warehouse has thousands of metres of fabric in rolls from £1 to £30 a metre including weaves, prints, velvets and linings. They also stock ready-made curtains plus all the trimmings, poles and tie-backs. The company has a making-up service and about a third of their business is now dedicated to blinds with a bespoke service as well as ready-made blinds.

Fabric World

287-289 High Street, Sutton, Surrey, SM1
Tel: 020 8643 5127
Tube: Morden   Rail: Sutton
Open: Mon-Sat 9am-5.30pm

Over 3,000 rolls of cut-price designer fabrics in stock, both from the UK and imported from all over the world. There are plenty of bargains to be found here with discounts of as much as 75% on certain clearance fabrics. The shop also has a making-up workroom and an interior design service.

Also at:
6-10 Brighton Road, South Croydon, Tel: 020 8688 6282

South London Fabric Warehouse

Unit F2 Felnex Trading Estate,
Hackbridge Road, Hackbridge, Wallington, Surrey, SM6
Tel: 020 8647 3313
Rail: Hackbridge
Open: Mon-Fri 9am-5.30pm, Sat 9am-6pm, Sun 10am-4pm

This large (18,000 square feet) warehouse is on two floors and is located between Croydon and Sutton. They stock competitively priced brands from the UK and abroad by the roll with prices from £2.99 to £30 a metre. There is a curtain-making service available as well as ready-made curtains and a wide choice of blinds, poles, tracks and all the trimmings. The company also offers a selection of bed linen, towels and cushions.

DIY and Equipment

Builders' Merchants

North

Buildbase
40 Muswell Hill Road, N6
Tel: 020 8883 9722
Website: www.buildbase.co.uk
Tube: Highgate
Open: Mon-Fri 7.30am-5pm, Sat 8am-12noon

This company has offers on all kinds of building materials from bricks to bathroom suites. It is particularly good value for its selection of garden stone with pallets containing 12.6 square metres of Indian sandstone for under £300. If you require stone for the garden this is probably the best place in London to find it.
Branches :
Oakleigh Road South, New Southgate, N11 Tel: 020 8361 3637
10-14 Crossway, Stoke Newington, N16 Tel: 020 7254 1117
Blackpool Road, Peckham, SE15 Tel: 020 7639 0138

Mr C. Demetriou DIY
132 Balls Pond Road, N1
Tel: 020 7354 8210
Tube: Highbury & Islington
Open: Mon-Fri 9am-5pm, Sat 9am-4pm, Sun 10am-3pm

This shop is an unusual mix of old and new DIY equipment and materials. The stock comes from all kinds of sources including auctions and markets and there is also part-exchange on power tools. The shop seems small from the outside, but extends back a long way. Mr Demetriou lives for his shop and even shows up for a few hours on Christmas Day to sell batteries to the kids in the neighbourhood for their new toys.

E.D. Elson Ltd
304 Essex Road, N1
Tel: 020 7226 6422
Tube: Angel or Highbury & Islington
Open: Mon-Fri 8am-5pm, Sat 9am-5pm

This shop offers a good value mix of decorating and building materials and tools. There is also has a small timber yard at the back of the store where wood can be cut to size.

M.P. Moran & Sons Ltd

(map 4)

293/301 Kilburn High Road, NW6
Tel: 020 7328 5566
Website: www.mpmoran.co.uk
Tube: Kilburn
Open: Mon-Fri 7am-5.30pm, Sat 7am-4pm

Moran's is a huge independent building suppliers offering plumbing and electrical equipment, painting and decorating materials, power and hand tools, all kinds of glass cut to size and a large timber yard which is situated just around the corner. All materials are competitively priced with regular promotions. Also at:

Rear of 5-23 Iverson Road NW6 (Timber Yard), Tel: 020 7328 5566
449-451 High Road, Willesden NW10, Tel: 020 8459 9000
198-200 Kennington Park Road SE11, Tel: 020 7735 9291

N & C Tile Building Materials

Unit 1a-b Alexander Place, Lower Park Road N11,
Tel: 020 8361 6050
Website: www.nichollsandclarke.com
Tube: Arnos Grove
Open: Mon-Fri 7.30am-5pm, Sat 8.30am-12.30pm

Nicholls & Clarke have been trading for over a hundred years, expanding to become a large building materials manufacturer as well as retailer. Since the closure of their Shoreditch branch the company now only has outlets on the outskirts of London but these are well worth visiting for good value building materials.

Also at:
Unit 14 Meridian Trading Estate, Bugsby Way, Charlton SE7
Tel: 020 8269 5960

Chris Stephens Ltd

545-561 Holloway Road N19
Tel: 020 7272 1228
Tube: Holloway
Open: Mon-Fri 7am-6pm, Sat 8am-6pm

This huge shop has four departments specialising in bathrooms, tiles, plumbing, paint and wallpaper. The shop is not fancy but provides excellent value across the board and is probably the cheapest place in London for bathroom furniture and fittings (see Bathrooms on page 136) and also offers cheap DIY equipment, tiles and paints.

West

Nu-Line Builders Merchants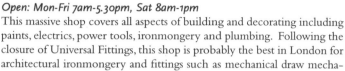
315 Westbourne Park Road, W11
Tel: 020 7727 7748
Tube: Ladbroke Grove
Open: Mon-Fri 7am-5.30pm, Sat 8am-1pm

This massive shop covers all aspects of building and decorating including paints, electrics, power tools, ironmongery and plumbing. Following the closure of Universal Fittings, this shop is probably the best in London for architectural ironmongery and fittings such as mechanical draw mechanisms for which they produce a regular colour catalogue. Nu-Line also has a large timber yard.

Mail Order

Screwfix Direct
Tel: 0500 414141
Website: www.screwfix.com
Open: Mon-Fri 7am-10pm, Sat-Sun 8am-8pm

Screwfix is a very good value building material mail order service which is very popular in the building trade, but also welcomes amateur DIY accounts. They produce a regular catalogue and the website is regularly updated and easy to use. The only draw back is the delivery time which can be as much as 14 days, so give yourself a little time to order if you are planning delivery for a particular project.

Paint & Wallpaper

Central

Leyland Paint

167-169 Shaftesbury Avenue, WC2

map 1

Tel: 020 7836 7337
Website: www.leylandsdm.co.uk
Tube: Leicester Square
Open: All branches Mon-Fri 7am-6pm, Sat 7.30am-5.30pm

Leyland are a specialist paint outlet selling their own and other brands of paint at competitive prices. Leyland also offer a paint mixing service.

Branches:

371-373 Edgware Road, W2 Tel: 020 7723 8048
19-29 Balls Pond Road, N1 Tel: 020 7275 2975
2-4 Great Eastern Road, EC2A Tel: 020 7377 8510
314-316 Old Brompton Road, SW5 Tel: 020 7370 6600
6-8 Warwick Way, SW1 Tel: 020 7828 8695
683-685 Finchley Road, NW2 Tel: 020 7794 5927
89-90 Farringdon Road, EC1 Tel: 020 7278 8933
347-349 King's Road, SW3 Tel: 020 7352 4742
7-15 Camden Road, NW1 Tel: 020 7284 4366
361-365 Kensington High Street, W14 Tel: 020 7602 9099
9 The Mall, Ealing Broadway, W5 Tel: 020 8566 0481
25 Goodge Street, W1 Tel: 020 7636 2995
314-316 Old Brompton Road, SW5 Tel: 020 7370 6600

North

Colour Centre

29a Offord Road, N1
Tel: 020 7609 1164
Website: www.colourcentre.com
Rail: Caledonian Road & Barnsbury
Open: Mon-Fri 8am-5pm, Sat 9am-1pm

This large warehouse sells a huge range of paints and decorating materials and offers trade prices to all its customers. It is a particularly good place to try for unusual things like anti-graffiti paint. For those with less exacting requirements, they also stock standard emulsions and wood paints and offer a colour matching service. Following the closure of Foxell & James this is the best paint outlet in town.

Dave's DIY
296-8 Firs Lane, N13
Tel: 020 8807 3539
Rail: Palmers Green
Open: Mon- Fri 7.30am-4.30pm, Thurs 7.30am-1pm

This company sells paints and wallpapers to the trade but also offers the same discounts to the public. There are many brand name wallpapers, and considerable savings to be found on most items. The store also has a wide range of paints and offers three paint-mixing systems.

West

Askew Paint Centre
99-103 Askew Road, W12
Tel: 020 8743 6612
Tube: Stamford Brook
Open: Mon-Fri 7am-5pm, Sat 8am-4pm

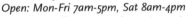

(map 5)

This shop offers great value paints with Dulux, Leyland and Sanderson all kept in stock. They also provide a mixing service. It might be a long way to go just for paint, but could be worth the journey as there are a number of DIY shops on nearby Uxbridge Road.

East

Bargain Wallpapers
203 Plashet Road, E13
Tel: 020 8470 7261
Tube: Upton Park
Open: Mon-Sat 10am-7pm, Sun 10am-4pm

This no-nonsense shop offers great value for wallpapers with prices starting from only £1 per roll, and they also sell brand name paints for below the usual price. Among the good deals are 2.5 litre tins of Dulux gloss for £9. A terrific place to come for decorating bargains.

Discount Decor
159 High Street, Walthamstow, E17
Tel: 020 8521 1999
Tube/Rail: Walthamstow Central
Bus: 123, 212, 275, W12
Open: Mon-Sat 9.30am-6pm, Sun 10.30am-3pm

This shop has deals on brand name paints and wallpapers and can mix colours from the Dulux and Berger paint ranges. The shop also offers good deals on small power tools.

Power Tools

West

Ideabright Ltd

770-776 Fulham Road, SW6

map 9

Tel: 020 7736 4014

Website: www.directbrandtools.com

Open: Mon-Sat 8.30am-5.30pm, Sun 10am-1pm

This local DIY merchants has an extensive power tools department with numerous special offers such as the two models of AEG drill which were reduced by 20% from the usual retail price. They also operate an easy-to-use website which is regularly up dated.

South

S.J. Carter Electrical Tools Ltd

74 Elmers End Road, Anerley, SE20

Tel: 020 8659 7222

Website: www.carterstools.co.uk

Rail: Birkbeck

Open: Mon-Fri 8am-5pm, Sat 9am-1pm

Carters are a large, well stocked and very competitively-priced tool shop. They sell both hand and power tools, have a mail order service and hire tools. As well as a great range of equipment, Carters also will attempt to match any price and also has regular special offers such as the Irwin Marpels chisel set recently reduced to £60.84 from an original price of £110.79.

A. Gatto & Son

206-12 Garratt Lane, SW18

map 8

Tel: 020 8874 2671

Rail: Earlsfield

Open: Mon-Fri 9am-5pm, Sat 9am-12noon

This tool distributor has been in business since 1933 and is happy to deal with the public. From past experience the staff are both friendly and willing to offer help and advice to the amateur who may well be daunted by the array of power tools on display. There are also plenty of bargains to be found here among the routers, drills and saws making this one of the best places in London to get a new power tool.

London Power Tools and Fixings

190 Lower Road, Rotherhithe SE16
Tel: 020 7237 9884
Website: www.londonpower.co.uk
Tube: Canada Water/Surrey Quays
Open: Mon-Fri 7.30am-5pm, Sat 8.30am-3pm

This shop stocks lots of different brands, but is one of the largest Bosch power tool retailers in the country and has the entire range in stock, all sold at significant discounts. On a recent visit a Bosch hammer drill was only £45 (exc VAT), while a De Walt router was only £108 (exc VAT) – a significant discount on the usual retail price. The company offers free delivery in the London area.

East

Toucan Tools Co.

373-375 Church Road, Leyton, E10
Tel: 020 8556 6060
Website: www.toucantools.co.uk
Tube: Leyton
Open: Mon-Fri 8am-4.40pm, Sat 8am-2.30pm

This large tool suppliers stocks all the major brand names at competitive prices and usually has a few special offers. Recently they had a promotion on a Makita circular saw for £92.50 (inc VAT) and a 12v cordless drill from the same manufacturer for £99 (inc VAT), which was half the usual price. The company will deliver free in the London area, has a large ironmongery and lock department, and will also repair tools.

C W Tyzack

79/81 Kingsland Road, E2
Tel: 020 7739 7126
Tube: Old Street
Open: Mon-Fri 8am-5.30pm, Sat 8am-1pm

C W Tyzack is a very well-stocked DIY store with a particularly wide selection of power tools. The prices are competitive and they have regular promotional discounts as well as a catalogue. The shop is usually busy and the staff do not have the time to discuss things in detail, so it's a good idea to know what you're looking for before visiting.

Outside London

Croydon Powertool Centre

Units 9 & 10 Roman Industrial Estate,
Tait Road, Croydon, CR0
Tel: 020 8683 0550
Open: Mon-Fri 8am-5pm, Sat 9am-1pm

This large shop buys tools in bulk and sells to the trade and public at large discounts. On a recent visit a Makita MTA II drill was on offer for only £39 (inc VAT) – reduced from the usual price of £50. They offer free delivery in the London area regardless of the amount spent, so give them a call for their best price.

They also have a sister company:
Lakedale Power Tools, 217-223 Plumstead High St SE18,
Tel: 020 8854 9894

Gill & Hoxby

131-137 St Mark's Road
Enfield, Middlesex, EN1
Tel: 020 8363 2935
Open: Mon-Fri 8am-5.30pm, Sat 8.30am-2pm

This shop boasts the largest display of power tools in the country and stocks every major and minor name, from professional equipment by Makita and DeWalt to tools made for domestic use by the likes of Black & Decker and Bosch. The company buys in bulk and sells at considerable discounts to the public. The savings you make on larger items may make the trip to Enfield worthwhile.

Impact Power Tools Ltd

Unit 10, Trowers Way
Holmthorpe Industrial Estate, Redhill, Surrey, RH1
Tel: 01737 772 436
Website: www.impactpt.co.uk
Open: Mon-Fri 8.30am-5.30pm, Sat 8.30am-12.30pm

DIY bores will gag at the bargains available at this large power tool warehouse. It has a comprehensive price list and offers free delivery for orders over £100. Recent bargains included a Bosch 14.4v cordless drill for only £89.95 (exc VAT) and an AEG heavy duty combi drill for just £139 (exc VAT). Phone for a specific price on an item or ask them to send you a price list.

Domestic Appliances

Kettles, toasters, microwaves, fridge freezers and washing machines vary in price from store to store. Comparing like with like is often difficult with subtle changes introduced with each new model number. If you're not too fussy about the latest model and can do without some of the extra special features you can get a bargain. For a large choice start by looking in big outlets like John Lewis, Argos, B&Q, Dixons, Homebase, Currys, Comet or Powerhouse to work out what you want and then compare prices in any of the shops below before you make your decision. If you're prepared to go for a machine that is 'graded', i.e. scratched or dented or an ex-showroom model, there are even greater savings to be made. Check out delivery charges, guarantees and whether installation and removal of your old machine is included.

North

CES

936-938 High Road, N12
Tel: 020 8343 8288
Tube: Woodside Park
Open: Mon-Fri 9am-6pm, Sat 9.30am-5.30pm

CES do most of their work with landlords, providing new and reconditioned fridges, washing machines and cookers for rented accommodation. The prices are very competitive with fridges from £69 and fridge freezers from only £89 with all domestic appliances guaranteed for six months. CES will also deliver free in the London area.

Glotech

660 & 646-648 High Road, N12
Website: www.glotech.co.uk
Tel:0800 3777 789
Tube: East Finchley/Woodside Park
Open: Mon-Sat 9am-6pm

This company (formerly known as Finchley VAC Centre) occupies several shops on Finchley High Road with 660 dealing in slightly damaged or scratched new appliances – mostly Indesit and Ariston. The store at 646-648 High Road deals in new machines straight from the manufacturers at prices you'll find hard to beat. All sorts of white goods can be found here: American fridges, old fashioned ranges, washing machines and dishwashers. Ask about their special offers.

London Domestic Appliances
4 Mordaunt Road, NW10
Tel: 020 8961 5695
Tube: Harlesden
Open: Mon-Sat 9am-6pm (closed Fri 12noon -3pm)

This long-established shop offers new, graded (slight seconds) and re-conditioned white goods. Reconditioned washing machines sell for £100-£175 and graded models are sold for £200-£350. Reconditioned fridges go here for £60-£75 and graded ones from £110-£165. London Domestic Appliances are Corgi registered for gas appliances.

Magnet Discount Warehouses Ltd
79 Fore Street N18
Tel: 020 8807 9211
Tube: Seven Sisters
Open: Mon-Sat 9am-6pm

These large stores offer good value on domestic appliances with all major brands found here including Bosch, Siemens and Whirlpool. The stores hold stock of their goods and so delivery is prompt and they are also willing to price match if you find the same product cheaper.
Also at: 17 Lymington Avenue N22, Tel: 020 8889 3600

Shantel AV Ltd
11-13 Long Lane, Finchley, N3
Tel: 020 8371 6671
Website: www.shantelav.co.uk
Tube: Finchley Central
Open: Mon-Sat 10am-6pm

Shantel AV is a friendly local electrical retailer that offers great value and service on a wide range of domestic appliances. Prices start from £200 for a Beco washing machine which includes delivery, installation and the removal of the old machine and the same service is available for a Bosch machine at only £249. The fridges are great value with a 50s style Baumatic fridge freezer for £299 and a large American style Whirlpool for £599. The shop also sells TVs and Hi-Fi's (see Electronics section on page 110).

Yes Domestic Appliances

161 Holloway Road, N7
Tel: 020 7700 5700
Tube: Holloway Road
Open: Mon-Sat 9am-7pm

This well organised shop sells cookers, fridges and washing machines that are either new, reconditioned or slight seconds. On a recent visit they had some great deals with a reconditioned Hoover WMS 38 washing machine for only £140, and a slightly scratched Bosch Classix machine that has never been used for only £250. Among the cookers was a very nice looking twin oven Zanussi with stainless steel finish for only £240. All the goods come with a 6 months guarantee, free delivery and free fitting and they also offer a very reasonable repair service.

West

Buyers & Sellers

120-122 Ladbroke Grove, W10
Tel: 020 7243 5400
Website: www.buyersandsellersonline.co.uk
Tube: Ladbroke Grove
Open: Mon-Fri 9am-5.30pm (Thurs 9am-6.30pm), Sat 9am-4.30pm

Buyers and Sellers adopt a travel agency approach to selling household appliances with a busy office/showroom, hundreds of brochures, helpful staff and a determination to offer the lowest possible price. Established over thirty years ago they can supply anything from the cheapest to the most sophisticated machines, integrated or free standing. Everything is fully guaranteed and delivery is fast. Worth calling in or phoning with the model number of the machine you fancy to get a comparative quote.

Cooker Centre Ltd

420 Edgware Road, W2
Tel: 020 7723 6444
Tube: Edgware Road
Open: Mon-Sat 8.30am-5.30pm

Friendly, family-run business offering 'massive' discounts and immediate delivery on new kitchen appliances. Located at the Maida Vale end of the Edgware Road near to Church Street market, the firm has a fast turn-around of discounted goods, many going to local builders and rental agencies. They are not averse to haggling and will try to beat any price if you find the same item cheaper elsewhere. All goods are fully guaranteed.
Also at: 69 Cricklewood Broadway NW2, Tel: 020 8452 8709

Hot & Cold Inc

13-15 Golborne Road, W10
Tel: 020 8960 1200/1300
Tube: Westbourne Park
Open: Mon-Fri 10am-6pm, Sat 10am-4.30pm

One of the countries best known discount outlets specialising in good quality built-in ovens, hobs and hoods, American fridge freezers and ranges. They also stock sinks, numerous taps, washing machines, fridges and vacuum cleaners. There are always considerable savings on end-of-line items such as the Bosch Quantum Speed built-in microwave and oven for only £499.50 (reduced from £635), the Siemens stainless steel oven reduced by £100 to only £399.50 and the large Siemens larder fridge for £749.50 (originally £837). The staff are helpful and produce price-lists to show you all the latest discounts. If you're in search of a particular item, they can usually order it quickly if it isn't in stock. All goods are in perfect condition and are fully guaranteed.

Kitchen Tech

163 King Street, W6
Tel: 020 8748 8770
Open: Mon-Sat 10am-6pm

This shop specialises in new cookers and fridges and is particularly good value for the Baumatic brand. Among the good deals a Baumatic built-in oven and separate hob was only £299 and a large stainless steel range cooker by the same company was only £729. Other good deals included a quality Lofra cooker which had been reduced by £100 to only £499. Kitchen Tech also offer a reasonably priced selection of washing machines from brands such as Hotpoint, Indesit and Whirlpool. The company has a fast and efficient same-day delivery and installation service.

Also at:
123 The Vale, Acton, W3 Tel: 020 8749 7606

Sun Hill Electric
117 Fulham Palace Road, W6
Tel: 020 8748 1861
Tube: Barons Court/Hammersmith
Open: Mon-Sat 9am-6pm

All makes of fully reconditioned appliances (cookers, fridge/freezers, washing machines) guaranteed for 3 months or, for an extra £20, a year. There are around 500 machines usually in stock (there's a garage-full at the back), including Bosch, Neff, AEG and Hotpoint. Expect to pay about £100 for a 2 year old Bosch washing machine (£380 new) or £120 for a four year old Zanussi fridge/freezer (£300 new).

South

Iceland Clearance Centre
120-132 Camberwell Road, SE5
Tel: 020 7708 4347
Tube: Elephant & Castle
Open: Mon-Sat 9am-5.30pm, Sun 10am-4pm

Clearance centre for shop-soiled, slightly damaged or discontinued fridges and fridge freezers from Iceland showrooms countrywide sold at 20% below the new price. If you are looking for top brands like Bosch and AEG you will be disappointed here, but they do have a reasonable stock of the cheaper brands such as Hotpoint, Whirlpool and their own brand Kyoto. The centre also has a small selection of other household items such as cookers and microwaves.

East

Discount Appliance Centre

44 Amhurst Road, E8
Tel: 020 8986 9296
Train: Hackney Central
Open: Mon-Sat 10am-6pm

This established retailer offers a wide range of quality new washing machines, dish washers, fridges and cookers at very competitive prices. Recent deals included a Siemens WL1400 washing machine for £499 (reduced from £600) and a large Bosch fridge freezer reduced by £100 to only £399. At the back of the store they display the graded (slight seconds) goods which are sold at even greater discounts. As well as good value they also offer a free, same-day delivery service.

Power Giant

353 Hoe Street, E17
Tel: 020 8520 2300
Tube: Walthamstow
Open: Mon-Sat 10am-7pm

Graded washing machines and fridge freezers at a fair price. They largely stock Hotpoint and Indesit but will attempt to source other brands if they do not have a particular item in stock.

Also at: Barking Road E13, Tel: 020 8470 4488

RGA Appliances Ltd

22 Stoke Newington High Street, N16
Tel: 020 7254 9742
Rail: Stoke Newington
Open: Mon-Sat 9.30am-6.30pm

This store largely sells new washing machines, fridges and dishwashers, but there are occasional graded (slightly damaged) products that are sold at a considerable discount. On a recent visit they had a slightly marked Whirlpool dishwasher for £199 (new price £279) and among the new goods a Bosch washing machine for £279 (new price £299).

Also at: 572 Green Street, E13 Tel: 020 8552 0056

Fabrics & Haberdashery

Below are reviewed many of the most interesting and good value fabric and haberdashery shops in the capital. Several of the shops offer both furnishing and dress fabric, but we have also included more specialist outlets dealing only in household fabrics. Berwick Street and Goldhawk Road are renowned for their many fabric shops and these areas have been reviewed collectively as budding dress makers will probably visit the area and compare the prices and stock of all the outlets on the street.

Central

Alexander Furnishings
51-61 Wigmore Street, W1
See review in the Curtains section (page 160).

Barber Green
Room 18, 33-35 St John's Square, EC1
Tel: 020 7608 0362
Tube/Rail: Farringdon
Open: By appointment
Bargain hunters should call these tailors in advance of a visit to arrange to check out the remnants and end-of-line fabrics such as lace, velvet, woollens and trimmings that they sell to the public at a hefty discount. If you slip out of bargain shopping mode, keep in mind that the tailors at this busy workshop also make wonderful, tempting, high-quality bespoke clothing.

Russell & Chapple
68 Drury Lane, WC2
Tel: 020 7836 7521
Website: www.randc.net
Tube: Covent Garden
Open: Mon-Fri 9am-5.30pm
Suppliers to the surrounding theatres, Russell and Chapple have an excellent selection of hard-to-find fabrics at extremely competitive prices. While domestic seamstresses may find little need for the flame retardant fabrics, there are several that are very practical. Cotton duck suitable for upholstery costs £3.70 per metre and muslin costs just £1.90 per metre.

Berwick Street, W1

Tube: Piccadilly or Oxford Circus
Open: Mon-Sat 9am-5pm

map
1

Berwick Street is famous for its fabric shops which do much of their trade with the film and theatre businesses of Soho. The fabric shops are unique, but all of them share a slightly theatrical atmosphere derived from the clients and the characters that run them. In terms of bargain shopping all the outlets here offer good value and most have remnants and clearance fabrics available. Any dressmaker looking for inspiration and good value fabrics should spend an afternoon visiting the cloth shops of Soho.

Other outlets on Berwick Street:

Cloth House

47 Berwick Street, W1
Tel: 020 7437 5155
98 Berwick Street, W1
Tel: 020 7287 1555
www.clothhouse.com

The Berwick Street Cloth Shop

14 Berwick Street, W1
Tel: 020 7287 2881

Borovick Fabrics Ltd

16 Berwick Street, W1
Tel: 020 7437 2180
www.borovickfabricsltd.co.uk

Broadwick Silks

9-11 Broadwick Street, W1
Tel: 020 7734 3320

Textile King Ltd

81 Berwick Street, W1
Tel: 020 7437 7372

Soho Silks

22 D'Arblay Street, W1
Tel: 020 7434 3305

Textile King

Textile King

The Berwick Street Cloth Shop

The Cloth Shop

North

Bargain Centre

93 Upper Street, N1
Tel: 020 7226 1741
Tube: Angel
Open: Mon-Sat 10am-5.30pm, Sun 10am-1pm

(map 3)

This pleasant little fabric shop has been on Upper Street (in various locations) since the 1960s – long before the estate agents and cafés which now predominate. The friendly staff undertake alterations as well as selling inexpensive suit fabric and linings. Prices start from as little as £3 per metre for a suit lining and suit fabrics are sold for £12-30. A great place to find tweeds, pinstripes and plain wools and wool blends for a fraction of the West End price.

Empee Silk Fabrics Ltd

31 Commercial Road, Edmonton, N18
Tel: 020 8887 6000
Website: www.wholesalefabrics.co.uk
Tube: Whitehart Lane
Open: Mon-Thurs 9am-5.30pm, Fri 9am-3pm, Sun 8am-2pm

This well-stocked fabric warehouse once occupied several shops on Brick Lane, but has moved to this larger site in north London in recent years. Empee offer such good value that they have managed to keep many of their loyal customers who now make the journey to get all kinds of material from plain cotton fabric for £1 per metre to fine silks from £5.25 per metre. The staff are very friendly and helpful and always prepared to do a deal. The store is largely wholesale, but they welcome individual customers with a minimum purchase of 10 metres per fabric. Take a look at their website to get some idea of their stock.

Martin's Fabric

24-26 South Mall, Edmonton Green Shopping Centre, N9
Tel: 020 8807 4222
Rail: Edmonton Green
Open: Mon-Wed, Fri-Sat 10am-5pm, Thurs 10am-2pm

Sheeting, upholstery and curtain fabrics are the forte here where fabrics are piled high and sell for as little as £1 a metre. A great place for budget-conscious DIY enthusiasts looking for curtain and upholstery fabric. They also sell a good range of ready-made curtains, net curtains and blinds.

Rolls & Rems

9 The Concourse,
Edmonton Green, N9
Tel: 020 8803 6532
Rail: Edmonton Green
Open: Mon-Sat 9am-5.30pm

As the name suggests, this small chain of fabric shops sells rolls of fabrics as well as a good selection of remnants. The choice is top-notch with plenty of printed and plain natural fabrics from £1 per metre as well as synthetics like fake fur at £4 per metre and a selection of bridal fabrics. The company also has a good selection of curtain fabric and all the stitching accoutrements from patterns to zippers.

Also at:
21 Seven Sisters Road, Holloway N7, Tel: 020 7263 3272
111 High Street, Lewisham SE13, Tel: 020 8852 8686

Sew Fantastic!

107 Essex Road, N1
Tel: 020 7226 2725
Tube: Angel
Open: Mon-Wed, Fri-Sat 10am-5.30pm

map 3

A great little local fabric shop selling everything you might need. The owner is helpful and informative. There are plenty of fabrics of all kinds for reasonable prices with material suitable for dressmaking and upholstery. Bargain hunters should check out the large box of remnants for just £1 a piece. As well as fabrics, they also sell buttons, ribbons, patterns and other sewing essentials.

West

The Cloth Shop
290 Portobello Road, W10
Tel: 020 8968 6001
Website: www.clothshop.net
Tube: Ladbroke Grove
Open: Mon-Sat 10am-6pm

Set among the market stalls of Portobello, this small shop is crammed full of amazing, mostly plain, fabrics with nothing over £15 a metre and plenty of fabric bargains such as Gingham for £2.95 per metre and coloured muslin for the same price. The shop has lots of linens, muslins, calicoes, and Indian cottons ideal for making up into stylish upholstery and curtains as well as a small range of clothing fabrics. They also stock a wide selection of antique household linen from Europe, Welsh wool blankets and antique Indian throws and cushions. To get a better idea of the shop have a look at their website. For those who can't make it to Portobello, the shop has a fast and efficient mail order service.

Shaukat Fabrics
168-172 Old Brompton Road, SW5
Tel: 020 7373 8956
Tube: Gloucester Road
Open: Mon-Sat 10am-6.30pm

This large shop has a cosy atmosphere which is largely provided by the reams of fabric that are piled high and sold at a very reasonable price. They are the only London outlet for Liberty remnants with 90cm wide reams for £6.99 per metre – a huge saving on the original price. As well as fabrics, Shaukat also sell great quality bags and bedding – see pages 94 and 149 for further details.

Goldhawk Road

Goldhawk Road, W12
Tube: Shepherd's Bush
Open: Mon-Sat 9am-5pm

The small part of Goldhawk Road between Shepherd's Bush Road and Shepherd's Bush Market is full of fabric shops selling largely dress material at very low prices. The shops listed below are some of the most prominent on the street, which together offer an unrivalled choice of fabric. It's a good idea to visit the area and compare prices to find exactly what you're looking for at the best price.

Other outlets on Goldhawk Road:

Classic Textiles
44 Goldhawk Road, W12
Tel: 020 8743 3516

A-One Fabrics
50/52 Goldhawk Road, W12
Tel: 020 8740 7349

U.K. Textiles
47 Goldhawk Road, W12
Tel: 020 8749 4077

Toni Textiles
51 Goldhawk Road, W12
Tel: 020 8743 1488

A to Z Fabrics
53a Goldhawk Road, W12
Tel: 020 8222 6566

South

Atlantic Silk Fabric

28 Electric Avenue, SW9
Tel: 020 7274 6040
Tube/Rail: Brixton
Open: Mon-Sat 9am-5.30pm

This shop sells silks as well as every other fabric you might want, from African prints to plain cotton shirting with stock sourced from around the globe. They've got a small selection of remnants as well as fabrics as cheap as £1 per metre. As expected, they also sell trimmings, buttons, and patterns as well as handing out free advice.

Rolls & Rems

111 High Street, Lewisham, SE13
Tel: 020 8852 8686
See entry in North London (page 185) for full details.

Yemmy Textiles & Fashion

115 Peckham High Street, SE15
Tel: 020 7635 6700
Tube/Rail: Elephant & Castle, Oval; Peckham Rye (Train)
Open: Mon-Sat 9.30am-7pm

Yemmy spent many years selling multi-coloured, brightly hued African fabrics in one of the arcades at Brixton Market, but has since moved to Peckham High Street. The shop may have moved, but the prices are still competitive, with good bargains to be had in the discontinued lines.

East

Bhopal Fabrics

98 Brick Lane, E1
Tel: 020 7377 1886
Tube: Aldgate
Open: Daily 9am-6pm

(map 12)

Like many Brick Lane area fabric shops, customers are required to buy at least five metres of fabric here. Elegant, vibrant silks start at just £5 per metre. The stock is varied and there is a particularly good selection of Indian fabrics in plain, bright colours or with pretty embroidery. A great place to find some ethnic chic.

Z. Butt Textiles 2001

24 Brick Lane, E1
Tel: 020 7247 7776
Tube: Aldgate East
Open: Mon-Fri 9am-6pm, Sun 9.30am-2.30pm

This is an established fabric outlet on Brick Lane offering great value fabrics and a lot of choice. Among the bargains are blue cotton drill for £2.95 per metre, 65" width calico for 95p per metre and quality velvet for £4.95 per metre. They have recently introduced a range of Salwar Karneez Asian outfits which range in price from £5-25. The outfits consist of three very large pieces of fabric amounting to as much as 7.5m – making them popular for home decoration. The pashmina shawls also sell well with prices starting from as little as £1.99 and going up to a very modest £3.99. The shop has a good reputation and is popular with designers who emerge laden with reams of fabric.

Epra Fabrics

52/56 Brick Lane, E1
Tel: 020 7247 1248
Tube: Aldgate East/Shoreditch
Open: Mon-Fri 9am-5.30pm, Sun 9am-2pm

Epra is a large fabric store with a wide selection of very cheap fabrics. Prices start at 75p per metre for simple calico and go up to a very modest £3.25 per metre for a kitsch synthetic fur fabric. They have a selection of curtain materials which are kept in a separate room and lots of colourful fabrics for children's clothes and furnishing. The shop does a good deal of wholesale business and has a minimum order of 10 metres per fabric, so it's a good place to visit for curtaining and other big projects.

Hardwick Textiles

369 Green Street, E13
Tel: 020 8472 1284
Tube: Upton Park
Open: Mon-Tues, Thurs-Sat 11am-6pm

Hardwick's has been on Green Street since before the First World War and has survived by offering great fabric at a very competitive price. The shop sells suiting, special occasion fabrics and linen and offers great value with the proprietor aiming to sell at half the price of high street retailers. Wool suiting goes for around £12 per metre and the shop does a roaring trade in Italian pure cotton shirt material with 300 different designs and prices starting from £3.85 per metre. Located just opposite Upton Park tube, this classic material shop is definitely worth making a special journey to visit.

Hussain Fabrics
123 Green Street, E7
Tel: 020 8548 4601
Tube: Upton Park
Open: Daily 10am-8pm

Plenty of fabrics from curtaining to dress material are available at this modest shop. The prices are very competitive with some fabrics going for as little as £2 per metre. Hardwick Textiles is just down the road.

Mermaid Fabrics
364 Mare Street, E8
Tel: 020 8985 3694
Rail: Hackney Central
Open: Mon-Sat 9.30am-5.30pm
See main entry in the Curtain and Blinds section (page 164).

Nasseri Fabrics (Formerly Fabrics le Prestige)
41 Wentworth Street, E1
Tel: 020 7375 2706
Tube: Aldgate/Aldgate East
Open: Mon-Fri 9.30am-5.30pm, Sun 9am-3pm

One of several shops along Wentworth Street that specialises in West African fabrics. The fabric here varies from the vibrant to the gaudy but the prices are low with a minimum order of six yards per fabric.

Outer London

Corcoran & May
31-35 Blagdon Road,
New Malden, Surrey, KT3
See main entry in Curtains and Blinds section (page 165).

Jersey Vogue
14 Station Road, Edgware, Middlesex, HA8
Tel: 020 8952 7751
Tube: Edgware
Open: Mon-Fri 9am-5.30pm, Sun 9.30am-1pm

Jersey Vogue has been providing the public with end-of-season fabrics from major manufacturers for over 30 years. The prices are very competitive with quality denim and corduroy for £4-5 per metre and some fabrics for only £1 per metre. The company's two warehouses hold thousands of reams of fabric making Jersey Vogue worth a special visit.

Furniture

This chapter concentrates on all the new furniture shops in London that offer great value, as well as mentioning several of the regular furniture sales which are great places to find discounted end-of-season stock and slight seconds from prestigious furniture companies such as Habitat and SCPR. If you are willing to buy second-hand furniture take a look at the Auctions (page 276) and Junk Shops (page 339) sections of this book as well as some of the larger charity shops such as the huge British Heart Foundation store in Wandsworth (page 317).

Central

Martin Barnett Furniture Ltd
68 Marylebone Lane, off Wigmore Street, W1
Tel: 020 7487 2997
Website: www.martinbarnett.co.uk
Open: Mon-Sat 10am-6pm, Sun 12noon-5pm

Martin Barnett offer a wide range of good value furniture with several 'flat pack' furniture kits which allow buyers to furnish a two-bedroom flat for £2,900 or a one-bedroom flat for £1,995. The company is popular with landlords seeking to meet the demands of the high-paying tenants of west and central London. The company offers sofas, chairs, dining room tables, rugs, blinds, curtains and mirrors – all at prices below those of other West End retailers. Give them a call or visit their website to find their latest designs and special offers.

Emporio Home
5-7 Tottenham Street, W1
Tel: 020 7580 8444
Website: www.emporiohome.co.uk
Tube: Goodge Street
Open: Mon-Tues, Wed, Fri 10am-6pm, Thurs and Sat 10am-6.30pm, Sun 12noon-6pm

This is the only London store of Emporio Home, which offers great value furniture for the bedroom, dining room and lounge. All the sofas in their 'Designers Choice' range come with at least a five-year construction warranty and ten years warranty for all sofas made-to-order. There are discounts to be found on a wide range of their furniture with recent deals including a pine dining room table and four chairs for only £299 (reduced from £655). Visit the website to get more information about their deals and see some of their designs.

Futon Company

169 Tottenham Court Road, W1T
Tel: 020 7636 9984
Website: www.futoncompany.co.uk
Tube: Tottenham Court Road
Open: Mon-Sat 10am-7pm7, Sun 11am-5pm

The Futon Company is a chain of stores that offers well-made and sur-prisingly good value futons. The prices in the store are very competitive and Futon Company also have regular sales – in the summer and winter – when futons are reduced by as much as £200. Have a look at their website for all the latest offers.

Branches at:
102 Chiswick High Road W4, Tel: 020 8995 2271
59 Muswell Hill Broadway N10, Tel: 020 8883 5657
60-62 London Road KT2, Tel: 020 8546 4868

SCP Ltd

135-139 Curtain Road, EC2
Tel: 020 7739 1869
Website: www.scp.co.uk
Open: Mon-Sat 9.30am-6pm, Sun 11am-4pm

SCP are famous for their high quality, contemporary furniture and acces-sories for the home and office. The company hold twice yearly (summer and winter) sales at both their sale outlets and once a year their warehouse is opened to the public for a one day sale where surplus stock is reduced to clear. Visit their website to find details of the next SCP sale with the one day warehouse sale a particular favourite for bargain hunters.

North

Big Bed & Pine Co
125 Essex Road, N1
Tel: 020 7359 9614
Tube: Angel or Highbury & Islington
Open: Mon-Sat 9am-5pm

This shop sells beds and quality pine and oak furniture. A 4"6 pine bed frame with a quality mattress was excellent value for only £199, while a single pine frame is £99 with a mattress for £49. All the chests are very well made with solid wood backs and drawers and are very competitively priced with a medium chest of drawers for £229 and a large one for £259. As well as having very good prices the shop will also stain the furniture to your liking, deliver in the London area, and, when necessary, assemble the furniture – all without charge. A great value shop.

Heal's Warehouse Sale
Unit 11 Lea Valley Trading Estate
Harbet Road, Edmonton, N18
Website: www.heals.co.uk

This annual warehouse sale is held at Heal's Edmonton warehouse. It is here that the company sells all its slight seconds and remainder stock at up to 75% discount. The sale usually takes place at the end of May, but dates vary so check their website for information about the next sale.

Ixia Leather Sofas
22 White Conduit Street,
Islington, N1
Tel: 020 7689 0013
Website: www.ixiainteriors.co.uk
Open: Mon-Sat 10am-6pm, Sun 11am-4pm

Ixia have three showrooms in London displaying their wonderful range of good value leather sofas. The chunky three-seater Torino sofa was very well priced at only £759 and matching armchairs are available for an equally modest £359. If you are on a smaller budget they also offer the same designs in fabric at considerably lower prices with a large cloth sofa for only £529. They offer free delivery within two weeks for those inside the M25. Readers can also get a further 5% discount if they mention Bargain Hunters' London when placing their order.
Branches at:
67 Gap Road, Wimbledon, SW19
Greenwich Covered Market, College Approach, Greenwich, SE10

West

Alma Home

12-14 Greatorex Street, E1
Tel: 020 7377 0762
www.almahome.co.uk
Tube: Aldgate East
Open: Mon-Fri 9am-6pm, Sat-Sun 10.30am-4pm

A 60 year old leather company that branched out into making trendy leather and suede home furnishings six years ago. The retail showroom is next to the factory. Enterprising and imaginative in their use of a huge variety of skins, they supply major stores like Liberty, the Conran Shop and Harrods with console tables, cushions, bean-filled stools and cubes and are currently working on producing suede blinds. Mongolian sheepskin rugs cost from £100; seating from £125. They offer regular special promotions at discounts of between 20% and 30%. They have just opened a flagship store at 8 Vigo Street, W1, but for the major discounts visit the Greatorex Street branch.

Lombok Clearance Store

Unit 2 The Gasworks,
2 Michael Road, SW6
Tel: 020 7751 8550 (Fri & Sat only)
Website: www.lombok.co.uk
Open: Sat 10am-5pm

(map 9)

Lombok is well known for the its eastern-inspired furniture, mirrors and cushions which are made to a very high standard and are usually beyond the pocket of most people when sold on the high street. Less well known is that Lombok sell their clearance stock, returns and slight seconds at their large warehouse every Saturday with over 100 items to be found there every week. At a recent sale an uphostered Planter's chair made damp in transit was reduced from £465 to £279, last season's cushions were reduced from £25 to £5 and clearance bed linen was reduced by 50%. The sales are always well attended so it's a good idea to get there early to avoid missing a bargain. Visit the website to find out more about the Lombok range.

Maison du Monde

273-279 The High Street, Acton, W3
Tel: 020 8993 5559
Website: www.maisondumonde.com
Tube: Acton Town
Open: Mon-Sat 10am-6pm, Sun 11am-5pm

This large warehouse outlet, tucked away in an industrial estate in Acton, imports furniture from India, Indonesia and Morocco and sells direct to the public at considerable discounts. They have a particularly good stock of dining room table and chairs with prices starting from £199 and a solid wood chest of drawers for the bedroom can be found here for only £275. The store's website is a useful resource and offers the opportunity to buy on-line.

Retro Sofas

225 Munster Road, SW6
Tel: 020 7381 9027
Email: sales@retrosofas.co.uk
Website: www.retrosofas.co.uk
Rail: Pasons Green
Open: Sat 10am-5pm or by appointment

Retro Sofas offer a wide range of fabulous leather sofas and armchairs at very competitive prices. Their website is very easy to use and shows the full range with measurements so that you can plan your purchase in advance. Expect to pay around £795 for a 3-seater leather sofa that would cost several hundred more at larger furniture stores.

Sofas to Go

Sofa Workshop, 8 High Street,
Ealing Broadway Centre, W5
Tel: 020 8579 0693
Website: www.sofaworkshop.com
Open: Mon-Sat 9.30am-6pm, Thurs till 7pm, Sun 11am-5pm

Sofas to Go is the national clearance centre for the Sofa Workshop chain of stores. Sofa Workshop are great value but at the clearance centre, ex-display models and returns are sold for a fraction of the usual price. On a recent visit a 2-seater sofa in durable red cloth was reduced from £395 to £200 because the sofa was in less than perfect condition. Sofa Workshop has over thirty stores nationwide so this clearance centre is kept well stocked with bargain sofas, chairs and sofa beds. Visit their website to see the range of designs available and then give the clearance store a ring to see what they have in stock.

South

Bucks Warehouse

125 Evelyn Street, SE8
Tel: 020 8692 4447
Tube: Surrey Quays
Open: Wed-Fri 10am-6pm, Sat 10am-5pm, Sun 10am-4pm

Trailer loads of good quality furniture arrives weekly at this large warehouse in Surrey Quays where you can pick up all sorts of furniture bargains. Three quarters of the stock is from a well-known store famous for its undies. The stock is from ex-photo shoots, slightly marked, end of range or ex-display; with almost everything discounted by between 45% and 55%. There's a huge selection of beds (doubles from £140), sofa beds (from £420), as well as upholstered furniture.

Dwell Clearance Shop

Unit 16 Merton Industrial Park,
Lee Road, SW19
Tel: 08700 600 180
Website: www.dwell.co.uk
Open: Mon-Fri 9am-6pm, Sat 10am-7pm, Sun 11am-5pm

Dwell are a fashionable, contemporary furniture outlet that offer great design at affordable prices from their stores in Balham and Islington. They also run a clearance shop from an industrial park in Merton that sells all kinds of returns, slightly damaged goods and seconds at discounts of as much as 90% from the usual retail price. Take a look at their website to get some idea of the quality and design of the the furniture and other household items available.

London Warehouses Ltd

Unit 2A Endeavour Way
Wimbledon, SW19
Tel: 020 8947 9878
Website: www.londonwarehouse.co.uk
Open: Sat-Sun 10am-5pm

London Warehouses specialise in clearing the unwanted returned stock from many well known high street furniture showrooms. The 7,000 sq ft warehouse is open every weekend for the public to find tables, chairs, sofas and cabinets from the likes of Marks & Spencer, Habitat and Sofa Workshop at a fraction of the usual retail price. The quantity and quality of stock may vary depending on their suppliers, so its a good idea to give them a call first to see what they have in stock.

East

Bohemia

55 Brushfield Street, Old Spitalfields Market, E1
Tel: 020 7375 3283
Website: www.retrotrading.co.uk
Tube: Liverpool Street
Open: Tues-Sat 12noon-5pm, Sun 10am-6pm

This extensive shop in the heart of Spitalfields Market has a great selection of retro furniture and houseware at prices considerably less than you would pay at some similar outlets in the West End. Recently they were selling original Elda chairs for £2,100 which retail new for £3,500 and an Ercol room divider for £450 which retails in some retro shops for £850. Bohemia has a particularly good selection of lighting from the 50s to the 70s with plenty of exceptional pieces at affordable prices. There is a quick turnover of stock so it's always worth a visit to see what they have available.

Poetstyle Ltd

Unit 1 Bayford Street Industrial Units,
Bayford Street, Hackney, E8
Tel: 020 8533 0915
Website: www.sofachairs.co.uk
Tube: Bethnal Green
Rail: London Fields
Open: Mon-Fri 8am-5.30pm, Sat 10am-5pm

Jack Cohen's grandfather started this family upholstery business in the late 19th century. The company has survived all these years by offering great quality furniture at a very reasonable price. The showroom is in the middle of the factory so you can see the latest designs and also get a view of the sofas, sofa beds and armchairs being made in their workshop. Customers can specify the dimensions of the furniture, choose any fabric available or supply their own material and the company can also build a sofa to any design. If you are rather fond of your existing tatty sofa, Poetstyle offer a great value refurbishment service. Sofa beds start from £440 and go up to a very reasonable £580. A price list and brochure illustrating their thirty or so designs is available on request.

Unto This Last

230 Brick Lane, E2
Tel: 020 7613 0882
Website: www.untothislast.co.uk
Tube: Liverpool Street or Old Street
Open: Daily 10am-6pm

Unto This Last derives its name from a book by John Ruskin advocating local crafts workshops instead of industrial manufacture. The name is as clever as the furniture which is cut from large boards on a computer programmed machine which manages to use as much of the board as possible and in this way keeps costs down. The furniture is not only efficiently manufactured but also beautifully designed and available in a variety of colours and materials – visit their website to see the full range of their products. In terms of bargains everything here is great value with a solid wood stool for only £30, dining room chairs for £75 and large sideboards starting from £290; and similar value can be found among their range of beds, lighting and accessories. Compared to similar quality furniture in high street shops, Unto This Last is fantastic value and has the added advantage of manufacturing on-site and to the customer's specific requirements. John Ruskin would have been proud.

Little Book of Furniture Ltd

107a Commercial Street, Old Spitalfields Market, E1
Tel: 020 7247 4445 / 020 7247 4448
E-mail: ibofurniture@aol.com
Website: www.littlebookoffurniture.com
Tube: Liverpool Street
Open: Sun-Thurs 10am-6pm, Fri 10am-5pm, Sat 11am-5pm

This business designs, makes and sells quality, eco-friendly sofas and chairs – all made in their London workshop and sold to the public at very competitive prices. The sofas are great looking and a leather 3-seater starts from £795, with armchairs in leather for £545. To get an idea of the quality and designs available phone for one of their colourful catalogues, view their website or, better still, visit one of their showrooms.

Also at:
93 The Stables, Camden Market, NW1 Tel: 020 7267 6699

Unto This Last

Poetstyle Ltd

The Furniture Café

Kitchenware, Cutlery & Homewares

Central

Denny's

55a Dean Street, W1
Tel: 020 7494 2745
Tube: Piccadilly Circus
Open: Mon-Fri 9.30am-6pm, Sat 10.30am-4.30pm

Denny's sells mostly chefs' and waiters' clothes at cheap prices, but there are also a few items that can be used in a domestic kitchen such as a white bib apron for £3.63 and white cotton damask napkins for £1.50 each. To encourage the budding chef, pick up a child's chef hat for £6.47. High quality knives from Henckels, Victorinox and others go for about 15% off the normal price, but you should still expect to shell out for these professional blades. It is worth noting that because this is largely a trade shop, all the above prices exclude VAT.

Leon Jaeggi & Sons

77 Shaftesbury Avenue, W1
Tel: 020 7580 1974
Tube: Leicester Square/Piccadilly Circus
Open: Mon-Sat 9am-5.30pm

Most amateur, domestic chefs will never need any of the heavy-duty, professional equipment sold here. However, the shop's excellent range of smaller items are of wider interest. A dozen simple wine glasses cost £7.50 and plain white china plates go for as little as £1.85 each and bowls for £2.50 each. Plate clips for holding a wine glass on a plate cost 36p each and sponges are just 90p. To host a really professional dinner party, pick up the table crumb sweeper for £12. The enthusiastic amateur chef will certainly find dozens of inexpensive items to buy for their next culinary adventure. Prices are quoted without VAT.

Pages

121 Shaftesbury Avenue, W1
Tel: 0845 373 4017
Tube: Leicester Square/Piccadilly Circus
Open: Mon-Sat 9am-6pm

Bigger than nearby Leon Jaeggi & Sons, Pages stocks the same types of things, but has a larger selection. From prepping to cleaning up, the shop is full of gadgets and major appliances to make the job easier. If you fancy white porcelain dishes, they carry a large and diverse stock of tableware from makers like Revol. A giant iron frying pan costs just £18. Keen home bartenders might find the wine racks, cocktail shakers and ice crushers tempting. Expect to pay at least 25% less than high street prices.

David Richards & Sons

10 New Cavendish Street, W1
Tel: 020 7935 3206
Tube: Baker Street/Bond Street
Open: Mon-Fri 9.30am-5.30pm, Sat 10am-5pm

Established over 35 years ago this shop sells silverware direct to the public at wholesale prices. Silver photo frames start from £25. Miniature silver animals are one of their best sellers and are priced from £45-£2,500 and silver wine coasters cost £85 each with silver mounted decanters from £110. This is a great place to search for gifts and wedding presents. They offer a repair service which includes getting rid of 'chips' in glasswear, and they can also engrave anything you buy.

North

A & K Warehouse Ltd

152 Camden High Street, NW3
Tel: 020 7267 3805
Tube: Camden Town
Open: Mon-Sat 9am-6pm, Sun 11am-5pm

This family-run shop is an oasis of domestic good sense among the fashion outlets of Camden High Street. Here you can kit out your kitchen with basic, good value items from glass jugs to buckets and tea towels. The front of the shop is small and often obscured by street traders, but inside it is much larger and well stocked.

Pandora's Box

54 Penton Street, N1
Tel: 020 7837 9297
Tube: Angel
Open: Mon-Sat 10am-5pm

(map 3)

This business started life as a stall on Chapel Market but has moved to a smart shop in one of the back streets of Islington in recent years. The shop continues to sell kitchen equipment to the catering trade, but also welcomes custom from individuals looking for professional kitchenware at trade prices. It's a great place to find good value glassware, cutlery, crockery and top quality food processors.

Reject Pot Shop

56 Chalk Farm Road, NW1
Tel: 020 7485 2326
Tube: Camden Town
Open: Tues-Sun 11am-5.30pm

Reject Pot Shop has been selling a great selection of simple white crockery with slight and often difficult-to-spot defects to the public for many years. The crockery is made with the intention of decorating it with patterns and any slight blemish in the glaze will show up when decorated, so must be rejected. Many people find the plain white look attractive and with fine bone china plates for only £3.50, white mugs for 75p and a 12-piece porcelain dinner service for only £15, it's possible to get good quality kitchenware at a budget price. In recent years the shop has expanded its range of kitchenware with some great value cutlery and considerable discounts on the Sunnex range of caving knives. The store also sells a range of cheap blinds which are ideal for the kitchen.

West

Hansens

306 Fulham Road, SW10
Tel: 020 7351 6933
Website: www.hansens.co.uk
Tube: Fulham Broadway
Open: Mon-Fri 9am-5.30pm

This huge shop is dedicated to professional cooking, but anyone can take advantage of the reasonable prices and wonderful selection of goods. Every little gadget, dish and appliance a chef might ever need is here from cheap plasticware to expensive, heavy-duty appliances. This is a good west London alternative to Pages and Leon Jaeggi & Sons in the centre of town.

Lords Home Care

119-121 Westbourne Grove, W2
Tel: 020 7792 2471
Tube: Notting Hill Gate
Open: Mon-Fri 8am-6pm, Sat 9am-6pm, Sun 12noon-5pm

This shop caters for all your kitchenware needs and sells many other useful household items. It is probably the cheapest store of its kind in the area and on a recent visit had angle-poise lamps for £20, large galvanised steel flower pots for £19.99 and portable BBQs from £22. A really useful shop in a generally very expensive part of town.

South

Chomette
See main entry in the Factory Shops section (page 325).

Dentons Catering Equipment
2-4 Clapham High Street, SW4
Tel: 020 7622 7157
Tube: Clapham North
Open: Mon-Fri 8.30am-5.30pm, Sat 8.30am-1pm

In business for over 65 years, this shop is family run and stocks more than the amateur chef will ever need. They cater to the restaurant and professional catering trade, but also offer good deals to ordinary punters. Among the interesting utensils were good quality stainless steel pans from Genware that started from £15 (exc VAT) and a large Bourgeat non-stick frying pan for only £13.95 (exc VAT). Dentons publishes a catalogue and also regular sales catalogues which can be sent out on request.

Villeroy & Boch
See main entry in the Factory Shops section (page 326).

What!!! Stores
Unit 4, Surrey Quays Road,
Surrey Quays, SE16
Tel: 020 7252 1441
Tube: Surrey Quays
Open: Mon-Sat 9am-6pm, Sun 10am-4pm

This huge, 27,000 square foot warehouse behind Surrey Quays Shopping Centre sells all kinds of things for the home from cheap food to garden furniture. It might best be described as a cross between Woolworths and B&Q. Among the bargains on a recent visit was a wooden garden table and chairs for £99.99, reasonable quality non-stick frying pans for £6.99 and a one-ring portable camping stove for just £8.99. Despite the rather unusual name of the store and the unprepossessing nature of the warehouse, there are plenty of bargains to be found here, making it worth a visit if you are in the area. The excellent sports store, Decathlon, is just across the road (see pages 218 and 257).

East

Kitchen Warehouse

12 Bacon Street, E1
Tube: Liverpool Street
Open: Daily 9am-5pm

This large warehouse is crammed with used professional kitchenware and kitchen furniture. Among the bargains on a recent visit was a huge stainless steel counter unit for £120 and massive industrial cookers and mixers for a fraction of the original price. The best deal was good quality second-hand bar and bracket shelving which was sold for about half the new price. Just about the best place in London to get cheap kitchen equipment and next door are two very good junk shops – see page 348 for further details.

Pot Luck

84 Columbia Road, Shoreditch, E2
Tel: 020 7722 6892
Tube: Liverpool Street or Old Street
Open: Fri 10am-3pm, Sun 8am-12.30pm

There's no such thing as perfect china and this shop, opened by Linda Solomon over 25 years ago, sells what are called 'blanks' in the trade, though you'd never guess there was anything wrong with them. All the bone and porcelain china on sale is white with plenty of bargains to be found such as bone china plates for £3 (£8.25 in some department stores), 4 expresso cups with saucers for £5.99 and side plates for only £1 each. As well as china tableware, Pot Luck also has a good selection of glass vases with many for under £10. The shop does most of its business with hotels and restaurants, but on Fridays and Sundays it is open to the public and is best combined with a visit to the Columbia Road flower market on Sunday.

Picture Frames and Mirrors

Nelly Duff

156 Columbia Road, E2
Tel: 07984 690 339
Website: www.nellyduff.com
Tube: Bethnal Green or Old Street
Open: Mon-Fri by appointment, Sat 2pm-6pm, Sun 9am-3pm

Nelly Duff is a stylish little gallery selling a great selection of modern art to the denizens of east London. As they often sell their art work framed they also run a framing service which offers a number of contemporary styles of frame considerably cheaper than many high street framers. I recently had a large poster framed by Nelly Duff for £176 which was £30 cheaper than I was quoted anywhere else for a similar frame. Phone them with the frame size you need or visit their shop at the weekend. Sunday is the best day if you want to combine your frame shopping with a visit to Columbia Road Market.

John Hinds

240 Camberwell Road, SE5
Mob: 07958 737242
E-mail: john.hinds64@googlemail.com
Open: Mon-Fri 9am-6pm and by appointment

John Hinds runs his own workshop making quality frames at competitive prices. All the frames are in solid wood, come in a range of designs and are handmade to your own specifications. The workshop does a lot of commissions for artists, so you can be sure that this is a place to find great value frames. Most customers visit the workshop and collect their finished frames, but delivery can be arranged on request.

London Scenes & Framing Ltd

Abbey Road Motorist Centre
131-139 Belsize Road, NW6
Tel: 020 7328 6915
Train: Kilburn High Road
Open: Mon-Fri 9am-6pm, Sat 10am-6pm

This established picture framers has many corporate clients in the city of London, but also offers a good value framing service to individual customers. It is one of the few companies in London to have a 50" wide heat sealing machine for the strengthening of posters and offers a wide range of styles and finishes of frame depending on your budget.

The London Picture Centre

287-289 Hackney Road, E2
Tel: 020 7739 6624
Website: www.thelondonpicturecentre.co.uk
Tube: Bethnal Green
Open: Mon-Fri 8am-5pm, Sat 10am-4pm, Sun 10am-2pm

This company have branches in east and west London offering great value ready-made and made-to-order picture frames and mirrors in a wide variety of designs. A recent bargain was the 40" x 30" mirror with a 1.5" silver frame for only £60 and there is usually a good choice of clearance items at equally competitive prices.

Branches at:
709 & 723 Fulham Road, SW6
Tel: 020 7731 4883
18 Crawford Street, W1
Tel: 020 7487 2895
75 Leather Lane, EC1
Tel: 020 7404 4110

G. Thornfield Ltd
(Day by Day Art & Interiors)

321 Gray's Inn Road, WC1
Tel: 020 7837 2996
Tube: King's Cross
Open: Mon-Fri 8am-6pm, Sat 9am-2pm

This store opened in 1953 and used to offer a wide range of paints, fabrics and wallpapers, but has in recent years become a specialist gallery and picture framers. There are a good selection of ready-made quality frames at reasonable prices and Thornfield are particularly good value when it comes to made-to-order frames and mirrors and offer additional services such as mount cutting and canvas stretching. If you are looking for a quality bespoke frame they are well worth giving a call.

Kids

Kids' Toys, Clothes & Equipment

Buying second-hand can sometimes prove a false economy, but in the case of children's clothing and equipment it makes very good sense because the little darlings outgrow things so quickly. Below are reviewed the best shops specialising in such second-hand items in the London area; many are also useful places for selling your children's things when finished with. Markets and car boot sales (pages 351 and 357) and charity shops (page 287) are also rewarding hunting grounds for children's things.

North

JoJo Maman Bébé

map 11

3 Ashbourne Parade,
1259 Finchley Rd, NW11
Tel: 020 8731 8961
Website: www.JoJoMamanBebe.co.uk
Tube: Golders Green
Sales: January, April and July each year

This company holds summer and winter sales of their own brand of children's, baby and maternity clothes at their North and South London sites. The clothing is good quality with lots of natural fibre garments and there are savings of 30%–75%. Most garments are sold at about half–price, but there are also items sold to clear and most maternity wear is sold for £5 or less. The company also stocks a range of children's toys and equipment. Phone for details of their next sale.

Also at: 72 Bennerley Road SW11, Tel: 020 7924 3144
82 Turnham Green Terrace, w4 Tel: 020 8994 0379
Unit 30 Putney Exchange, Putney High Street, Sw15 Tel: 020 8780 5165

Junior Style

Alphaville 2, 14 Shepherdess Walk, N1
Tel: 020 7689 3925
Website: www.juniorstylesales.co.uk
Kids designer and brand-name clothing for 0-12yrs
Open: 4 sales per year
For a full review see the Designer Warehouse Sale section (page 69).

Rub-a-Dub-Dub
15 Park Road, N8
Tel: 020 8342 9898
Rail: Hornsey
Open: Mon-Sat 10am-5.30pm, Sun 11.30-4pm

This is a new shop which sells only new kids' clothing and equipment. Although you will not get the kind of bargains you can find buying second-hand, the stock is very competitively priced. Among the good deals are Baby Bjorn Slings for £45 (usual price £50) and Maxi Cosi Car Seats for £95 (usual price £100). The best deal was the Trip-Trap high chair which was £99 (usual price £109). A great place to stock-up on equipment for your little sprogs.

Simply Outgrown Nursery Equipment & Toys
360 Lordship Lane, N17 (opposite Lordship Recreation Ground)
Tel: 020 8801 0568
Tube: Wood Green
Open: Mon-Fri 10.30am-5pm, Sat 10.30am-4pm

This shop buys and sells nearly-new baby equipment and toys. All goods are clean, checked for safety and under 2 years old. Specialising in toys and equipment and being pretty fussy about the goods they buy, this is one of the best places in London to kit out a nursery on a budget.

West

The Little Trading Company
7 Bedford Corner, The Avenue, Chiswick, W4
Tel: 020 8742 3152
Tube: Turnham Green
Open: Mon-Fri 9am-5pm, Sat 9am-4.30pm

Located in the back streets of Chiswick, this wonderful children's dress agency is easily missed. It's worth taking the trouble to visit because it's the main repository for high quality used clothes, toys, shoes and equipment from the surrounding leafy avenues. The shop also offers children's haircuts by appointment from £10.50.

Pixies
14 Fauconberg Road, W4
Tel: 020 8995 1568
Tube/Rail: Gunnersbury
Open: Mon-Fri 10am-4.30pm, Sat 10am-3pm (term time);
Wed-Fri 10am-4.30pm, Sat 10am-3pm (school holidays)

This shop is crammed to the gunnels with good quality new and used kids' clothes and equipment, but nevertheless manages to appear tidy and well-ordered. Situated in a rather upmarket part of west London the shop gets more than its fair share of designer labels, but they are all affordably priced and there are always cheaper garments to suit those on a tight budget. Recent bargains included Bumbo Seats for £15 (£30 new) and good condition Mini Boden dresses from £6.75. Pixies are particularly strong on seasonal kids' gear and do a roaring trade in ski-wear in the winter and sun shades and UV protector suits in the summer months. A great little shop.

South

The Anerley Frock Exchange
122 Anerley Road, SE20
Tel: 020 8778 2030
See main entry in Dress Agencies section (page 87).

Jo Jo Maman Bébé
72 Bennerley Road, SW11
Tel: 020 7924 3144
See main entry in West London (page 208).

East

Merry-Go-Round
12 Clarence Road, E5
Tel: 020 8985 6308
Rail: Hackney Central
Open: Mon-Sat 10am-5.30pm, Sun 11am-5pm

This children's clothing and equipment agency is located in a rough area, but inside the shop it is reassuringly clean and well organised. The stock includes a great selection of clothes, toys, books and equipment, extending over two floors. Among the bargains on a recent visit were a large cot for £50, denim jackets for only £4, a wide choice of wellington boots for £3 and cotton baby-grows for £1. The basement is dedicated to children of 3 years and above, with a similar mix of clothing, books and equipment. One of the best value children's shops in town.

Other outlets for kids' things:

David Charles
1 Thanes Works,
Thane Villas, N7
Tel: 020 7609 4797
See main entry in the Designer Sale section (page 68).

Choice
Unit 11, Arcadia Centre, Ealing Broadway, W5
Tel: 020 8567 2747
See main entry in the Street Fashion section (page 29).

La Scala
39 Elystan Street, SW3
Tel: 020 7589 2784
La Scala has lots of stylish clothing for children up to the age of 6.
See the main entry in the Dress Agencies section (page 86).

Mail order / Internet

www.amalaika.com
Tel: 0870 0428 955

A family-run firm that sources last season's designer kids' wear from many different places and sells them via their website. The site is regularly updated with the latest offers and they are also contactable by phone if customers want to deal with a human rather than a computer. A great little online shop.

www.babyjumbles.co.uk

This is a very well organised website with a vast selection of babies' clothes all categorised by age and illustrated with a photograph. The postage charges are very low, making this a reasonable site for buying kids' clothing.

www.funkycrocodile.com

A well organised website with a good choice of new and 'gently worn' designer kids' wear. There are plenty of great value clothes to be found here and the search engine allows you to find exactly what you are looking for quickly and easily.

www.milliemoos.com
Tel: 0870 0428 955

This is the sister site of amalaika.com, specialising in used kids' clothes with plenty of designer labels as well as high street brands. The prices are very competitive and there are always lots of special offers and clearance items.

214...Bikes
225...Books
236...CD's, DVD's and Vinyl
248...Photography
259...Travel

Leisure

Bikes

It's difficult to find new bikes at a discount as high street shops tend to sell new bikes at similar prices. One way to get a bargain is to buy your bike in the autumn – when new models are introduced and the superseded ones are cleared at considerable discounts. Below are featured many bike shops that say they will better the price offered by other outlets and it is a good idea to use this promise to beat the price down. The number of price-competitive bike websites has greatly increased in recent years and this section has been expanded to include places like Chain Reaction and Bonthrone Bikes which hold a vast selection of new bikes. A good tip when buying a new bike is to get the bike with all the specifications you want. The bike shop wants your business and will usually be willing to change the saddle, tyres and other peripherals at no extra cost. If you don't object to shopping at a large retailer, the French sports retailer Decathlon offers fantastic value with its own range of bikes and very good value bike parts and accessories. One important rule when buying a bike is to avoid very cheap new bikes with unrecognisable brand names. These bikes look OK to the novice cyclist, but are badly made and not worth buying. If you don't know a good bike from a bad one it's a good idea to bring a bikie friend with you to give advice.

If you want a real bargain then it's best to buy second-hand and there are lots of places to look. There are quite a few specialist second-hand bike outlets in London which are reviewed below, but they are not the cheapest places in town. I found that some of the best deals were to be found at new bike shops that sell part-exchange bikes. These bikes are sold to clear and the retailer is not trying to make a profit from them so they are often great value. If you fancy being a bit more adventurous you could try R. F Greasby Auctioneers which sells bikes on behalf of the Metropolitan Police (see their entry on page 281). There are also cycle jumbles which are mysterious events where second-hand bikes and parts are sold to more serious cycle enthusiasts. To find out more about cycle jumbles check the classified pages of Cycling Weekly where they are intermittently advertised. I have also included the community web notice board www.gumtree.com which is a simple way of buying and selling second-hand and always has a few bikes for sale.

Dialabike

30 Strutton Ground, SW1
Tel: 020 7233 4224
Tube: St James's Park
Open: Mon-Fri 10am-5.30pm

This one-man business is particularly good for second-hand bikes with usually about 20 bikes in stock. All bikes are sold fully serviced, with a three month guarantee and prices range from £450 for a good condition Cannondale F400 (RRP £800) to a basic mountain bike for a very modest £80. Well worth checking out for second-hand bike bargains.

On Your Bike

52-Strutton Ground, SW1
Tel: 020 7378 6669
Tube: London Bridge
Open: Mon-Fri 7.30am-7.30pm, Sat 10am-6pm, Sun 11am-5pm

This shop only deals in new bikes, but occasionally sells off its used hire bikes at very good prices. The sale of these bikes is rare and occasional but it's worth giving them a call to see if there are any such bikes coming up for sale.

Pedal It

18 Newington Causeway, SE1
Tel: 020 7407 9115
Tube: Elephant & Castle or Borough
Open: Mon-Sat 8am-7pm, Sun 10am-5pm

This is one of the few shops in London specializing in second-hand bikes with around 100 bikes from which to choose. Prices range from £50 for a basic urban workhorse to around £500 for a top of the range mountain bike or racer. Recent bargains included a Ridgeback Genesis for £160 (around £300 new) and a very smart Cannondale Cad5 for £350 (around £1,000 new). This shop is well worth a visit for a good value second-hand bike and offers a further 10% discount for London Cycle Campaign members.

North

Camden Cycles

251 Eversholt Street, NW1
Tel: 020 7388 7899
Website: www.camdencycles.co.uk
Tube: Mornington Crescent
Open: Mon-Fri 9am-7pm, Sat 9am-6pm, Sun 11am-5pm

map
2

Camden Cycles is a recent arrival to the area and is one of the best places in London to get a good second-hand bike. Outside the store are a variety of old bikes for around £50, but inside there is a wide range of better quality mountain and road bikes. On a recent visit stock included a Ridgeback Cyclone for only £155 and a fabulous Claud Butler 7005 for only £200 – these bikes were in good condition and were over £400 when new. A definite must for the bargain hunting cyclist.

Chamberlaines

75-77 Kentish Town Road, NW1
Tel: 020 7485 4488
Tube: Camden Town
Open: Mon-Sat 8.30am-6pm

This local bikeshop has been trading for over 100 years and usually has a few second-hand, part-ex bikes as well as offering great value new bikes with regular promotions on particular models. On the last visit to the store they were offering a new GT Aggressor mountain bike for only £200 and had a second-hand Giant Rock SE for only £90.

West

Mend-a-Bike

19 The Arches,
33 Munster Road, SW6
Tel: 020 7371 5867
Tube: Parsons Green or Putney Green
Open: Mon-Fri 9am-7pm, Sat 9am-6pm

map
9

This large bike workshop has been selling good quality new and used bikes for over 30 years. It is a particularly good place to find ex-showroom bikes and slight seconds at 20-25% discount. Prices range from a Lemond Versaille carbon frame racer with a slight scratch for £1,000 – reduced from £1,400, to a Trek 7.0 mountain bike for £180– reduced from £230. All bikes come with a 3 month guarantee and used bikes are fully serviced. The shop also offers an excellent repairs service.

Brick Lane Bikes

Mend-a-Bike

Camden Cycles

Edwardes

Swim, Bike, Run (formerly Bonthrone Bikes)

917-919 Fulham Road, SW6
Tel: 020 7731 5005
Website: www.bonthronebikes.co.uk
Tube: Fulham Broadway
Open: Mon-Sat 10am-7pm, Sun 11am-5pm

map 9

This large sports showroom in southwest London is dedicated to triathlon equipment but offers a great selection of bikes as it is part of the sports company which owns the web retailer Bonthrone Bikes (see online section). There is a wide range of bikes on offer from basic town bikes to high-end racing bikes for serious cyclists and triathletes. The best deals are to be found towards the end of September when manufacturers bring out their new designs and previous models are sold at a discount.

South

Decathlon

Surrey Quays Road
Canada Water Retail Park, SE16
Tel: 020 7394 2000
Website: www.decathlon.co.uk
Tube: Surrey Quays
Open: Mon-Fri 10am-8pm, Sat 9am-7pm, Sun 11am-5pm

Decathlon are an established French sports retailer who have two large retail outlets in Surrey Quays offering all kinds of sporting goods from bikes to camping equipment. Decathlon sell only their own brand of bikes, but they are good quality and excellent value. The entry level mountain bike 'b'Twin' comes with a lightweight aluminium frame, Shimano gears, V-brakes and front-suspension for only £199, which is excellent value. For those on an even more limited budget Decathlon offer several models of basic town bike for under £100. All bikes come with a full manufacturers' warranty and a free first service within three months of purchase. For more about Decathlon see the sports section (page 257).

De Ver Cycles

630-634 Streatham High Road, Norbury, SW16
Tel: 020 8679 6197
Website: www.devercycles.co.uk
Rail: Streatham Hill
Open: Mon-Sat 10am-6.30pm (closed Wed and Sun)

De Ver Cycles is a great bikeshop run by former British cycling champion Maurice Burton. The store offers a range of cycles from standard town bikes to £3,000 racing machines. Bargain hunters should have a look at the 20 or so part-exchange, second-hand bikes for anything from £30 to £200. If you are after a shiny new bike at a discount you should wait for their October sale which offers substantial discounts on superseded models. De Ver Cycles sometimes offer special deals through e-Bay – to find out more view their website which has a link to the site.

Edwardes

221/225 Camberwell Road, SE5
Tel: 020 7703 5720 / 020 7703 3676
Tube: Kennington
Open: Mon-Sat 8.30am-6pm

This family business has been trading since 1908 and now occupies four shop fronts on Camberwell Road stocking many reputable makes like Scott and Ridgeback, as well as serious racing bikes from names like Pinello and Giant. They have regular sales and always have bikes on promotion, recently offering a full-suspension Saracen for £199 (reduced from £300). They also accept bikes in part-exchange which means that they always have about twenty second-hand cycles for those on a budget. A friend of mine bought a very clean Orbea Hybrid for £100 which is still going strong.

Leisure ● Bikes

The London Bicycle Repair Shop

2-3 Benson House, Hatfields, SE1
Tel: 020 7928 6898
Tube: Southwark
Open: Mon-Fri 9am-6pm, Sat 10am-4pm

This small shop offers a good value repair service and usually has a few second-hand bikes for sale. The used bikes range from a worn, but road-worthy, town bike for as little as £40, to a high-spec mountain bike that has been lovingly re-built for £250. There are also occasional returns sourced from bike distributors which are repaired and sold at discount prices. The shop is run by bike enthusiasts and is well worth giving a call to see what bikes they have in stock.

Recycling

110 Elephant Road, SE17
Tel: 020 7703 7001
Tube: Elephant and Castle
Open: Mon-Fri 9am-6.30pm, Sat 9am-6pm, Sun 11am-4pm

This large showroom has a grunge atmosphere with thumping bass music and the scent of tobacco smoke and bike oil in the air. This is the kind of shop where you would expect to get a bargain, but it actually appears a little expensive with old upright bikes for no less than £70 and second-hand kids' bikes for around £25. There were a few good deals to be found including a good condition Cannondale 'Badboy' for £350 (retail price £700) and a Brompton L6 for £325 (retail price £600). All the bikes are sold serviced and come with a one month guarantee.

Smith Bros

14 Church Road, SW19
Tel: 020 8946 2270
Tube: Wimbledon Broadway
Open: Mon-Sat 9.30am-5.30pm

This small shop has a great selection of second-hand, part-ex bikes with plenty to choose from for both adults and kids. Prices start from £29 for a used kid's bike and go up to about £150 for a good quality mountain bike. Although Wimbledon is quite a trek for many Londoners there are enough offers here to make it worth giving them a call to see what they have in stock.

East

Barclays for Bikes
515 Kingsland Road, E8
Tel: 020 7241 3131
Rail: Dalston

This local bike workshop offers a good repair service and occasionally sells second-hand bikes at reasonable prices. On a recent visit they were selling a good condition Giant Hybrid for only £140.

The Bike Station
1 Upper Walthamstow Road, E17
Tel: 020 8520 6988
Rail: Wood Street Walthamstow
Open: Mon-Sat 9am-6pm

This small local bike shop offers new bikes at reasonable prices, but usually has a few second-hand. In the spring and summer months there are a few more part-exchange bikes for sale, all of which have been checked and serviced before being sold.

Brick Lane Bikes
118 Bethnal Green Road, E2
Tel: 020 7033 9053
Website: www.bricklanebikes.co.uk
Tube: Liverpool Street
Open: Mon-Fri 9am-7pm, Sat 11am-7pm, Sun 11am-6pm

(map 12)

This recent arrival to the Brick Lane area is one of the best bike shops in London, selling all kinds of new bikes but with a special emphasis upon fixed-wheel track bikes. At the back of the store is an open yard where the repairs are carried out and a small selection of used bikes is on display. Among the bargains to be found on a recent visit was a worn but still sound Peugeot road bike with tri-bars and a good set of expensive Continental racing tyres for only £150 and a more mundane but road -worthy Raleigh hybrid town bike for £98. A bike shop run by bike enthusiasts and one that offers a value repair service.

Ditchfields

792-794 High Road, E10
Tel: 020 8539 2821
Tube: Leyton
Open: Mon-Sat 9.15am-5.30pm

This local bikeshop has occasional second-hand part-ex bikes. The bikes can range from hardly-used ladies' hybrids for £160 to a worn but still usable shopping bike for only £35.

Everything Cycling

530 Forest Road, E17
Tel: 020 8521 5812
Tube: Walthamstow Central or Blackhorse Road
Open: Mon-Sat 10am-5.30pm, Closed Thurs

This shop has been trading for over fifty years and usually has a few part-ex bikes on offer for between £59 and £150. On a recent visit there was a good condition Trek mountain bike for only £120. Stock of second-hand bikes varies, so give the shop a call to see what they have available.

Heales Cycles

477 Hales End Road, E4
Tel: 020 8527 1592
Rail: Highans Park
Open: Mon-Fri 9am-6pm, Sat 9am-5.30pm

This shop has a changing stock of part-ex bikes and is a good place to look for second-hand quality mountain bikes. On a recent visit they had a very smart Cannondale racer for £495, which was a bargain given the new price of over £1000.

Out of Town

Ciclos Uno

37 New North Road,
Hainault, Ilford, Essex, IG6
Tel: 020 8500 1792
Website: www.ciclosuno.com
Open: Tues, Thurs, Fri-Sat 9am-4pm

This shop is not for the everyday cyclist as it specialises in top quality racing bikes, but if you are looking for a serious racing machine on a budget this is definitely a good place to visit. They always have a selection of used racing bikes to choose from and can offer great deals on bike parts as well as detailed advice about anything to do with serious cycling.

Bicycle Repair

Brick Lane Bikes

118 Bethnal Green Road, E2
Tel: 020 7033 9053
www.bricklanebikes.co.uk
Tube: Liverpool Street
Open: Mon-Fri 9am-7pm, Sat 11am-7pm, Sun 11am-6pm

This shop not only sells new and used bikes (see page 221), but also offers a good value bike repair service. A full service starts from £29.50 which is great value compared with many high street bike shops.

Mend-a-Bike

19 The Arches, 33 Munster Road, SW6
Tel: 020 7371 5867
Open: Mon-Fri 9am-7pm, Sat 9am-6pm

As well as selling great value bikes (see page 216), Mend-a-Bike also undertake all kinds of repairs at a competitive price.

Perlie Rides

28 Southborough Road, E9
Tel: 020 8525 5694
Website: www.perlierides.com

Perlie Rides is a bike workshop that carries out all repairs and can carry out collections and inspections from home or office on request. The workshop is well organised and they can source all replacement parts and offer great value considering the quality of work.

Internet & Mail Order

www.bonthronebikes.co.uk

Customers can visit the website to get an idea of the range of bikes and click on the discount page for the latest offers. The best deals are to be found in the autumn when the discount pages of the site have a good selection of superseded models on sale. Bonethrone pride themselves on offering good value and will try to match any price for the same product – phone their sales staff on 01753 830 118 to discuss any such price issues. Bonthrone offer full manufacturer guarantees on all products and a 10% discount on all accessories bought when buying a bike.

www.chainreactioncycles.com

Chain reaction is one of the largest specialist cycle warehouses and has an established reputation for good service. The website is easy to use and has a great many special offers on accessories such as a Giro Monza cycle helmet for £34.99 (RRP £49.99). The site is also very competitive for new bikes – a recent visit to the site found a GT Avalanche 1.0 mountain bike for only £339.99, which is about as cheap as you can find such a bike.

www.davehinde.veriovps.co.uk
Tel: 0870 990 9826

If you don't know a bottom bracket from a hub then this site will be of little interest, but for bike enthusiasts this is a great value site for sourcing parts for road and mountain bikes. Dave Hinde are particularly good value for top quality bike wheels and also hand-build wheels at very competitive prices. The website is simple to use but gives little detail. The staff are helpful should you need to give them a call.

www.gumtree.com

Gumtree is a simple-to-use website which acts as a massive jumble sale with thousands of goods for sale by members of the public. Just log onto the site and put the word 'bike' in the key word search and you will find a great range of bikes for sale with anything from a hi-tech racing bike for £300 (originally £700) to a simple hybrid town bike for £70. Most of the goods for sale have a photo so the prospective buyer can get an idea of what they are buying.

Books

There are lots of places in London to find cheap second-hand books and below are reviewed some of London's best second-hand bookshops as well as a few of the most interesting remainder and cheap new bookshops. For those in search of real bargains it's always best to pay attention to the tables outside most bookshops. It is from such tables that booksellers clear surplus stock at a discount and hope to attract passing custom. Other places to seek out cheap reading matter include London's street markets, the best being Camden Passage (on Thursdays) and Riverside Walk (on the Southbank), as well as the larger markets like Spitalfields and Portobello (see markets section on page 351). Charity shops (page 287) are another source of cheap, interesting books, with the Oxfam Books and Music on Marylebone High Street (page 291), Oxfam Books (pages 292, 298, 312 and 315) and Books for Amnesty (pages 300 and 313) being the best in the capital. Bloomsbury Book Auctions (page 284) is a good place to look for rare and collectable books.

Central

Any Amount of Books

56 Charing Cross Road, WC2
Tel: 020 7836 3697
email: charingx@anyamountofbooks.com
Website: www.anyamountofbooks.com
Tube: Leicester Square
Open: Mon-Sat 10.30am-9.30pm, Sun 11.30am-8.30pm

A deceptively large general bookshop with enough quality second-hand paperbacks to catch the bargain hunter's eye. The £1 trays on the pavement are always worth a browse and there is a good selection of bargain stock housed in the basement.

Bookends

108 Charing Cross Road, WC2
Tel: 020 7836 3457
Tube: Leicester Square
Open: Mon-Fri 9am-9pm, Sat 9.30am-6.30, Sun 11am-3pm

This long-established discount bookshop is the only branch of Bookends in London and offers great deals on all manner of shop-soiled and remainder books. The stock covers a wide range of subjects, from paperback fiction to art history, with all books sold at a considerable discount.

Bookhouse

24 Torrington Place, WC1
Tel: 020 7436 3286
Tube: Goodge Street
Open: Mon-Sat 10am-7pm, Sun 12noon-6pm

This outlet has a stylish interior and looks very upmarket, but is in fact a remainder bookshop offering a wide range of books at well below the retail price. It is particularly strong on art, design, architecture and history and has an ideal location, close to a large Waterstone's and just a few doors from an organic supermarket and café.

Book Warehouse

120 Southampton Row, WC1
Tel: 020 7242 1119
Tube: Russell Square
Open: Mon-Fri 8.30am-10pm, Sat 9am-10pm, Sun 10am-9pm

The most central branch of a chain of remainder discount bookshops that offer a wide range of books at considerable discounts. The shops are particularly strong on large, glossy books concerning art, design, architecture, gardening and cookery. They also sell CDs, cards and stationery.

Other branches in London:

38 Golder's Green Road, NW1
Tel: 020 8458 0032

72-74 Notting Hill Gate, W11
Tel: 020 7727 4149

295A Regent Street, W1
Tel: 020 7636 6011

41 Strutton Ground, SW1
Tel: 020 7976 0577

158 Waterloo Road, SE1
Tel: 020 7401 8528

101 King St, Hammersmith, W6
Tel: 020 8222 8862

Quinto

Henry Pordes

Quinto

Judd Two

82 Marchmont Street, WC1
Tel: 020 7387 5333
Tube: Russell Square
Open: Mon-Sat 11am-7pm, Sun 12am-6pm

This is a fantastic bookshop ranging over two floors with an emphasis on the humanities, but also featuring lots of quality fiction. Remaindered books are discounted for 20-50% and even greater discounts are to be found from tables on the pavement. The shop also offers a 10% discount for students.

Henry Pordes Books Ltd

58-60 Charing Cross Road, WC2
Tel: 020 7836 9031
Website: www.henrypordesbooks.com
Tube: Leicester Square
Open: Mon-Sat 10am-7pm, Sun 1pm-6pm

Henry Pordes is an established bookshop on Charing Cross Road selling second-hand, antiquarian and remaindered books on every conceivable subject. The real bargains are to be found in the basement where paperbacks are sold for as little as £2 and there are always bargain boxes by the door with books priced for £1-£2. A great place to rummage for book bargains.

Quinto

48a Charing Cross Road, WC2
Tel: 020 7379 7669
E-mail: sales@haycinemabookshop.co.uk
Tube: Leicester Square
Open: Mon-Sat 9am-9pm, Sun12am-8pm

An established feature of the West End book scene, covering most academic subjects and a good range of fiction. Although it makes no claim to be a bargain outlet, Quinto offers enough choice to reward the eager bargain hunter. There are over 20,000 books in stock and there are weekly deliveries of second-hand books from their warehouse.

Quinto of Great Russell Street

63 Great Russell Street, WC1
Tel: 020 7430 2535
E-mail: sales@quintogrs.co.uk
Tube: Tottenham Court Road
Open: Daily 10am-6.30pm

Over 50,000 second-hand academic and remaindered books in all subjects. There's a selection of 50p bargain books outside and regular sales offer up to 50% discount.

Skoob Russell Square

86 Brunswick Centre, WC1N
Tel: 020 7278 8760
Website: www.skoob.com
Tube: Russell Square
Open: Mon-Sat 10am-8pm, Sun 11am-5pm

Not the cheapest bookshop in London, but rated by many as the best. Skoob has recently returned to the Brunswick after a two year break. It has a wide range of books with a particular emphasis on academic subjects including maths, philosophy, engineering and the arts. In addition to the 70,000 books on display, all titles from Skoob's even bigger online catalogue can be delivered to the store for inspection within a day or two. A spacious air-conditioned shop next to the Waitrose rear entrance.

Soho Original Bookshop

(map 1)

11-12 Brewer Street, W1
Tel: 020 7494 1615
Website: www.sohobooks.co.uk
Tube: Piccadilly Circus
Open: Mon-Sat 10am-1am, Sun 11am-11pm

This chain of bookshops sell new books at about 10% discount or in many cases £1 off the published price, as well as quality remaindered books at much greater discounts and a 3-for-2 books section. The stores have a particularly good stock of art, fashion, style, fiction, erotica and travel books. Those of a prudish disposition should avoid the basement which is stocked with top-quality porn.

Branches at:
23/25 Leather Lane EC1, Tel: 020 7404 3594
124 Middlesex Street E1, Tel: 020 7377 5309
63 Cowcross Street EC1, Tel: 020 7251 8020
231 Kilburn High Road, NW6, Tel: 020 7328 9026
9 Caledonian Road, NW1, Tel: 020 7278 4335

Unsworths Booksellers

101 Euston Road, NW1
Tel: 020 7383 5507
E-mail: books@unsworths.com
Website: www.unsworths.com
Tube/Rail: King's Cross and St Pancras
Open: Mon-Sat 10am-6.30pm, Sun 12noon-5pm

This shop is ideally located opposite the British Library and carries a large stock of literary and academic titles. The emphasis is on the humanities, with classics and history being especially well represented. The prices are low, usually 50-90% off the published price. An excellent shop for the high-brow bargain hunter.

North

Archive Second-hand Books and Music

83 Bell Street, NW1
Tel: 020 7402 8212
Tube: Edgeware Road & Marylebone
Open: Mon-Sat 10.30am-6pm

If you like bookshops to be musty establishments piled to the ceiling with books, this shop will not disappoint. The varied stock fills two floors and the cheaper stuff can be found on the pavement outside for as little as 50p. The music referred to in the shop's name is not records but a basement full of printed music and related books. This shop is disorderly but fun and a great place to shop for second-hand book bargains.

Books Ink

159 Stoke Newington High Street, N16
Tel: 020 7249 8983
Rail: Stoke Newington
Open: Mon-Sat 10am-5pm

Books Ink have two discount book outlets in London which offer a great selection of new stock at considerable discounts. They are particularly good for fiction, cookery and children's books and on a recent visit offered a great choice of classic fiction from Dostoevsky to Zola for £2.50 a copy. They also sell greetings cards, stationery and a limited range of discounted CDs.

Also at: 134 High Street, Walthamstow, E17 (page 235)

Church Street Bookshop

142 Stoke Newington Church Street, N16
Tel: 020 7241 5411
Rail: Stoke Newington
Open: Mon-Fri 11.30am-6pm, Sat 11am-6pm and Sun 11.30am-6pm

A second-hand bookshop with a fine stock of well-priced books, and a particularly impressive stock of paperback fiction. They usually have a good choice of review copies and several boxes of books for £1 each or 3 books for £2. The excellent Ocean Books is just opposite.

Keith Fawkes

1-3 Flask Walk, NW3
Tel: 020 7435 0614
Tube: Hampstead
Open: Mon-Sat 10am-5.30pm, Sun 1pm-6pm

The books in this shop are reasonably priced, but the conversation, advice and bookish atmosphere are priceless and free. A blissful refuge from the hustle and bustle of Hampstead High Street. Recently an independent trader with some connection to the shop has begun selling bric-à-brac outside on an irregular basis which only adds to the appeal of the shop for bargain hunters.

Ocean Books

127 Stoke Newington Church Street, N16
Tel: 020 7502 6319
E-mail: oceanbooksn16@yahoo.co.uk
Rail: Stoke Newington
Open: Mon-Sat 11.30am-6pm, Sun 12noon-6pm

This establishment may look small from the street but offers a well-chosen selection of second-hand books at reasonable prices. The back room of the shop is now dedicated to records.

Walden Books

38 Harmood Street, Camden, NW1
Tel: 020 7267 8146
email: Walden_books@tiscali.co.uk
Website: www.ukbookworld
Tube: Camden Town/Chalk Farm
Open: Thurs-Sun 10.30am-6.30pm

map 2

Situated just off busy Chalk Farm Road, this is a great place to escape the Camden crowds and browse for second-hand books. The stock is well chosen and very reasonably priced with bargain tables outside offering paperbacks for as little as 50p.

West

Book & Comic Exchange

14 Pembridge Road, W11
Tel: 020 7229 8420
Tube: Notting Hill Gate
Open: Daily 10am-8pm

(map 7)

This busy store offers a wide range of paperback fiction and reference books. The turnover is fast and books are regularly discounted if they fail to sell. The bargain basement has books all marked down to 50p.

Bookthrift

22 Thurloe Street, South Kensington, SW7
Tel: 020 7589 2916
Website: www.bookthrift.co.uk
Tube: South Kensington
Open: Mon-Fri 10am-8pm, Sat 11am-7pm, Sun 12noon-7pm

This well organised discount store offers great deals on a wide range of subjects, but is particularly strong on glossy, large format books about art, design, architecture and photography. Bookthrift is just a few doors away from the wonderful Polish restaurant, Daquise.

Gloucester Road Bookshop

123 Gloucester Road, SW7
Tel: 020 7370 3503
E-mail: manager@gloucesterbooks.co.uk
Tube: Gloucester Road
Open: Mon-Fri 9.30am-10.30pm, Sat-Sun 10.30am-6.30pm

This is a friendly second-hand bookshop offering lots of book bargains. The shop has a good reputation for art, history and literature, but if you're after cheap paperback fiction look at the stands outside, where prices start from only 20p. They publish a regular catalogue.

Notting Hill Books

132 Palace Gardens Terrace, W8
Tel: 020 7727 5988
Tube: Notting Hill Gate
Open: Mon-Wed, Fri and Sat 10.30am-6pm, Thurs 10.30am-1pm

A small shop, but packed full of discounted and second-hand books on a variety of serious subjects from art to travel. The small selection of quality fiction is half the publisher's price and there are trays of bargain books outside.

Tlon Books

Chelsea Farmers' Market, Sydney Street, SW3
020 7823 3769
Website: www.tlon-books.demon.co.uk
Tube: Sloane Square or South Kensington
Open: Daily 11am-6pm

This small branch of Tlon Books offers quality second-hand books at reasonable prices. See the main review for further details (page 234).

World's End Bookshop

357 King's Road, SW3
Tel: 020 7352 9376
Tube: Fulham Broadway/South Kensington
Open: Daily 10am-6.30pm

This is a fine little bookshop with a broad general stock. There are lots of discounted titles sold from tables outside with prices starting from 50p. Between Saturday and Monday there's a further 20% off all titles. Don't forget the two charity shops on the same corner.

South

Bookmongers

439 Coldharbour Lane, SW9
Tel: 020 7738 4225
Tube/Rail: Brixton
Open: Mon-Sat 10.30am-6.30pm

This second-hand bookshop has been offering a great value selection of books to the people of Brixton for many years. The stock is wide ranging and very well organised with plenty of discounted titles to catch the bargain hunters' eye. One of the best second-hand shops south of the river and located near the excellent Rosie's café on Market Row.

Marcet Books

4A Nelson Road, Greenwich, SE10
Tel: 020 8853 5408
Website: www.marcetbooks.co.uk
email: info@marcetbooks.co.uk
Rail/DLR: Greenwich
Open: Daily 10am-5.30pm

In one of the alleyways leading off Greenwich Craft Market, this is a small shop packed with a good choice of mostly second-hand books but with some discounted new titles.

My Back Pages

8-10 Balham Station Road, SW12
Tel: 020 8675 9346
Tube/Rail: Balham
Open: Mon-Fri 10am-8pm, Sat 10am-7pm, Sun 11am-6pm

This long-established and well-run bookshop offers second-hand and some discounted new books as well as a good selection of review copies. The shop is well organised and offers books on all kinds of subjects from academic text books to popular fiction. There are always bargains to be found with prices starting from under £1 for a tatty but still readable paperback.

The Junk Shop & Spread Eagle Bookshop

9 Greenwich Street, SE10
Tel: 020 8305 1666
Website: www.spreadeagle.org
Rail/DLR: Greenwich
Open: Daily 10am-6pm, closed for lunch 1-2pm

Since the closing of the Spread Eagle Bookshop the stock from the shop has been incorporated into this large and rambling junk shop. There are about 3,000 books among the antiques and bric-à-brac with lots of bargains to be found in the general stock and plenty of books reduced to clear. Well worth having a browse if you're in Greenwich. For more information about the shop see the Junk Shop section (page 347).

Tlon Books

Unit 316, Ground Floor, Elephant & Castle Shopping Centre, SE1
Tel: 020 7701 0360
Website: www.tlon-books.demon.co.uk
Tube: Elephant & Castle
Open: Daily 11am-6pm

A gem of a second-hand bookshop set in the unpromising surroundings of this pink monstrosity of a shopping centre. The shop is well laid out and has a decent general and academic stock. The selection of paperback fiction of all kinds is impressive and prices are competitive. Tlon Books now has a store in Chelsea (see page 233).

East

The Bargain Bookshop
135 Station Road, E4
Tel: 020 8524 9002
Website: www.bookservice.biz
Rail: Chingford
Open: Mon-Sat 9am-5.30pm, Easter to Christmas open Bank Holidays and Sundays 11am-3pm

This shop is just one minute's walk from Chingford Station and offers a good selection of discounted and full price new books. This is a remarkably friendly and helpful local bookshop with enough bargains to justify the name.

Books Ink
134 High Street, Walthamstow, E17
Tel: 020 8520 8551
Tube: Walthamstow
Open: Mon-Sat 9.30am-5.30pm

The second branch of this excellent discount book retailer.
See the main entry in North London (page 230).

Bookfairs and Events

Amnesty International Book Sale
Conway Hall
Red Lion Square, WC1
Tel: 020 7383 2680
e-mail: amnesty.x@btconnect.com

Amnesty run these large book sales every six to eight weeks offering an incredible range of books at bargain prices. The atmosphere is feverish with large crowds gathering to rummage among the thousands of books mostly priced at £1. The sale takes place in the historic Conway Hall in Bloomsbury which gives the event a wonderful atmosphere. For information about the next sale, phone the above number or contact one of the two Amnesty Bookshops in London (pages 300 and 314).

CDs, Records, Tapes & DVDs

There are numerous new and used outlets for vinyl, CD's and DVDs in the London area. They range from smart modern retail chains like Borders to the more modest vinyl shops catering for the music enthusiasts who have fought the trend to ditch their record collections.

Central

Borders Books and Music

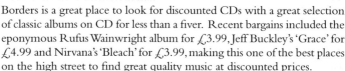

197-213 Oxford Street, W1
Tel: 020 7292 1600
Open: Mon-Sat 8am-11pm, Sun 12noon-6pm
Website: www.bordersstores.co.uk

Borders is a great place to look for discounted CDs with a great selection of classic albums on CD for less than a fiver. Recent bargains included the eponymous Rufus Wainwright album for £3.99, Jeff Buckley's 'Grace' for £4.99 and Nirvana's 'Bleach' for £3.99, making this one of the best places on the high street to find great quality music at discounted prices.

Branches at:
120 Charing Cross Road, WC2 Tel: 020 7379 8877
Unit MSU1-2, 26 Parkfield Street, Islington, London, N1 Tel: 020 7226 3602

Brill

27 Exmouth Market, EC1
Tel: 020 7833 9757
Tube: Angel or Farringdon
Open: Mon-Fri 9am-6pm, Sat10am-6pm

Brill is an appropriate name for this music shop that is also a café. The CDs are all reasonably priced, there is always a good choice of second-hand stuff for between £2.99 and £6.99 and they also serve a mean cappuccino.

Cheapo Cheapo Records

53 Rupert Street, W1
Tel: 020 7437 8272
Tube: Piccadilly Circus
Open: Mon-Sat 11am-10pm

This huge second-hand music shop is still going strong after many years trading in Soho. They sell an incredible range of CDs for as little as £2 each, vinyl from £2 and DVDs for £6 each. Cheapo Cheapo Records remains true to its name by offering even bigger discounts for multiple purchases with unbeatable deals like 5 DVDs for £20. Be prepared to hunt as the selection is enormous and presentation is not one of the shop's strong points.

Harold Moores Records and Video

2 Great Marlborough Street, W1F
Tel: 020 7437 1576
email: sales@hmrecords.demon.co.uk
Tube: Oxford Circus
Open: Mon-Sat 10am-6.30pm, Sun 12noon-6 pm

This established classical record shop is renowned for its basement of well catalogued and priced, used and collectable CDs and vinyl. They are particularly good for jazz and classical music with vinyl starting from £2.50 and going up to £400 for some rare collectables. CDs sell for about half the new price, starting from as little as £3. This shop also offers an efficient mail order service.

MDC Music & Movies

Royal Festival Hall, SE1
Tel: 020 7620 0198
Website: www.mdcmusic.co.uk
Tube: Embankment or Waterloo
Open: Daily 10am-10pm

This smart, modern outlet offers a wide choice of classical and jazz CDs and a wide choice of world cinema DVDs at very competitive prices. The shop is particularly good value for box sets of CDs with bargains such as a 10 CD Miles Davis collection for only £9.99 and a box containing the complete works of Bach for only £90. For those on a more limited budget the shop has up to 15 browsers containing sale items with lots of film DVDs for as little as £3.99. A great place to look for film and music bargains and their website is also a useful resource.

Leisure • CDs, Records, Tapes & DVDs

Music & Video Exchange

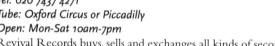

95 Berwick Street, W1
Tel: 020 7434 2939
Website: www.mveshops.co.uk
Tube: Leicester Square
Open: Daily 10am-8pm

This branch of the Music and Video Exchange group specialises in rock, pop, soul, folk and dance music. There are plenty of bargains to be had with prices starting from as little as £1 and usually a few bargain bins to rummage through.

Revival Records

30 Berwick Street, W1
Tel: 020 7437 4271
Tube: Oxford Circus or Piccadilly
Open: Mon-Sat 10am-7pm

Revival Records buys, sells and exchanges all kinds of second-hand CDs and vinyl. Just about every kind of contemporary music can be found here although you will have to rummage among the racks for your favourite artist because their cataloguing system is not yet developed. A great shop to rummage for music bargains…

Sister Ray

34-35 Berwick Street, W1
Tel: 020 7734 3297
Website: www.sisterray.co.uk
Tube: Oxford Circus or Tottenham Court Road
Open: Mon-Sat 9.30am-8pm

(map 1)

This shop is well organised and tries to keep its prices for back catalogue CDs at below those of the larger high street stores. About 20% of their stock is second-hand CDs and vinyl but they only stock rarer stuff that they cannot get new. A great music shop with enough bargains to make it worth a visit.

North

Alan's Records

218 High Road, East Finchley N2
Tel: 020 8883 0234
Tube: East Finchley
Open: Tue-Sun 12noon-6.30pm

Alan Dobrin has been running this vinyl and CD shop for many years and has accumulated a varied stock of 10-15,000 predominantly second-hand records from the 1950s to the present day, plus 3,500 CDs and tapes. Reggae, soul and jazz are the shop's particular specialities but every kind of music is covered. There is a high turnover of stock and there are always reduced price bargains for between 50p and £3 on display outside. A shop well worth visiting.

Audio Gold

308-310 Park Road, N8
Tel: 020 8341 9007
Website: www.audiogold.co.uk
Tube: Finsbury Park then W7 bus
Open: Mon-Sat 10.30am-6.30pm

This shop is best known for second-hand hi-fi equipment, but it also sells a great selection of vinyl with all kinds of music covered from classical to dance, all neatly arranged and competitively priced. For hard-core bargain hunters they also have clearance racks with records being sold for only £1. A great place to browse for good value vinyl, they also serve a great coffee.

Leisure • CDs, Records, Tapes & DVDs

Flashback

50 Essex Road, N1
Tel: 020 7354 9356
Website: www.flashback.co.uk
Tube: Angel
Open: Mon-Sat 10am-7pm Sun 12noon-6pm

This shop has an excellent collection of second-hand music, film DVDs and vinyl. The basement is devoted to vinyl, where anything from Krautrock to hip hop can be found, with a special accent on rare and collectable items. Prices for vinyl start from £1. Upstairs is where the CDs are kept, with an equally impressive selection of music and recent releases for around £7. There's an impressive selection of film DVDs from £4. They give a good deal if you want to trade in your old records and CDs, but can be quite picky – ultimately a good thing for the overall quality of the stock. While many CD/vinyl outlets have closed in recent years, Flashback has expanded and now has a smaller store in Crouch End.
Also at: 144 Crouch Hill, Crouch End, N8 Tel: 020 8342 9633
Open: Mon-Sat 10am-7pm, Sun 11am-5pm

Haggle Vinyl

114-116 Essex Road, N1
Tel: 020 7704 3101
Website: www.hagglevinyl.com
Tube: Angel
Open: Mon-Sat 9am-7pm, Sun 9am-3pm

If you are one of those that still treasure your vinyl collection and keep your turntable dust-free and in working order, then this shop will prove a useful place to add to your collection. They claim to have over 21,000 albums and taking a look at the packed display units and large piles of records on the floor it is easy to believe. Among the stock is every type of music from the 50s onwards with a particular emphasis upon soul, reggae and jazz. The records on the floor are usually £2, while those in the units can range from £8 to as much as £200 for a signed collectable. Haggle often has boxes outside with records reduced to clear.

Beats Workin'

Alan's Records

Music & Video Exchange

Out On The Floor

Music & Video Exchange

208 Camden High Street, NW1
Tel: 020 7267 1898
Website: www.mveshops.co.uk
Tube: Camden Town
Open: Daily 10am-8pm

This is one of the largest and best stocked record shops in town with two floors offering CDs, vinyl, DVDs and videos. They claim to have an emphasis on contemporary music, but in reality every kind of music is represented here and the less favoured styles, like classical and folk, are often sold at greater discounts. All stock is competitively priced and they keep a corner of the ground floor and the entire basement for bargain items. In the bargain areas all LPs are less than £5, with many for as little £1, there are piles of CDs for 50p each and the novel idea of 10 singles for £1 (the packs of 10 are wrapped so you can't see what you get). Even in the main areas there are numerous records that have been reduced in price to below £5. If you have kept your video player, this shop still sells videos for only £1-£2.

Music & Video Exchange

281 & 208 Camden High Street, NW1
Tel: 020 7267 0123
Website: www.mveshops.co.uk
Tube: Camden Town
Open: Daily 10am-8pm

This second branch of the Music and Video Exchange in Camden serves as a clearing store for the larger store at number 208. The prices are cheap and the range and volume of CDs, vinyl, videos and DVDs enormous. A great place to look for music and film bargains.

Ocean Books

127 Stoke Newington Church Street, N16
Tel: 020 7502 6319
E-mail: oceanbooksn16@yahoo.co.uk
Rail: Stoke Newington
Open: Mon-Sat 11.30am-6pm, Sun 12noon-6pm

This small bookshop has now dedicated its small back room to vintage vinyl. The stock is always well chosen and there are usually a few bargains to be found.

Out On The Floor

10 Inverness Street, NW1
Tel: 020 7267 5989
Tube: Camden Town
Open: Daily 10am-6.30pm

Three floors of collectable and second-hand vinyl, with an emphasis on soul, funk, reggae, indie, rock and pop. The stock is very well organised with most CDs and LPs for around £7 and plenty of 60s and 70s vinyl bargains in the basement. They buy good condition stuff and also offer part-exchange. Out On The Floor also now sell posters and T-shirts.

West

Honest Jon's Records

278 Portobello Road, W10
Tel: 020 8969 9822
Website: www.honestjons.com
Tube: Ladbroke Grove
Open: Mon-Sat 10am-6pm, Sun 11am-5pm

Specialising in reggae, jazz, world music and dance, bargain hunters can find a plethora of good quality CDs and vinyl here with both new and used stock. Not everything is dirt cheap since some of their stock is highly prized, but there are always a few items to clear and usually a few bargain boxes.

Intoxica

231 Portobello Road, London W11
Tel: 020 7229 8010
Website: www.intoxica,co.uk
Tube: Ladbroke Grove
Open: Mon-Fri 10.30am-6.30pm, Sat 10am-6.30pm, Sun 10am-5pm

This store specialises in vinyl from the 50s to 70s with particular emphasis on jazz, soul, blues, psych and beat. This is a great place for vinyl addicts to get their fix and there is always a sale bin kept well stocked with clearance records for as little as 50p. A fantastic record shop with a useful website and well run mail order service.

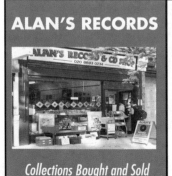

Music & Video Exchange

www.mveshops.co.uk
Tube: Notting Hill Gate
Open: Daily 10am-8pm

General:
38 Notting Hill Gate, W11
(Bargain Basement)
Tel: 020 7243 8573

Classical:
36 Notting Hill Gate
Tel: 020 7229 3219

Computer Games:
40 Notting Hill Gate
Tel: 020 7792 9393

Soul & Dance:
42 Notting Hill Gate
Tel: 020 7221 2793

Videos:
Stage & Screen
34 Notting Hill Gate
Tel: 020 7221 3646

This chain of shops has colonised a sizeable chunk of Notting Hill Gate with a variety of music, video and computer game outlets. The shops are plain, the staff a little surly, but the selection of vinyl and CDs is enormous. The general store at 38 Notting Hill Gate also has videos and a bargain basement with discounted CDs and vinyl. For even more discounts don't forget the store at no.40 which sells discounted video games, but also thousands of clearance LPs for 50p. Although many of the albums are worthless dross, there are enough little gems to make the search worthwhile. If you like classical music, the Classical Music Exchange at 36 is a good place to look for bargains, with many quality LPs, CDs and tapes gradually reduced in price until they sell. Stage & Screen at 34 specialises in second-hand videos, with films for £1-£14. Bring ID if you want to trade your old vinyl or CDs.

South

Beanos

7 Middle Street
Croydon, Surrey
Tel: 020 8680 1202
Website: www.beanos.co.uk
Rail: East Croydon
Open: Mon-Fri 10am-6pm, Sat 9am-6pm

Beanos was the largest second-hand record shop in Europe, but has suffered in recent years from internet competition and the rise of new computer formats. The store has been forced to restructure and is now only trading in music on the first floor of its vast store and turning the other floors into an indoor market area with lots of traders and a café. The ground floor shop is still a great place to visit for CD and vinyl bargains and it is hoped that this great establishment will thrive its smaller incarnation.

Music & Video Exchange

Dance/General
23 Greenwich Church Street, SE10
Tel: 020 8858 8898
Rail/DLR: Greenwich
Open: Daily 10am-8pm
See the main entry in West London (page 245).

Rat Records

348 Camberwell New Road, SE5
Tel: 020 7274 3222
Website: www.ratrecordsuk.net
Tube: Oval
Open: Mon-Sat 10.30am-6.30pm

This is one of south London's best kept secrets with second-hand vinyl and CDs, piled high and sold cheap. There are at least 500 fresh records arriving every Saturday including soul, reggae, hip-hop, R&B, jazz, rock, indie, folk, blues and much more. Most CDs are sold for £5 or less, with many reduced to clear for £3 or less. The vinyl starts for as little as £2 and is never more than £8. Well worth going out of your way to visit.

East

Beats Workin'

93-95 Sclater Street, E1
Tel: 020 7729 8249
Website: www.beatsworkinrecords.com
Tube: Aldgate East/Liverpool Street
Open: Tues-Sun 11.30am-7.30pm

Beats Workin' is a welcome recent arrival to the Brick Lane area – buying and selling second-hand vinyl and CDs. The design of the shop is clean and modern and the stock is well ordered and eclectic with anything from Hendrix to Abba available for between £4.99 and £6.99. The staff are helpful and there are turntables on hand for you to check your vinyl before buying. A great place to shop for music bargains.

CD & Vinyl Fairs

There are a number of organisations that run CD & Vinyl Fairs in London, where many independent traders gather at a large venue to sell to the public. These events are great entertainment and there are always plenty of bargains to be found. Below are the details of the main companies organising events in the London area:

VIP Events

Website: www.vip-24.com
Tel: 0116 277 1133

This organisation runs the majority of music fairs in the capital and their website gives details of all forthcoming events. The fairs are either held at the Camden Electric Ballroom or at the Olympia Exhibition Centre. The two day event at Olympia is held twice a year and attracts a vast array of vinyl and CD traders.

Dollar Promotions

Website: www.dtrecords.co.uk
email: fairs@dtrecords.co.uk

Dollar Promotions hold regular CD and vinyl fairs specialising in soul and dance music. View their website for information about forthcoming dates.

Photography

Photography has been revolutionised by the growing popularity of digital cameras which now dominate the market and have deprived many traditional camera shops of their trade. The shops below are largely specialist camera stores, but digital photography has opened the market to more general electronics retailers. Morgans is one such computer retailer that has expanded its activities to incorporate digital cameras and the store gets a review in this chapter. There are other similar stores to be found just 10 minutes walk from Morgans, on Tottenham Court Road, and details of these can be found in the Electronics section of the book (see page 115).

Camera Equipment

Central

Aperture Photographic

44 Museum Street, WC1
Tel: 020 7242 8681
Website: www.apertureuk.com
Tube: Tottenham Court Road
Open: Mon-Fri 11am-7pm, Sat 12noon-7pm

Aperture Photographic is the only camera shop that doubles as a café. The shop specialises in new and used camera equipment with an emphasis upon high-end professional cameras and accessories with names like Nikon, Canon, Leica and Hasselblad all to be found here. On a recent visit they had a good condition used Canon ID MkII for £1450 which is a bargain considering the new camera retails for around £3,000. There are plenty of second-hand offers for more modest pockets and the website is updated daily with all the current new and used stock. Unlike Jessops they also serve an excellent cappuccino.

Camera World

14 Wells Street, W1
Tel: 020 7636 5005
Website: www.cameraworld.co.uk
Tube: Oxford Circus/Tottenham Court Road
Open: Mon-Fri 9am-6pm, Sat 10am-5pm

This shop offers a large selection of digital cameras, SLR cameras and lenses, camerabags and accessories at very competitive prices. There are regular sale items and they recently offered the discontinued Nikon D50

SLR digital camera with 18–55mm lens for only £299 (inc VAT). Camera World also offers a digital and 35mm printing service which takes two working days. The website offers refurbished and clearance items sold with full guarantees at considerable discounts.

Jacobs Digital

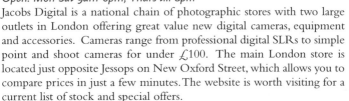

74 New Oxford Street, WC1
Tel: 020 7436 5544
Website: www.jacobsdigital.co.uk
Tube: Tottenham Court Road
Open: Mon-Sat 9am-6pm, Thurs till 8pm

Jacobs Digital is a national chain of photographic stores with two large outlets in London offering great value new digital cameras, equipment and accessories. Cameras range from professional digital SLRs to simple point and shoot cameras for under £100. The main London store is located just opposite Jessops on New Oxford Street, which allows you to compare prices in just a few minutes. The website is worth visiting for a current list of stock and special offers.

Also at: 124-6 Cannon Street, EC4 Tel: 020 7621 1621
Open: Mon-Fri 8.30am-6pm

Jessops

63-69 New Oxford Street, WC1
Tel: 020 7240 6077
Website: www.jessops.com
Tube: Tottenham Court Road
Open: Mon-Sat 9am-6pm, Thurs till 8pm

Jessops is the largest camera chain in the UK and has a good reputation. They sell every type of camera plus all the accessories and offer to match any local price. They often have special offers on cameras and equipment making them a good first point of call for photographers. They also offer a developing and printing service.

Branches at:
67 Great Russell Street, WC1B Tel: 020 7831 3640
Unit 1, Cannon Street Station, EC4N Tel: 020 7623 1381
113 Fenchurch Street, EC3M Tel: 0207 481 4777
46 Fleet Street, EC4Y Tel: 020 7353 4125
43 Strutton Ground, Victoria, SW1 Tel: 020 7222 0521
Unit 28, Whiteleys Centre, 133-165 Queensway, W2 Tel: 020 7221 1784
Unit 8, No 1 The Poultry, EC2R Tel: 020 7248 2780
120 Moorgate, EC2M Tel: 020 7588 4831
10 New Broadway, Ealing, W5 Tel: 020 8840 7734

Leisure ● Photography

39-41 High Street, Putney, SW15 Tel: 020 8788 6648
360 Kensington High Street, W14 Tel: 020 7602 5311
443 The Strand, WC2R 0QU Tel: 020 7379 6522
154 Tottenham Court Road, W1T Tel: 020 7387 7001
89 King Street, Hammersmith, W6 Tel: 020 8741 2670
42 Upper Street, Islington, N1 Tel: 020 7354 4144
85 St. Johns Road, Clapham Junction, SW11 Tel: 020 8228 0419
Unit 1A The Eye, High Holborn, WC1 Tel: 020 7405 3364
Unit R1330 Cabot Place, East Canada Square, E14 Tel: 020 7719 1999
Opening times vary, call branch for details. For other branches view their website.

R G Lewis Ltd

(map 1)

29 Southampton Row, WC1
Tel: 020 7242 2916
Fax: 020 7831 4062
Tube: Holborn
Open: Mon-Fri 8.30am-5.30pm, Sat 9.30am-3.45pm

R.G. Lewis has been trading since before the war but has only recently moved to this new location on Southampton Row. The new premises still have a traditional feel with lots of wood and glass display units and the same personal service. The shop specialises in Leica cameras but also has a range of second-hand cameras at very competitive prices. Among the bargains found here on a recent visit was a Leica III with lens for only £269. They also sell an extensive range of vintage cameras as well as digital cameras from £50 to £800. All the used goods come with a 6 month warranty and they offer a mail order service.

London Camera Exchange

(map 1)

98 Strand, WC2
Tel: 020 7379 0200
Website: www.lcegroup.co.uk
Tube: Covent Garden
Open: Mon-Fri 9am-5.30pm, Sat 11am-5pm

This shop sells new and used cameras and equipment and is one of the few stores in London to offer part-exchange. There are usually around 150 cameras in stock at any one time with about 20% of these being digital and the rest film. The second-hand goods are all sold on a 16 day trial period and those over £200 have a 6 month warranty.

Microglobe

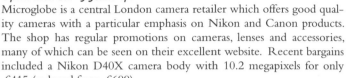

3 Galen Place (off Bury Place), WC1
Tel: 020 7240 6774
Website: www.microglobe.co.uk
Tube: Tottenham Court Road
Open: Mon-Sat 9.30am-6pm

Microglobe is a central London camera retailer which offers good quality cameras with a particular emphasis on Nikon and Canon products. The shop has regular promotions on cameras, lenses and accessories, many of which can be seen on their excellent website. Recent bargains included a Nikon D40X camera body with 10.2 megapixels for only £415 (reduced from £699).

Morgan

64-72 New Oxford Street, WC1
Tel: 020 7255 2115
Website: www.morgancomputers.co.uk
Tube: Tottenham Court Road
Open: Mon-Fri 10am-6.30pm, Sat 10am-6pm, Sun 11am-5pm

Morgan have established their reputation as a computer outlet, but have in recent years expanded into other electronic goods including digital cameras. The range of digital cameras is now extensive and there are plenty of bargains including a 7.1 megapixel Samsung NV7 for only £164.49 and the Nikon D70 digital SLR with lens for only £446.49. A great shop to seek out camera bargains and just opposite Jessops and Jacobs for an easy price comparison. For more details about their computers and other electronic goods see page 100.

North

Nicholas Camera Company

15 Camden High Street, NW1
Tel: 020 7916 7251
Website: www.nicholascamera.com
Tube: Mornington Crescent
Open: Mon-Sat 10am-6pm

A great little camera shop with lots of new and used SLR digital and film cameras at reasonable prices and a more limited range of darkroom equipment. They are particularly strong on professional and collectors equipment and the website is detailed and easy to use.

Photocraft
4 Heath Street, NW3
Tel: 020 7435 9932
Tube: Hampstead
Open: Mon-Sat 9am-5.30pm

A general photographic store, which has a large range of second-hand cameras sold on commission, rather than bought in and then sold with a mark-up. This makes the possibility of finding a quality bargain very likely. Although no guarantees are available on used gear, refunds or repairs can be offered if purchases are brought back within two weeks.

West

Film Plus
Unit 5 Westway Centre
69 St Marks Road, W10
Tel: 020 8969 0234
Website: www.filmplus.com
Tube: Ladbroke Grove/Notting Hill Gate
Open: Mon-Fri 8am-7pm, Sat 10am-12.30pm

A shop for the professional photographer, specialising in equipment rental. They have a small selection of second-hand cameras, and while happy snappers probably won't find anything to fit the bill here, serious photographers may well get lucky.

Photo Optix
187 Kings Road, SW3
Tel: 020 7351 7178
Website: www.digistor.co.uk
Tube: Sloane Square
Open: Mon-Sat 9am-5pm, Sun 11am-5pm

Photo Optix are a chain of stores which offer competitive pricing on new cameras, but also regularly receive ex-display models which are refurbished and sold with full warranties at about half the usual retail price.

Branches at:
Lakeside Shopping Centre, West Thurrock Tel: 01708 890 348
34 Broadway, Victoria, SW1 Tel: 020 7222 7828
8 Oak Road, Ealing Broadway Centre, W5 Tel: 020 8840 7028
1b The Broadway Centre, Hammersmith, W6 Tel: 020 8563 7073

Mac's Cameras

262 King Street, W6
Tel: 020 8846 9853
Tube: Ravencourt Park
Open: Mon-Sat 8.45am-5.45pm

A large camera shop that sells film cameras, cine cameras and super 8 equipment. If you are still committed to film rather than digital equipment then this shop is well worth a visit. A recent bargain was a Pentax 645N with two lenses for £1499 which was a bargain considering this professional equipment cost over £3,000 new and was in mint condition.

Outer London

Mr Cad

68 Windmill Road, Croydon
Surrey, CR0 2XP
Tel: 020 8684 8282
E-mail: sales@mrcad.co.uk
Website: www.mrcad.co.uk
Rail: East Croyden, West Croyden
Open: Mon-Fri 9am-5pm, Sat 10am-4pm

Europe's largest used camera store with 9000 sq ft of used bargains offering studio lighting, darkroom equipment, lenses and cameras from 35mm to 10x8. There are lots of good deals available and a very efficient mail order service.

Photomarket

397B High Street, Wembley
Middlesex, HA9
Tel: 020 8903 0587
E-mail: sales@photomarket.co.uk
Website: www.photomarket.co.uk
Tube: Wembley Central
Open: Mon-Sat 9am-5.30pm

This large photographic retailer has a fine stock of second-hand film cameras and accessories, details of which can be found on their easy-to-use website. New cameras and equipment – including a good range of digital cameras – are sold at very competitive prices, with special offers on certain items. Photomarket welcomes part-exchange.

Websites/Mail Order

Below are some of the most interesting web retailers but they will not always be the cheapest. A simple price comparison can be done with price comparison websites that will compare the price of a camera among many web retailers to find the best price. Among these search engines Moneysupermarket.com is quick and easy to use with a wide selection of retailers from which to choose.

www.cameraking.co.uk

Order Line: 020 8965 1722
Open: Mon-Fri 9.30am-6.30pm, Sat 9.30am-1.30pm

An easy-to-use website with lots of good deals on Nikon, Leica and Canon cameras and accessories. Recent bargains included a Leica V-Lux 1 10 megapixel digital SLR for only £579.95. The offers are always changing so check on the site for all the latest deals.

Lee's Cameras

PO Box 35519, London, NW4 1YF
Tel: 020 8202 9918
E-mail: sales@leescameras.demon.co.uk
Website: www.leescameras.demon.co.uk
Open: Mon-Fri 10am-5pm

Lee's Cameras is now run as a mail order business offering a large stock of cine cameras, accessories and slide projectors. If you are still using 35mm film for slides and cine film, view their website or give them a call.

R K Photographic

www.thedarkroom.co.uk
Tel: 01707 643 953

R K Photographic used to have a store in Finchley, but in recent years have moved out to a business park in Potters Bar and most of their business is now mail order. The website is excellent and clear and the company still offers excellent value for the serious photographer with a good stock of used equipment and regular promotions on new products.

Camera Repair

Camera Care
20 Hanway Street, W1
Tel: 020 7436 8655
Tube: Tottenham Court Road
Open: Mon-Fri 9.30am-6pm, Sat 10am-5pm
Repairs are done on site to cameras, i-pods, digital video cameras, computer equipment, TVs and hi-fi's. All repairs are guaranteed.

London Camera (map 6) Repair Centre
72 Golborne Road, W10
Tel: 020 8968 5554
Tube: Westbourne Park or Ladbroke Grove
Open: Mon-Fri 11am-7pm
An established camera repair shop which offers a 6-month guarantee on all work and also sells a limited stock of second-hand cameras

Sendean Camera Repair
9-12 St Anne's Court, W1
Tel: 020 7734 0895
Tube: Tottenham Court Road
Open: Mon-Fri 10.30am-6pm
Good quality camera repairs at reasonable prices, with a selection of second-hand equipment as well. Same-day estimates can be given on most repairs and they provide a same day cleaning service for digital camera CCDs.

Darkroom Supplies

Process Supplies

13-25 Mount Pleasant, WC1
Tel: 020 7837 2179
Website: www.process-supplies.co.uk
Tube: Farringdon
Open: Mon-Fri 9am-5.30pm

Process Supplies offers reductions on film, paper, chemicals and process-ing accessories, most of which is sold at trade prices. As well as provid-ing a great value service for those that use traditional film cameras the store now offers all the accessories for digital photography from printer cartridges to memory cards. A great shop and one that has managed to adapt to the digital world.

R K Photographic

Website: www.thedarkroom.co.uk
Tel: 01707 643 953

RK sells all the main makes of enlargers, plus all darkroom accessories and a large range of papers.

Darkroom Hire

The Camera Club

16 Bowden Street, SE11
Tel: 020 7587 1809
Website: www.thecameraclub.co.uk
Tube: Kennington
Open: Mon-Fri 11am-10pm, Sat & Sun 11am-6pm

Once you have paid the annual membership fee of £99, you can make use of this club's extensive services. Facilities include a B&W darkroom for £4 per hour, and a studios for as little as £8 per hour. The club now has a Digital Suite for £3 per hour and runs courses all year round. The Camera Club is a not-for-profit organisation and offers excellent value for its members.

Sports Equipment

Decathlon
Surrey Quays Road
Canada Water Retail Park, SE16
Tel: 020 7394 2000
Website: www.decathlon.co.uk
Tube: Surrey Quays
Bus:
Open: Mon-Fri 10am-8pm, Sat 9am-7pm, Sun 11am-5pm

Decathlon are an established French sports retailer with two large retail outlets in Surrey Quays offering all kinds of sports and leisure goods. Just about every sport is catered for within the store from outdoor activities such as camping and cycling to martial arts and weight training. Decathlon sell other manufacturers but are particularly good value with their own range of sporting products which are unique to the store and always of good quality. The staff at Decathlon are remarkably friendly and enthusiastic and are always on hand to offer help and advice. There are regular sales at the Surrey Quays store and occasionally they run a second-hand department which sells customers unwanted sports goods at a discount. Decathlon is a definite first point of call for sporty Londoners looking for bargains.

Direct Dance Wear
Lancaster House, Dollis Hill Estate,
105 Brook Road, NW2
Tel: 020 8450 2456
Website: www.directdancewear.com
Tube: Dollis Hill
Open: Mon-Thurs 9.30am-5.30pm, Fri 10am-1.30pm, Sun 10am-1.30pm

This small retail outlet on the second floor of an uninspiring office block offers dancewear for adults and children at discount prices. They sell their own label to dance shops but you can buy from them direct. Children's leotards start from £8, children's ballet shoes from £7.50. They also stock jazz and tap shoes, tights and anything else you might need for dance classes.

Lillywhites

24-36 Lower Regent Street, SW1
Tel: 0870 333 9600
Website: www.sportsdirect.com
Tube: Piccadilly Circus
Open: Mon-Sat 10am-6pm, Sun 12noon-6pm

This sports superstore used to have a reputation as an upmarket sports department store, but in recent years it has begun to redefine itself as a sports discount outlet with the emphasis upon special offers and most of the ground floor dedicated to discounted sports and casual clothing. Even their website puts the emphasis upon the discounts with special promotions on Karrimor bags and shoes and lots of deals on current football kits. Recent deals included a tube of 4 Slazenger Wimbledon balls for only £2.99 and Reebok NBA Downtime trainers for £11.99 (reduced from £59.99). While athletes looking for specific equipment for their chosen sport might be disappointed with the change in the store, for general sports equipment it's a good place to visit.

Sports World

(map 1)

26-28 Oxford Street, W1
Tel: 0870 333 9566
Website: www.sportsdirect.com
Open: Daily 10am-8pm

This chain of sports stores has a reputation for offering very good value for a whole range of sports goods and casual wear. They were recently offering a wide range of Karrimor trainers for under £20 and are the cheapest place in town to buy tennis balls as Slazenger are part of the same company. Take a look at their website to find out about the latest offers. Branches at:

Unit 3, Gallions Reach Shopping Centre, Beckton, E6
Unit D Brent Cross Shopping Park, Tilling Road, Brent Cross, NW2
1110-1112 Whitgift Centre, North End, Croydon, Surrey, CR0
540-580 Enfield Retail Park, Enfield, Middlesex, EN1
Unit 1 Greenwich Shopping Park, Bugsby Way, Greenwich, SE7
Unit 2 The Arena Shopping Centre, Green Lanes, Harringey, N4
Unit 2 Southernwood Retail Park, 2 Humphrey Street, Old Kent Road, SE1
Unit A, Friern Bridge Retail Park, Pegasus Way, Friern Barnet, N11
427/429 North End Road, Fulham, SW6
99-101 High Street, Putney, SW15
16-18 Ludgate Hill, St Pauls, EC4M
154-156 Stoke Newington High Street, N16
Unit G18, The Plaza, 116-128 Oxford Street. W1D (Sports Direct)

Travel

Budget Airlines (from London)

The key to getting the great prices from any airline (including the low-cost, no-frills airlines) is to book as early as possible for the best choice of fares. Book online as most airlines give a slight discount for doing so and often send newsletters about sales and special promotions. Always check that all taxes and charges are included before comparing prices and remember that most of their telephone reservation numbers are toll calls. It's always worth checking British Airways' sales as their discounted flights often beat the low-cost airlines' fares.

Air Baltic
Tel: 09115980599
Website: www.airbaltic.com
Air Baltic is the Latvian national airline. From London, they fly to several destinations in the Baltic, Scandinavia, Russia and as far as Tel Aviv. They fly to Moscow, Saint Petersburg and Tallinn from £50. The airline also offers cheap hotel deals and discounts on group bookings.

Air Berlin
Tel: 0871 5000 737
Website: www.airberlin.com
From London Stansted, Air Berlin flies to every conceivable city in Germany as well as British inbound destinations such as Belfast, Manchester and Glasgow. The airline also flies to Mallorca and Alicante for as little as £24 (including food and drinks).

Air Comet
Tel: 020 7290 7887
Website: airpluscomet.com
One of the few low-cost airlines flying to destinations in South America and the Caribbean. Air Comet offers direct flights from London Gatwick to Madrid, from where they operate their flights. You can transfer onto destinations in Argentina, Columbia, Peru and the Caribbean. We found flights to Santo Domingo and Havana for as little as £250.

Aurigny
Tel: 0871 871 0717
www.aurigny.com
With flights to Alderney, Jersey and Guernsey from Gatwick and Stansted starting from just £29, Aurigny is the cheapest way to access the Channel Islands from London. Based in Guernsey, it has been running flights there since 1968.

Easyjet
Tel: 09058210905
Website: www.easyjet.com
Distinguished by their bright orange logo, Easyjet is one of the biggest no-frills airlines flying from Britain. They fly to over 100 cities in the UK, France, Spain, Switzerland, the Netherlands, Denmark, Italy, the Czech Republic, Greece, Germany and Portugal. They also operate a car rental service (0870 899 9900) and ski holiday travel booking service through their website or on Tel: 0845 070 0203. There is no office in London, so booking is best done by phone or on the website (you get a small discount for booking on-line). Join their mailing list to receive up-to-date route information. London Luton is their hub, but they also fly from Gatwick and Stansted.

Excel
Tel: 0870 320 7777
www.xl.com
Excel, also known as XL, bills itself as "the world's leading charter airline" and there is no doubt it has cornered the market for packages and flights to the most popular summer destinations. It serves all the main Greek and Spanish islands, Egypt, Barbados and the Mediterranean from Gatwick. Typical deals when I looked were £106 for a week's package in Mallorca and £79 return flight only to Paphos.

Flybe
Tel: 0871 522 6100
Website: www.flybe.com
Once called British European, Flybe has a large network of flights between destinations in the UK, Ireland, France, Spain, Switzerland, Belgium and Italy all sold at competitive prices. From London Gatwick they offer flights to Bergerac and UK destinations such as Belfast, Jersey, Isle of Man and Inverness.

German Wings
Tel: 0870 252 12 50
www2.germanwings.co.uk
A superb low-cost budget airline from Germany and a partner of Lufthansa, offering services from Cologne/Bonn, Hamburg and Stuttgart into Stansted and Gatwick. They specialise in offering tempting savings for events within the cities it serves, such as exhibitions in Cologne, boat trips in Hamburg and offers hotel accomodation from £15.

Iceland Express
Tel: 870 240 5600
www.icelandexpress.com
Iceland Express is a small airline offering affordable daily flights to Iceland, which is a notoriously expensive destination. Prices start at £69 from Stansted.

Meridiana
Tel: 084 5355 5588 (reservations) / 08702243711.
Website: www.meridiana.it
This low-fare Italian airline runs flights from London Gatwick to Florence and Olbia in Sardinia. Within Italy, their flights link all major cities and they also fly to Paris, Barcelona and Amsterdam.

Monarch
Tel: 087 0040 5040
www.flymonarch.com
Monarch flies sun-seekers to all the Iberian islands and other holiday destinations from Luton and Gatwick, and gives up to 40% discount on web offers, with fares as low as £10.

MyTravelite
Email: mytravelinfo@airtours.co.uk
Website: www.mytravelite.com
My Travelite offers "cheap flights to the sun" and operates from 22 airports in the UK to 60 destinations around the world. From London Gatwick, the airline flies to a great many Mediterranean islands. We found flights to the Balearic Islands for as little as £20 or to the Canary Islands for £30.

Niki

Tel: 08707388880
Website: www.flyniki.co.uk

Low fare alliance partner of Air Berlin founded by former formula one driver Niki Lauda. From London Stansted they fly to several cities in Germany, but also holiday destinations in Spain, Italy and France. Their website features a list of special offers to help you find the best deal.

Norwegian

Tel: 020 8099 7254
www.norwegian.no

Norway's own low-cost airline is offering flights from Stansted to five Norwegian cities. They fly daily to the coastal cities of Bergen and Trondheim, five times a week to Tromso and Stavanger, and the capital city Oslo thirteen times a week. Prices start at around £30 one-way including taxes.

Ryanair

Tel: 0871 246 0000
Website: www.ryanair.com

Ryanair always have some special fare offer whether it be £1 seats within the UK or £10 roundtrips to European destinations. Remember that these fares do not include airport taxes, which can significantly raise the fare. Keep abreast of sales by registering with them on their website. London Stansted is their hub, but they also fly from Gatwick and Luton.

SkyEurope

Tel: 0905 7222 747
www.skyeurope.com

SkyEurope was arguably the first airline to provide low-cost travel from London to the most popular destinations in the new European Union countries. It flies daily from Stansted to Bratislava, and provides a gateway to the Tatra mountain area at Poprad. Prices start from £19 one-way.

Sterling

Tel: 0870 787 8038
Website: www.sterling.dk

Scandinavia's first low-cost airline. From London Gatwick, there are cheap flights to Oslo, Stockholm and Copenhagen. From there you can fly to popular destinations in Italy, Spain, Greece and Eastern Europe.

ThomsonFly

Tel: 0870 1900 737
Website: www.thomsonfly.com

With flights to almost any beach destination in Turkey, Greece, Egypt and Spain, ThomsonFly is one of the largest low-cost airlines. Their city-break holidays are also popular and reasonably priced. Flights to Amsterdam, Venice and Prague start at around £30.

Transavia

Tel: 020 7365 4997
www.transavia.com/uk

Flies daily to Rotterdam from Stansted, with prices starting at £36.99 for a single flight.

VLM

Tel: 0871 666 5050
www.flyvlm.com

This airline flies out of London City Airport to the Benelux countries, Jersey and the Isle of Man. Major cities such as Amsterdam, Brussels, Rotterdam, Antwerp are served as well as Luxembourg, from around £53. This airline is ideal for its high frequency of flights for business travellers. On weekdays, they fly eleven times daily to Rotterdam, and six times to Amsterdam.

Wizzair

www.wizzair.com

Wizzair is a burgeoning low-cost airline based in Poland, operating daily services out of Luton to several destinations in eastern and central Europe. The main cities served directly are Budapest, Warsaw, Sofia, Zagreb and Split. Prices started from around £15 one-way, but as of May 2006, some routes were priced as little as £0.01 plus taxes.

Zoom Airlines

Tel: 0870 240 0055
website: www.flyzoom.com

Zoom Airlines is a low-cost airline based in Ottawa. They operate flights to Bermuda, New York and destinations in Canada from London. Daily flights from London Gatwick to New York for as little as £130.

Travel Agents

Cheap holiday packages are always available and finding them is often a matter of scanning publications such as Time Out and The Evening Standard and phoning around to get the best quote. You could also take a look at the travel pages on Teletext which offer lots of up-to-date flight bargains or check out their website: www. teletextholidays.co.uk. Below are reviews of many of the established discount travel agents to help you in your search. If you're under the age of 26, always ask about youth fares. Often they are up to 50% less than a full-priced economy fare.

Flight Centre
5 Regent Street, SW1
Tel: 020 7925 1114
Website: www.flightcentre.co.uk
Tube: Piccadilly Circus
Open: Mon-Fri 9.30am-6pm, Sat 10am-4pm

This international chain of travel agents sells discount flights to destinations all over the globe. They also promise to beat any lower fare that you find either at another agent or online. Besides flights, the company can also arrange lodging and transportation at your destination. For other branches throughout London telephone 0870 499 0040, or visit their website.

Going Abroad
417 Hendon Way, NW4
Tel: 0870 442 7557
Tube: Hendon Central
Open: Mon-Thurs 9am-8pm, Fri 9am-7pm, Sat-Sun 9am-6pm

Great for last minute deals and cheaply priced package holidays, specialising in Mediterranean and Caribbean offers.

Student Travel Centre

24 Rupert Street, W1
Tel: 020 7434 1306
Website: www.student-travel-centre.com
Tube: Piccadilly
Open: Mon-Fri 9am-6pm, Sat 10am-2pm

This company was recommended by a friend as a great value travel agents for students and those under 26. They offer flights throughout Europe and world-wide, tickets for Eurostar as well as accommodation and tours. Other services include travel insurance and car hire. A great value independent travel agent.

STA Travel

Website: www.statravel.co.uk
Call centre: 0871 468 0680 (Europe & Worldwide). Call this number rather than the individual branches.

STA Travel has over 51 branches in the UK and over 400 branches worldwide. They specialise in offering cheap flights, accommodation and tours to full-time students and those aged under 26. Some airlines have restrictions on the age of students for their reduced flight prices, so mature students will not be eligible for all deals.

Branches at:
33 Bedford Street, Covent Garden WC2
52 Grosvenor Gardens, Victoria SW1
24 Ludgate Hill EC4
11 Goodge Street W1
117 Euston Road NW1
University of London Union, Malet Street WC1
Imperial College, Sherfield Building SW7
King's College, Macadam Building WC2
London School of Economics, East Building WC2
Queen Mary and Westfield College, 329 Mile End Road E1
85 Shaftesbury Avenue W1
40 Bernard Street WC1
1 Campden Hill Road, W8
2 Hogarth Road, SW5
5 The Mall, W5
40, Bernard Street, WC1N

Teletext

Website: www.teletext.co.uk/holidays

Use your TV to find loads of last-minute holiday bargains. From the website, you can access discount flights, accommodation, holidays, ski breaks and cruises.

Thomas Cook

Website: www.thomascook.com
Tel: 0870 750 511

Thomas Cook is the oldest travel agency in the UK and has branches nationwide. They offer clubbing holidays, city-breaks and cheap holiday packages to destinations all around the world and within the UK. The agency also deals with travel insurance, car rental and villa lettings.

Branches in Central London:
29-30 St. James's St, London, SW1A
138 Shaftesbury Av, London, WC2H
108 Fleet St, London, EC4A
88-92 Baker St, London, W1U
49 London Wall, London, EC2M
186 Baker St, London, NW 1
21 Old Brompton Rd, London, SW7
39 Islington High St, London, N1

Travelwise

51 Fortis Green Road, N10
Tel: 020 8444 4444
Website: www.travelwiseuk.com
Tube: East Finchley or Highgate
Open: Mon-Sat 9am-6pm

This neighbourhood travel agency has been dispensing low-cost holidays for over twenty years. Specialising in packages to places like Greece, the Balearics and other warm climes, they are good at putting together inexpensive holidays whether they last two days or two weeks.

Bargain Travel Websites

www.bargainholidays.co.uk
This online travel agency has some very good offers and the quantity of holidays is impressive. A week in Cyprus recently cost £229. You can also search for flights both scheduled and charter.

www.cheapflights.co.uk
This search engine compares flights from all major carriers to find the best price. You can also search by destination or by low-cost airline. They also deal with holidays, cottages, hotels and short breaks.

www.deckchair.com
Another online travel agent booking everything from flights to holidays. The best deals are on last-minute fares. A week in the Canary Islands for £180 per person was a recent deal.

www.ebookers.com
Ebookers offer cheap and last-minute flights as well as travel insurance, last-minute holidays, hotels and car hire.

www.expedia.co.uk
Specialises in last-minute bookings for package holidays. Flights and lodging for seven nights in Dubai cost from £410.

www.holidaydeals.co.uk
One of the most basic, but fast, on-line bucket shops, good for last minute deals. Holiday destinations such as Barbados for £420 and Cuba for £419.

www.lastminute.com
The original and best of the online bucket shops. You can also find reduced tickets to London musicals, international music festivals and theme parks.

www.onlinetravel.com
In addition to city breaks, flights and hotels, Onlinetravel has a 'fare finder' facility that will help you find cheap prices regardless of when you fly. The company is part of lastminute.com.

www.openjet.com
Billing itself as 'the virtual airline', Openjet will help you locate the cheapest and most convenient flights from all the low-cost airline deals available online.

www.opodo.co.uk
An excellent resource for price-comparison shopping for the major airlines. They often have good deals.

www.priceline.co.uk
Originally from the States, Priceline conceived the novel idea of letting customers name their price for flights, hotels and car rentals. Give it a try.

Leisure ● Travel

www.pricerunner.com
A useful price comparison website, mainly for household goods but excellent for flights. London to Rome gave me 137 flights within 20 seconds.

www.skydeals.co.uk
Plenty of flight deals to choose from as well as flight search capabilities. Recent deals included Gatwick to Mexico for £385.

www.skyscanner.net
Users enter their budget and timeline. Skyscanner tells them where they can afford to go.

www.travelocity.co.uk
One of the first and still one of the best. Travelocity searches 95% of the flights or seats available and returns good results. Their "Fare Watcher" will e-mail you with offers on destinations that you can select.

www.wegolo.co.uk
Wegalo operates with low cost airlines and offers the possibility of combining out and inbound flights with different airlines.

Travel Insurance

Getting insurance from your travel agent is convenient, but you often pay well above the market price for that convenience. As with flights and accommodation it's best to phone around and compare prices. Money Supermarket (www.moneysupermarket.com) is a handy search tool for comparing insurance quotes. If you're travelling light STA offer good rates. Below are some other alternatives.

Columbus Direct (www.columbusdirect.co.uk) Tel: 0845 330 8518

Direct Travel Insurance (www.direct-travel.co.uk) Tel: 0845 605 2700

Essential Travel (www.essentialtravel.co.uk) 0870 343 0024

JS Insurance (www.jsinsurance.co.uk) Tel: 0870 755 6101

Flexi Cover-Direct (www.flexicover.com) Tel: 0870 990 9292.

Worldwide Travel Insurance (www.worldwideinsure.com) Tel: 0870 112 8100

Other Useful Addresses:

Air Travel Advisory Bureau (Lupus Travel)
5 High Street,
Royal Tunbridge Wells,
Kent, TN1
Tel: 018 9255 3500
Website: www.atab.co.uk
Open: Mon-Fri: 9am-6pm

Association of British Travel Agents (ABTA)
68-71 Newman Street, W1
Tel: 020 7637 2444
Website: www.abta.com

Association of Independent Tour Operators (AITO)
133A St Margarets Road, Twickenham, TW1 1RG
Tel: 020 8744 9280
Website: www.aito.co.uk

Leisure • Travel

Bargain Hunting by Outlet

Architectural Salvage 272

Auctions 276

Charity Shops.............. 287

Factory Shops............. 323

Independent Designers .. 328

Junk Shops 339

Markets 351

Car Boot Sales 357

Pawnbrokers............... 361

Architectural Salvage

Below are some of the best value architectural salvage outlets in and around London. There is also an architectural salvage organisation which provides up-to-date information about architectural salvage dealers in the UK via their website – www.salvo.co.uk.

Central

LASSCO
Brunswick House,
30 Wandsworth Road, SW8
Tel: 020 7394 2100
Website: www.lassco.co.uk
Tube: Vauxhall
Open: Mon-Sat 10am-5pm

This is one of London's largest salvage yards and one of several Lassco outlets. The shop specialises in architectural salvage including fireplaces and chimneypieces as well as interior and exterior doors, ranging in period from Georgian to the 1930s. Among the other things to be found here are lighting, door furniture and room panelling.

Also at: 41 Maltby Street, SE1 Tel: 020 7394 2103
3 Pigeons, London Road, Milton Common, Oxfordshire, OX9 2JN
Tel: 01844 277 184

North

The Architectural Forum
312-314 Essex Road, N1
Tel: 020 7704 0982
Tube: Angel
Open: Mon-Sat 8.30am-6pm
Website: thearchitecturalforum.com

This established salvage yard is divided into two small yards containing bathroom fittings, radiators, fireplaces, doors, some light fittings, wooden panelling and a large selection of paving stones. Among the bargains on a recent visit was a large, free-standing bath with ornate feet for £280, which needed some attention but was still a bargain given that such baths new are about £500.

Also at:
V&V Reclaimation, Tree Heritage, North Road, Hertford, SG14 2PW
Tel 01992 550 941, Website: www.vandv.co.uk

Brondesbury Architectural Reclamation

136 Willesden Lane, Brondesbury, NW6
Tel: 020 7328 0820
Rail: Brondesbury Park
Open: Mon-Sat 10am-6pm

A yard and showroom offering a wide range of antiques, architectural items and smaller artifacts.

Willesden Green Architectural Salvage

189 High Road, NW10
Tel: 020 8459 2947
Tube: Willesden Green
Open: Mon-Sat 9am-6pm

This small yard holds a surprisingly large stock of fireplaces, doors, radiators, stained glass windows and other smaller fixtures and fittings. A fully restored Edwardian fireplace was recently found here for £700, which is good value considering that in smarter establishments they sell for around £1,300.

South

Architectural Salvage

83 Haydons Road,
South Wimbledon, SW19
Tel: 020 8543 4450
Tube: South Wimbledon
Open: Tues-Sat 10am-5pm

This small shop and yard offers a reasonable selection of doors, fire places and sanitary ware.

Bellows

202 Garratt Lane, SW18
Tel: 020 8870 5873
Rail: Earlsfield
Open: Mon-Fri 9am-6pm, Sat 10am-5.30pm

Mr Wandle has been restoring and selling fireplaces from this small workshop for many years and has established an excellent reputation for the quality and value of his work. Cast iron fireplaces start from as little at £85 and the company can also renovate an existing fireplace for a very reasonable price if you want to stick with what you've got.

The House Hospital

9 Ferrier Street, SW18
Tel: 020 8870 8202
Rail: Wandsworth Town
Open: Mon-Sat 10am-5pm

A modern industrial warehouse site specialising in reconditioned cast iron radiators, but also offering doors, fireplaces, flooring and bathroom furniture among its stock.

Out of Town

Architectural Reclaim

Theobalds Park Road,
Crews Hill, Enfield, Middlesex
Tel: 020 8367 7577
Website: www.architecturalreclaim.com
Rail: Drews Hill
Open: Mon-Fri 8am-5pm, Sat-Sun 9am-3pm

This massive three acre site has anything from old telegraph poles and railway sleepers to Victorian garden furniture. Well worth a trip out of town to visit.

Salvo Fair

Knebworth House, Herts
Tel: 01225 422 300 / 020 8400 6222
www.Salvo-fair.com
Car: A1M, Junction 7
Open: Annual weekend event in last week of June.
Admission: £7

This annual event is a great place to find numerous architectural salvage specialists displaying their wares in the grounds of Knebworth House. There are lots of interesting things available from fireplaces to doors and plenty of good deals to be negotiated. As well lots of sellers there are numerous events, lectures and demonstrations concerning subjects such as restoration and traditional crafts. Those interested should refer to their website to find the dates for the next fair.

277...General Auctions
285...Car Auctions
286...Property Auctions

Auctions

Auctions

Auctions have the reputation for being fusty old institutions where fine art is sold to equally fusty old art dealers and dilettantes. The auctions reviewed below are quirky and idiosyncratic places, but tend to have more general goods such as cameras, bikes, household furniture, books, office equipment and much more. There are plenty of bargains to be found at these auctions and they are usually a lot of fun to visit. When visiting an auction it's a good idea to attend the viewing before the sale starts. This gives you time to inspect the lots you are interested in before bidding begins and to set yourself a maximum price for each item — this will hopefully prevent you from losing your head when bidding begins. This chapter also includes car and house auctions for those with more money to spend.

North

Centaur Auctions
Harbet Road, N18
Tel: 020 8803 9796
Fax: 020 8807 7111
Sales: Monthly on the first Sat of every month from 10am
Viewing: Fri 10am-4pm, Sat from 9am
Buyers' premium: 20%
Bidders' returnable deposit: £50

This established auction house deals largely in liquidated stock provided by bailiffs and the Inland Revenue and as such can include anything from office equipment to computers and kitchenware. There are always enough bargains here to justify sacrificing a Saturday morning lie-in.

Hornsey Auctions Ltd
54-56 High Street, N8
Tel: 020 8340 5334/8341 1156
Deliveries arranged (min charge £25)
Sales: Every Wed 6.30pm-9pm
Viewings: Tues 5pm-7pm and Wed 9am until the sale
Buyers' premium: 10%
Bidders' returnable deposit: £0

Hornsey Auctions has a rather grand exterior, but deals mainly with house clearances, probate and insolvency stock. The auction offers a good mix of items from boxes of bric-à-brac for a fiver, to imposing period furniture for over £300. It's a particularly good place to find large ornate mirrors for under £100.

Schools Connect Auction

The Auction House, Pegamoid Road, Edmonton, N18
Tel: 020 8345 6535
Website: www.tagpc.co.uk
Sales: Fortnightly Sats 11am-4pm
Viewing: Sat 9am-11am
Buyers' premium: 10% (+VAT)
Bidders' returnable deposit: £40

This hi-tech auction house has all kinds of equipment going under the hammer including fully operational PCs, printers, keyboards and other accessories. They also sell other items for the office such as photocopiers, telephones and office furniture. A recent sale included about 450 lots, some of which still had the manufacturers' warranty. Those without a warranty are sold with a 90 day guarantee. It's a good idea if you don't know much about computers to bring a technically-minded friend with you for guidance.

Southgate Auction Rooms

55 High Street, Southgate, N14
Tel: 020 8886 7888
Fax: 020 8882 4421
Sales: Mon from 5pm
Viewing: Sat 9am-12pm, Mon 9am-5pm
Buyers' premium: 15%
Bidders' returnable deposit: £30 (cash)

A general household auction, selling items on behalf of individuals. A good place to find basics for the home as well as some reasonably priced antiques.

North London Auctions

(map 10)

Lodge House,
9-17 Lodge Lane, N12
Tel: 020 8445 9000
Fax: 020 8446 6068
Sales: Mon from 5pm
Viewing: Sun 9am-1pm, Mon 9am-5pm
Buyers' premium: 15%
Bidders' returnable deposit: £10

A large auction house selling antiques, collectables and general household goods from a variety of sources. The quality of the stock tends to be high, and every 6 to 8 weeks they hold a sale of the classier items.

West

Chiswick & West Middlesex Auctions

31 Colville Road, W3
Tel: 020 8992 4442
Fax: 020 8896 0541
Sales: Tues 5pm-7pm for smaller items, 7pm onwards for furniture
Viewing: Sun 12noon-6pm, Mon 10am-6pm, Tues 10am-5pm
Buyer's premium: 15%
Bidders' returnable deposit: £0

This auction house has chandeliers dangling from the ceiling, rugs strewn on the floor and quantities of crockery, porcelain, silverware and furniture in between. The quality of the goods varies from genuine antiques to bric-à-brac.

Francis Smith

107 Lots Road,
Chelsea, SW10
Tel: 020 7349 0011
Fax: 020 7349 0770
Sales: Fortnightly Tues from 6pm
Viewing: Mon 9am-7pm, Tues 9am-6pm
Buyers' premium: 15% (+VAT)
Bidders' returnable deposit: £0

This auction room sells mostly antiques, but usually offers about 50 lots of more modern furniture among the 150 lots which go under the hammer every fortnight.

Lots Road Auctions

73 Lots Road, SW10
Tel: 020 7376 6800
Fax: 020 7376 6899
Website: www.lotsroad.com
Sales: Sun 2pm contemporary goods, 4.30pm antiques
Viewing: Thurs 2pm-7pm, Fri-Sun 10am-4pm
Buyers' premium: 17.02%
Bidders' returnable deposit: £0

map 9

As befits its location in the heart of Chelsea, this is a rather smart antiques auction with not much selling for under £50. There are bargains to be found, but this venue is definitely more suited to well-heeled wannabe bargain hunters, rather than those looking for cheap bric-à-brac.

Richmond & Surrey Auctions

Kew Road, Richmond, TW9
Tel: 020 8948 6677
Fax: 020 8948 2021
Sales: Thurs 6pm-8.30pm
Viewing: Wed 4pm-8pm, Thurs 10am-6pm
Buyers' premium: 15%
Bidders' returnable deposit: £0

This weekly auction usually has between 300 and 400 lots offering good quality modern and antique furniture, objets d'art, watches, silverware and paintings. The bidding is brisk at about 160 lots per hour, so don't wander too far from the saleroom.

South

General Auctions

63-65 Garratt Lane, SW18

map 8

Tel: 020 8870 3909
Fax: 020 8877 3583
Website: www.generalauctions.co.uk
Sales: Mon 11am for cycles, 12noon-5pm general goods,
(motor vehicles are sold at 2pm)
Viewing: Sat 10am-3pm
Buyers' premium: 12.5%
Bidders' returnable deposit: £50

As the name suggests this auction shifts a gallimaufry of goods, from designer clothing to cars. Many items come from the Inland Revenue, Customs & Excise and liquidators. This is a very good auction for finding quality second-hand bikes.

R.F. Greasby

211 Longley Road, SW17
Tel: 020 8672 2972
Fax: 020 8767 8616
Sales: Tuesdays from 10am
Viewing: Monday 2.30pm-6.30pm, 8.30am-10.30am on day of sale
Buyers' premium: 12.5% (plus VAT)
Bidders' returnable deposit: £100

All sorts of items turn up here as sales are held on behalf of the Metropolitan Police, London Transport, Customs and Excise and bailiffs. This is an excellent auction for bargain bikes, cameras, electronics, jewellery and office furniture.

Greenwich Auctions Partnership

47 Old Woolwich Road, SE10
Tel: 020 8853 2121
Sales: Sat 11am-3pm
Viewing: Fri 2pm-7pm, Sat 9am-11am
Buyers' premium: 10%
Bidders' returnable deposit: 0%

About 800 lots are sold under the glass roof of this large factory space on a typical auction day. It's a good auction for bargains, because much of the stock derives from house clearances and is therefore sold without a reserve price. There's a caff on site and Greenwich Park is just around the corner if you want a break. If you are going in the winter be sure to wear something warm.

Lloyds International Auction Galleries

Lloyds House, 9 Lydden Road, SW18
Tel: 020 8788 7777
Fax: 020 8874 5390
Website: www.lloyds-auction.co.uk
Rail: Earlsfield
Sales: Alternate Weds 3pm
Viewing: Wed 10.30am-2.45pm
Buyers' premium: 17.5%
Bidders' returnable deposit: £40

This established auction house holds regular sales for bodies such as the Metropolitan Police and Heathrow Airport. At these events you can find all kinds of bargains including bikes, cameras, computers, video recorders and even designer clothes. It's a good idea to get here early to view the lots before bidding. Auction dates are posted on Lloyd's website and you can even download the auction catalogue to prepare yourself in advance.

Rosebery's

74-76 Knight's Hill, SE27
Tel: 020 8761 2522
Fax: 020 8761 2524
E-mail: auctions@roseberys.co.uk
Website: www.roseberys.co.uk
Sales: Fortnightly usually on a Tues 12noon-5pm
Viewing: Sun 2.30pm-5.30pm, Mon 10am-7pm,
Tues 9.30am-11.45am
Buyers' premium: 15% (+VAT)
Bidders' returnable deposit: £0

This auction house alternates between a general auction and an antiques auction where the finer items are sold. The general auction is a great place to pick up furniture and things for the home, with plenty of bargains among the 700 or so lots. Rosebery's also hold specialist auctions covering subjects like Modern Design and Toys and Collectables.

East

Frank G. Bowen Ltd

73 Sceptre Road, E2
Tel: 020 7790 7272
Fax: 020 7790 7373
E-mail: mail@frankbowen.co.uk
Website: frankgbowen.co.uk
Sales: Alternate Thursdays from 11am
Viewing: Wed 12noon-4pm, Thurs 9.30am-11am on the day of sale
Buyers' premium: 10%
Bidders' returnable deposit: £0

This auction deals largely in commercial equipment from the Official Receiver, insolvency practitioners, bailiffs and the police. Lots can include commercial stock and equipment as well as cars.

Outer London

Bainbridge's

The Auction Room, Ickenham Road,
Ruislip, Middlesex, HA4
Tel: 01895 621 991
Fax: 01895 623 621
Sales: One Thurs per month from 11am
Viewing: Wed before the sale 1pm-7pm, Thurs 9.30am-11am
Buyers' Premium: 17.5%
Bidders returnable deposit: £0

This company trades in probate clearance and most items sell without a reserve. Sales can vary from valuable antiques to basic household goods, depending on the houses being cleared.

Parkins

18 Malden Road, Cheam, Surrey, SM3
Tel: 020 8644 6633
Fax: 020 8255 4703
Website: www.parkinsauction.co.uk
Sales: 1st Mon of the month 10am (antiques), 2nd & 4th Mons 10am
(general sales). Monthly Fri evening sale 7pm (small antiques)
Viewing: (Mon sale) Fri 2pm-4pm, Sat 10am-4pm, Mon 9am-10am,
(Fri sale) Fri 2pm-7pm
Buyers' premium: 10% (+ VAT)
Bidders' returnable deposit: £0

There are a number of different sales held at this auction house, with the general sale being of most interest to the bargain hunter. There are all manner of chattels to be found, and one or two bargains among the 200-400 lots.

Rosans & Company
Croydon Auction Rooms,
145-151 London Road, CR0
Tel: 020 8688 1123
Fax: 020 8681 3284
Sales: Sat (fortnightly) 10am-1.30pm
Viewing: Fri 9am-4.45pm, Sat 9am-10am
Buyers' premium: 10%
Bidders' returnable deposit: £20

This company usually deals in bankrupt commercial stock of all kinds. There are generally about 700 lots in each sale, with vehicles being sold at midday. The sales are occasionally held at the site of a bankrupt company, so get details before visiting.

Book Auctions

Bloomsbury Book Auctions
3-4 Hardwick Street, EC1
Tel: 020 7636 1945
Fax: 020 7833 3954
Sales: Thurs 1pm usually twice a month
Viewings: Tues 9.30am-5.30pm, Wed 9.30am-8pm,
Thurs 9.30am-1pm before the sale
Buyers' premium: 17.5%
Bidders' returnable deposit: £0

This auction is strictly for the collector, and those with an interest in books as objects as well as things to be read. The catalogue is the size of a novella and contains arcane descriptions like 'original decorative roan, gilt, uncut, some joints split'. A far cry from the usual 'box of books' seen in most auction catalogues. The prices are equally rarefied with most lots selling for over £50, and a commission of 17.5% on top of the hammer price. It's a great place to visit for an insight into the book world, but only an expert would be able to spot a bargain.

Car Auctions

As long as you're careful and put in a bit of effort, car auctions can be a good place to buy a second-hand car. It's important to choose the type of vehicle you want in advance, bearing in mind factors like the insurance group of the car, fuel consumption, reliability and repair bills. Monthly publications like Parker's Car Price Guide are a useful reference point for the general public, giving lots of important information as well as market prices for all makes and models.

Once you've determined the car you're looking for, and set yourself a budget, you can begin the hunt. If you're after a popular model, it may be worth looking out for a fleet car. These have been regularly serviced and the mileage is always genuine. The auctioneer will use the word 'direct' to describe any lot originating from this source. Many auctions use windscreen sheets and these should be studied carefully for details of the car's history. Above all, avoid any car sold without warranty. The warranty allows you an hour to try the car out and return it if something is wrong. If you have any problems contact the Motor Industry Federation (01788 576 465), although they can only help if the auction is a member. Provided you keep your head and remain patient the auctions listed below may be the place to find a four-wheel bargain. Good luck!

BCA Auctions
620 Great Cambridge Road, EN1
Tel: 020 8366 1144

Dingwall Motor Auctions
Beddington Farm Road,
Croydon, Surrey, CRO
Tel: 020 8684 0138

Manheim Motor Auctions
Waterside Way,
Plough Lane, SW17
Tel: 020 8944 2000

Thameside Motor Auctions
Wandsworth Bridge Road, SW6
Tel: 020 7736 0086

map 9

Property Auctions

If you're interested in buying a property by auction the companies listed below will send you details and a catalogue of their next sale. It is essential that you view the property and have valuations done before bidding. You'll need a 10% deposit on the day of the sale, and the financial ability to finalise the contract within 28 days. For those willing to do the leg work, there are incredible bargains to be found.

Allsop

100 Knightsbridge, SW1
Tel: 020 7494 3686
Website: www.allsop.co.uk

Andrews & Robertson

27 Camberwell Green, SE5
Tel: 020 7703 2662
Website: www.a-r.co.uk

Barnard Marcus

Commercial House,
64-66 Glenthorne Road, W6
Tel: 020 8741 9990/9001

Clive Emson Property Auctioneers

8 Cavendish Way,
Bearsted, Maidstone,
Kent, ME15
Tel: 01622 630 033
Website: www.cliveemson.co.uk

Countrywide Property Auctions

144 New London Road,
Chelmsford, CM2
Tel: 0870 240 1140

Drivers Norris

407-409 Holloway Road, N7
Tel: 020 7607 5001
Website: www.drivers.co.uk

Edwin Evans

253 Lavender Hill, SW11
Tel: 020 7228 5864
Website: www.edwinevansproperty.co.uk

FPD Savills

139 Sloane Street, SW1
Tel: 020 7824 9091
Website: www.fpdsavills.co.uk

Willmotts

12 Blacks Road, W6
Tel: 020 8748 6644
Website: www.willmotts.com

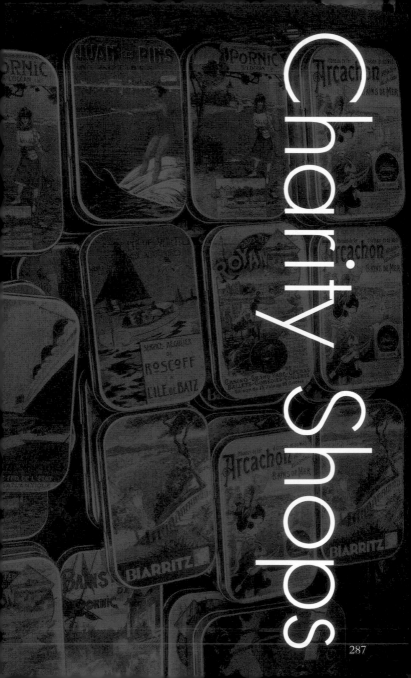

Charity Shops

Charity Shops

Central London
Covent Garden, WC2
Soho, W1
Marylebone, W1
Victoria, SW1
Goodge Street, W1
Faringdon, EC1

North London
Islington, N1
Stoke Newington, N16
Finchley, N3
North Finchley, N12
Golders Green, NW11
Highgate, N6
Holloway, N7
Muswell Hill, N10
Wood Green, N22
Camden Town, NW1
Hampstead, NW3
West Hampstead, NW6
Kentish Town, NW5
Cricklewood, NW2
Kilburn, NW6
St. John's Wood, NW8
Wembley, HA9

West London
Chelsea, SW10
Fulham, SW6
South Kensington, SW5
Kensington, W8
Bayswater/ Paddington, W2
Notting Hill, W11
Shepherd's Bush, W12
Hammersmith, W6
Chiswick, W4
Ealing, W5

South London
Brixton, SW2
Tooting, SW17
Barnes, SW13
Putney, SW15
Wandsworth/ Southfields, SW18
Clapham, SW11
Balham, SW12
Streatham, SW16

East London
Whitechapel, E1
Dalston, E8
Hackney, E8 & E9
Bethnal Green, E3

Outer London
Richmond, TW9
Twickenham, TW9
Covent Garden

Note: some charities, notably the Relief Fund for Romania and the YMCA, are given free accommodation for some of their shops in empty stores whose owners are in the process of trying to sell them. This means that a small number of the shops listed here may not still be there when you visit them. We have indicated which shops are temporary. In the case of Relief Fund for Romania and YMCA, they are very likely to have relocated to a nearby shop. The law has now changed to prevent charity shops from selling used electrical goods without them having been checked by a qualified electrician. We have indicated all shops that have checking procedures and still sell electrical goods.

Central

Covent Garden WC2

Tube: Covent Garden

Oxfam
23 Drury Lane
Tel: 020 7240 3769
Open: Mon-Sat 11am-6pm

(map 1)

This is a tidy charity shop, situated not far from the busy hubbub of Neal Street. There are two walls of books in very good condition ranging from £0.99-£2.00 with a display of top ten reads – on a recent visit there were piles of Sotheby's and Christie catalogues. Further back there are colour coded clothes rails, stocked with an above-average number of women's jackets including designers such as Paddy Campbell, Escada, Fenn Wright Mason and Jean Muir. Men's jackets are also plentiful and in good condition ranging up to £20.

Oxfam Original
22 Earlham Street
Tel: 020 7836 9666
Open: Mon-Sat 11am-6pm

(map 1)

This is a trendy Oxfam shop dedicated solely to clothes, with a mix of retro and modern. The menswear is on the ground floor, and sells packaged £1 boxer shorts, good condition casual trainers with their boxes and the usual jackets, t-shirts and trousers. On a recent visit there was a very stylish tweed Jigsaw blazer for £20. Downstairs is women's fashion, and there is even a futon for those wishing to relax after a hard day of bargaining. The staff at this store are largely fashion students from St.Martin's and The London College of Fashion. The shop is situated next to Earlham Market which is a good place to find new fashionable clothing.

Soho W1

Tube: Oxford Circus/Piccadilly Circus

Salvation Army Charity Shop/Cloud 9
9 Princes Street
Tel: 020 7495 3958
Open: Mon-Fri 10.30am-6pm,
Sat 11.30am-6.00pm

(map 1)

This charity shop has recently had a refurbishment; the downstairs is pretty much the same, selling old clothes and some bric-à-brac. Upstairs is much more like a high-street shop than it used to be, it is less vintage-like than before but there is still a good range of clothes and high-heeled shoes. Perks include floor-length faux fur coats, 1970s dresses and evening bags. The vintage range is at least half the price of Topshop's, situated just around the corner.

Marylebone W1

Cancer Research UK
*24 Marylebone High Street
Tel: 020 7487 4986
Open: Mon-Fri 10am-6pm,
Sat 10am-5pm, Sun 11am-5pm*

At a first glance this looks like any old charity shop, until you start burrowing through the rails where you will find labels such as Kenzo, MaxMara, Cath Kidson, LK Bennet and Hobbs. Prices are relatively high, with women's cashmere coats and suits at £100 and dresses not much below £20. Menswear is of a good quality, with stylish designer trousers including Joseph at around £20.

Oxfam Books and Music
*91 Marylebone High Street
Tel: 020 7487 3570
Open: Mon-Sat 10am-6pm,
Sun 11am-6pm*

This is a fantastic charity shop with somewhat of a Manhattan feel, with low hanging light shades and pine floorboards. The shop goes quite far back, there are stacks of books covering just about every subject and a case of collectables, such as H.G Wells and Shakespeare anthologies and a reasonable number of Penguin orange classics. There are music books for instrument players, old maps and postcards and a box of theatre programmes. They also have lots of vinyl records in plastic cases with genres including house, indie and rock and a whole case of classical vinyls and a fair collection of kids' books. This is definitely worth a visit.

Other charity shops in this area:

Geranium Shop for the Blind
*4 George Street
Tel: 020 7935 1790
Open: Mon-Sat 10am-4pm*

Sue Ryder
*2 Crawford Street
Tel: 020 7935 8758
Open: Mon-Sat 9am-4.30pm*

Victoria SW1

Crusaid
*19 Churton Street, SW1
Tel: 020 7233 8736
Open: Mon-Sat 10.00am-6pm
Sun 11am-3pm*

This shop is situated in the heart of Belgravia which explains the amount of designer donations given. Brands include Armani, Ralph Lauren, Christian Dior, Manolo Blahnik and Hermes. There is also a selection of books, CDs, bric-à-brac and a great range of ballgowns. An absolute must.

Retromania (FARA)

40 Tachbrook Street
Tel: 020 7630 7406
Open: Mon-Sat 10.30am-6pm,
Sun 11am-5pm

As its name suggests, this charity shop is an Aladdin's cave for all vintage lovers. Retro clothes from all the other FARA shops end up here, and there are racks full of ball gowns, dresses, shirts… you name it. A variety of shoes hang on the wall, and there is a particularly good collection of silk scarves, hats and ties. There is a rack dedicated to vintage designer clothes, such as Chanel, although prices start from about £50. If this is too much, try the sale rack outside which sells cheaper clothing for £5-£10. The menswear is in the back, as is the collection of retro vinyls and some old books. A real find.

Oxfam

15 Warwick Way
Tel: 020 7821 1952
Open: Mon-Sat 10am-5pm

Like all good Oxfam shops, only the best stock is displayed. The clothes are in excellent condition, with many top brands ranging from Christian Lacroix (a suit will set you back £30) to Topshop and Zara. Shoes and accessories are arranged neatly on shelves above the racks. Menswear is equally good, with many jeans and some designer shirts. Downstairs is dedicated to bric-à-brac, CDs (79p for a single and £1.99 for an album) and books.

Oxfam Books & Music

34 Strutton Ground
Tel: 020 7233 3908
Open: Mon, Wed, Fri 9.30am-5pm,
Tue, Thur 10am-5pm,
Sat 12pm-3pm
Nearest Tube: St. James' Park (10 minute walk from Victoria)

This is another great central Oxfam Books & Music store. Books cover a wide range of genres and political books are particularly common, due to the number of MPs that live nearby. The window is always crammed with interesting finds. Book collectors will not be disappointed, with plenty of first editions. There is a lot of fiction, including some orange penguin classics. Non-fiction subjects include Philosophy, History, Foreign Languages, Classics, Travel, Craft and even Beer.

Other charity shops in this area:

Sue Ryder

35 Warwick Way
Tel: 020 7630 0812
Open: Mon-Sat 9am-5pm

Trinity Hospice

85 Wilton Road
Tel: 020 7931 7191
Open: Mon-Sat 10 am-5pm
Sun 12pm-4pm

FARA

14 Upper Tachbrook Street
Tel: 020 7630 1774
Open: Mon-Sat 10am-6pm
Sun 11am-5

Goodge Street W1

Tube: Goodge Street

Oxfam
52 Goodge Street
Tel: 020 7636 7311
Open: Mon-Fri 10.30am-6pm,
Quite a good Oxfam with lots of Traidcraft goodies at the front, while downstairs holds tapes for 60p, CDs, console games and men's clothing.

YMCA
22 Goodge Street
Open: Mon-Fri 9.30am-6.30pm,
Sat 11am-6.30pm, Sun 2pm-6pm
This central London charity shop is well stocked with clothes, books, records and bric-à-brac. The shop is large and cluttered, but more fun to potter around as a result.

Other charity shops in this area include:

Octavia
24 Goodge Street
Tel: 020 7636 4201
Open: Mon-Sat 10am-6pm

Farringdon EC1

Tube: Farringdon

Age Concern
53 Leather Lane
Open: Mon-Fri 10am-3pm
Tel: 020 7831 4928
This is a brilliant little charity shop. The stock is well selected and of a good quality. Balls of wool sell for £1.20 and videos and albums are a cracking £1. The clothes are trendy and there is a particularly good selection of accessories including scarves, underwear, shoes and hats.

North

Islington N1

Tube: Angel/Highbury & Islington

Cancer Research UK

34 Upper Street
Tel: 020 7226 8951
Open: Mon-Sat 10am-6pm,
Sun 11am-5pm

map 3

A good quality charity shop, with a wide range of clothes, books, bric-à-brac and CDs. The clothes are generally of good quality and there are some designer labels if you hunt for long enough.

Marie Curie Cancer Care

318-320 St Paul's Road
Tel: 020 7226 0565
Open: Mon-Sat 9am-5.20pm

Marie Curie's biggest branch in London which sees around 52,000 customers a year, this store is deservedly loved by the local Islingtonites. Designer labels include Chanel, MaxMara, Gucci, Paul Costelloe and Paul Smith, but there are also very good high street donations from shops such as Gap, Zara and Topshop. There is a good collection of books, vinyls and bric-à-brac too, but be warned, Sundays and Mondays are the busiest days.

Oxfam

29 Islington High Street
Tel: 020 7837 2394
Open: Mon-Sat 10.30am-5.30pm,
Sun 11am-5pm

map 3

Despite the tiny shop front, this is a sizeable store, usually with a worth-while selection of books, clothing and household goods. They have a range of Fairtrade products around the till, ties are 99p, CDs £1.29 and singles 20p

Salvation Army Charity Shop

284 Upper Street
Tel: 020 7359 9865
Open: Mon-Sat 10am-5pm, Sun 11am-6pm

map 3

Although small from the front, the shop does extend quite far back and is well located among the boutiques of Upper Street. There is lots of bric-à-brac and children's toys, and clothing racks along one side of the shop. Clothing is of a good quality and there are bar-gains to be had, especially in the 50p tops basket and £1 rail at the front.

Sue Ryder

72 Essex Road
Tel: 020 7354 9050
Open: Mon-Sat 9am-5pm

map 3

This is a good little charity shop, with a well-dressed window and a range of stock. Clothing is all of a good quality with some high street and designer labels, and there is an extensive selection of CDs and re-cords at the back of the shop.

Stoke Newington N16

Bosnia Herzegovina Community Biblioteka

7 Cazenove Road
Open: Mon-Sat 10.30am-6.30pm
This is a small shop absolutely crammed mainly with clothes, and requires a bit of a rummage in order to find anything worthwhile. That said, not much is priced over the £5 mark. There are kid's clothes and upholstery material and curtains.

Other charity shops in this area:

All Aboard

2A Regent Parade,
Amhurst Park, N16
Tel: 020 8880 2458
Open: Mon-Fri 9.30am-5.30pm,
Sunday 10am-4pm

Scope

236 Stamford Hill
Tel: 020 8809 1306
Open: Mon-Sat 10am-6pm

Finchley N3

Tube: Finchley Central

Cancer Research UK

69 Ballards Lane
Tel: 020 8349 4962
Open: Mon-Sat 9am-5.30pm
This is a tidy and well laid out shop, with mainly women's clothes of a good quality and reasonable price. There is a wall of goods made by the charity as well as books and vinyl records for £1.

The ORT Shop

80 Ballards Lane
Tel: 020 8349 4554
Open: Mon-Thur 9.30am-6pm Fri 9.30am-3.00pm
This is a great store, with tons of bric-à-brac, especially glassware, located around the front. In womenswear there is a £7.50 and £4 rail. In menswear jackets are £7 and shoes are all £4.50. Paperbacks are 30p, hardbacks 50p, CDs and videos £2 and vinyl records £1.50. There is a boutique rail and an exceptional cashmere rail, where the jumpers are all cleaned and priced at around £20.

Other charity shops in this area

Norwood Ravenswood

66 Ballards Lane, N3
Tel: 020 8371 0006
Open: Mon-Fri 10am-5pm

Oxfam

55 Ballards Lane
Tel: 020 8346 3870
Open: Mon-Sat 10am-5pm

North London Hospice

Finchley Central _
15 Ballards Lane
Tel : 020 8349 0290
Open: Mon-Sat 9.30am-5pm

North Finchley N12

Tube: Woodside Park 9 (High road is 10 minute walk away)
Rail: North Finchley

Cancer Research UK
775 High Road
Tel: 020 8446 8289
Open: Mon-Sat 9.30am-5.30pm
Sun 11am-4pm
A nicely laid out store with reasonable prices and a range of homeware from the charity. There is a rack of women's party dresses and men's shirts priced at around £15, plus kids' ware and the usual collection of bric-à-brac.

North London Hospice
839 High Road
Tel: 020 8343 8841
Open: Mon-Sat 9.30am-5pm
This is a very good charity shop located just opposite to Relief Fund for Romania. There aren't many trendy donations, but there is a nice range of evening dresses, bric-à-brac and surprisingly, golf and tennis balls.

Relief Fund for Romania
824 High Road
Tel: 020 8445 9351
Open: Mon-Sun 10am-5.30pm
The cheapest shop in the area, and one of the best for the dedicated rummager. Women's clothes outnumber menswear, but there are plenty of both, as well as lots of kids' clothes. On a recent visit Mills & Boon books were selling for only 25p.

Other charity shops in this area:

Barnardos
802 High Road
Tel: 020 8445 5433
Open: Mon-Sat 9am-5.30pm

British Heart Foundation
718 High Road
Tel: 020 8446 0840
Open: Mon-Sat 9.30am-5pm

Golders Green NW11

Tube: Golders Green

All Aboard (map 11)
125 Golders Green Road
Tel: 020 8455 3184
Open: Mon-Fri 9.30am-5.30pm,
Sun 10.30am-4.00pm
In this little charity shop you'll find loads of clothes, bric-à-brac and books, as well as records and toys. Hardbacks go for £2 and paperbacks £1.

All Aboard (map 11)
616 Finchley Road
Tel: 020 8458 1733
Open: Mon-Fri 9.30am-6pm, Sun 10am-4pm
This is a very busy but well-stocked charity shop, full of clothes, records and books. On a recent visit there were rolls of 70s fabric and a pretty blue and white Wedgwood set for £30.

Jami

89 Golders Green Road
Tel: 020 8201 8074
Open: Mon-Thur 9.30am-
5.00pm, Fri 9.30am-3pm, Sun
9.00/9.30am- 4pm

(map 11)

This is a big shop and well stocked with quite good quality of clothes, but the emphasis is on price. All men's shirts, women's skirts and trousers are £2 and paperbacks and videos are 50p. On a recent visit there were transparent plastic umbrellas for £1.50.

Marie Curie Cancer

54 Golders Green Road
Mon-Sat 10am-5pm
Sun 9am-4pm
Tel: 020 8457 5859

(map 11)

This is a reasonably priced store with good stock, including a selection of party dresses for women, kid's clothing and videos for 99p.

North London Hospice

41 Golders Green Rd,
Golders Green
Tel: 020 8731 7807
Mon-Fri 10.30am-5.30pm, Sat
10.30am-6pm

(map 11)

A nice charity shop stocking all the usual, in particular there is a section for ladies with a fuller figure. Men's jackets average around £6 and there is a good selection of books and kids' toys.

Oxfam

1049 Finchley Road,
Temple Fortune
Tel: 020 8455 3830
Open: Mon-Sat 10am-5pm

(map 11)

In this little shop there is an excellent selection of quality books, with lots for under 50p, bric-à-brac and clothes. Two vinyl records cost 99p and greeting cards start at the same price.

Other charity shops in this area:

All Aboard

1111 Finchley Road,
Temple Fortune
Tel: 020 8458 7078
Open: Mon-Fri 9.30am-5.30pm
(Tues till 6.30pm), Sun 11am-3pm

(map 11)

Cancer Research UK

871 Finchley Road
Tel: 020 8458 6914
Open: Mon-Fri 9am-5pm,
Sat 9am-4.45pm

(map 11)

Norwood Ravenswood

84 and 87 Golders Green Road
Tel: 020 8209 0041
Open: Mon-Fri, Sun 10am-5pm

(map 11)

Highgate N6

Tube: Highgate

Cancer Research UK
72 Highgate High Street
Tel: 020 8341 6330
Open: Mon-Sat 9.30am-5.30pm,
Sun 11am-5pm
The standard of clothes here is very high, with brands such as Jaegar, Paul Smith and Armani. The shop is quite small, although well laid out and all accessories are neatly displayed in plastic boxes above the rails.

Other charity shops in this area include:

Highgate
329 Archway Road,
Tel: 020 8341 1188
Mon-Fri 10am- 5.00pm,
Sat 10am-5.30pm

RSPCA
335 Archway Road
Tel: 0208 348 5725
Mon-Sat 10.00am-5.00pm

Oxfam
80 Highgate High Street
Tel: 020 8340 3888
Open: Mon-Sat 10am-5pm,
Sun 11am-3pm

Oxfam Bookshop
47 Highgate High Street,
Tel: 020 8347 6704
Mon-Sat 10am-5pm,
Sun 11am-3pm

Holloway N7

Tube: Holloway Road

Scope
46 Seven Sisters Road
Tel: 020 7607 7779
Open: Mon-Sat 9am-4.45pm

Traid
375 Holloway Road
Tel: 020 7700 0087
Open: Mon-Sat 9am-5pm

Muswell Hill N10

Tube: Highgate (then bus)

Cancer Research UK
85 Muswell Hill Broadway
Tel: 020 8365 3788
Open: Mon-Sat 9.30am-5.30pm,
Sun 11am-5pm
This is a well spaced out and neat charity shop, with friendly staff and a fast turnover of clothes. Saturday is the best day for getting your hands on good quality gear, and donations are often given from the Gap nearby. On a recent visit there were cashmere jumpers behind the counter going for around £30.

North London Hospice
44 Fortis Green Road
Tel: 020 8444 8131
Open: Mon-Sat 9.30am-5pm
A traditional charity shop stocking lots of clothes, with some labels such as Jigsaw and a good selection of books and bric-à-brac.

OCTAVIA

Charity Shops • North

Octavia is the new name for the Notting Hill Housing Trust Shops

A programme of re-branding will transform the charity shops over the next few years, but the commitment to great value new and used goods will remain the same.

Look out for our stores:

SOUTH WEST

SW3	211 Brompton Road
	303 Kings Road
SW6	654a Fulham Road, Fulham
SW7	3 Bute Street, South Kensington
SW10	309 Fulham Road
SW13	3 Barnes High Street
SW15	288 Upper Richmond Road, Putney,
SW17	36 High Street, Tooting

WEST

TW1	394 Richmond Road, Richmond
W1	24 Goodge Street
W2	178 Queensway
W4	46 Turnham Green Terrace
W5	40 High Street, Ealing
W8	57 Kensington Church Street
	266 High Street Kensington
W12	76 Askew Road
NW3	33 South End Road, Hampstead
NW8	53 St John's Wood High Street

Sue Ryder
129 Muswell Hill Broadway
Tel: 020 8444 6061
Open: Mon-Sat 9am-5pm
This shop tends to be a little cheaper than some of the charity shops in the area and offers a particularly good selection of clothes. Videos sell for £1 and there is also a good selection of upholstery and bric-à-brac.

Other charity shops in this area:

Cancer Research UK
161 Muswell Hill Broadway
Tel: 020 8444 6688
Open: Mon-Sat 9.30am-5.30pm,
Sun 11am-5pm

Oxfam
233 Muswell Hill Broadway
Tel: 020 8883 2532
Open: Mon-Sat 10am-5.30pm

Wood Green N22

Tube: Wood Green

Cancer Research UK
7 High Road
Tel: 020 8365 7876
Open: Mon-Sat 9am-5pm
As in all other branches, this store has plenty of clothes, shoes, books and bric-à-brac. Prices are reasonable and the quality is good.

North London Hospice
212 High Road
Tel: 020 8365 8622
Open: Mon-Sat 9.30am-4.45pm
Quite a small shop, and you have to rummage a bit to find what you need, but nevertheless there is something for everyone. Prices are average and there is a range of books and bric-à-brac plus a great range of jewellery.

Oxfam
12a The Broadway
Tel: 020 8881 6044
Open: Mon-Sat 10am-5.30pm
This shop has a young, trendy feel about it, and you can often find interesting CDs. Bargains include CD for as little as 50p.

Camden NW1

Tube/Rail: Camden Town/
Mornington Cresent

Books for Amnesty (map 2)
241 Eversholt Street, NW1
Tel: 020 7388 0070
Open: Mon-Sat 10am-6pm
This is practically a mini-Waterstone's with two floors and a fantastic range of books. On the ground floor there are books reduced to 50p and a wide selection of genres such as American politics and religion. Towards the back there are also some vinyl records selling at £2. In the basement the shelves are dedicated to fiction and there are also books under the genres of gender and black history, which is fitting for the charity.

Help the Aged

63 Camden High Street
Open: Mon-Sat 9am-5pm
020 7388 7911

map 2

This is a very neat and well-lit charity shop, selling mainly clothes with some donations from the local high street, including New Look on a recent visit. Behind the desk there is clean (but slightly Bridget Jones-esque) underwear for sale.

Mind in Camden

20 Camden Road
Tel: 020 7916 0158
Open: Mon-Sat 10am-6pm

map 2

This is a very cool little shop, situated in a hip location just opposite the train station. The shop has a very well dressed window and clothing hangs on rails either side of the shop to allow for an easy-access central aisle. Ties, belts and pillowcases are 50p and twelve inch vinyl records sell for £1. Behind the door there is high quality gift wrapping which starts at 99p. If you are in the area and have some foreign currency lying about in your purse, drop it off to the staff who will be happy to accept your donation.

Scope

73 Camden High Street
Tel: 020 7380 1455
Open: Mon-Sat 10am-6pm, Sun 12pm-6pm

map 2

This busy, well-organised shop offers a wide selection of clothes and books and is particularly good for kids' clothing.

Other charity shops in this area:

Age Concern

35 Camden High Street
Tel: 020 7387 4328
Open: Mon-Sat 10am-5.30pm

map 2

British Heart Foundation

65 Camden High Street
Tel: 020 7387 2952
Open: Mon-Sat 9.30am-5pm

map 2

Cancer Research UK

81 Camden High Street
Tel: 020 7383 5910
Open: Mon-Sat 9.30am-5pm, Sun 11am-4.30pm

map 2

Oxfam

89 Camden High Street
Tel: 020 7387 4354
Open: Mon-Sat 10am-5.30pm

map 2

Sue Ryder

103-105 Parkway
Tel: 020 7424 0225
Open: Mon-Sat 9.30am-5.30pm

Sue Ryder

19 Hampstead Road, Euston
Tel: 020 7387 1691
Open: Mon-Sat 9am-5pm

Kentish Town NW5

Tube: Kentish Town
Rail: Kentish Town West

Help the Aged
247 Kentish Town Road
Tel: 020 7485 9245
Open: Mon-Sat 9.30am-5.30pm
This is a busy charity shop with a good selection of clothes, shoes and books. Men's jackets are of a high quality and cost around £7.99, kid's books are 29p and videos go for 49p.

Other charity shops in this area:

Oxfam
166 Kentish Town Road
Tel: 020 7267 3560
Open: Mon-Fri 10am-5pm

Pdsa
249 Kentish Town Road
Tel: 020 7485 6153
Open: Mon-Sat 9.30am-5.30pm

Hampstead NW3

Tube: Hampstead

Octavia
33 South End Road
Tel: 020 7435 3453
Open: Mon-Sat 10am-6pm, Sun 12pm-5pm

Oxfam
62 Gayton Road
Tel: 020 7794 4474

West Hampstead NW6

Tube/Rail: West Hampstead

The Children's Society
Tel: 0207 794 5374 (map 4)
240 West End Lane,
Open: Mon- Sat 10am-5pm
A good charity shop, with a stylishly dressed window. All clothes are colour co-ordinated and are relevant to the season. On a recent visit there was a whole rackful of indian slippers for £5 and some quality children's clothes.

Other charity shops in this area :

All Aboard
224 West End Lane (map 4)
Tel: 020 7794 3404
Open: Mon-Fri 10am-6pm (Thurs until 7pm), closed Saturday, Sun 10am-4pm

Cancer Research UK
234 West End Lane (map 4)
Tel: 020 7433 1962
Open: Mon-Sat 9.30am-5.15pm, Sun 11am-4.30pm

Children's Society
240 West End Lane (map 4)
Tel: 020 7794 5374
Open: Mon-Sat 10am-5pm

The Community Charity Shop
92 Mill Lane (map 4)
Tel: 020 7431 5250
Open: Mon-Fri 11am-5pm,

Marie Curie

216 West End Lane
Tel: 020 7431 5490
Open: Mon-Fri 9.45am-5.15pm,
Sat 10am-5.30pm, Sun 10am-
4.30pm

(map 4)

Oxfam

246 West End Lane
Tel: 020 7435 8628
Open: Mon-Sat 10am-6pm,
Sun 12pm-4.30pm

Scope Charity Shop

214 West End Lane
Tel: 020 7431 5531
Open: Mon-Sat 9.30am-5.30pm

Scope

139 Kilburn High Road
Tel: 020 7624 7798
Open: Mon-Sat 9am-5pm

(map 4)

Kilburn NW6

Tube: Kilburn Park
Rail: Kilburn High Road

Traid

109 Kilburn High Street
Tel: 020 7328 1453
Open: Mon-Sat 10am-6pm, Sun
11am-5pm

This Charity shop is the size of a
small warehouse, and has a similar
feel to T.K.Maxx. There are two
racks of beautiful salwar kameez
priced at around £10, and indian
fabric for £7.99. There is a whole
wall of coats; with tops, trousers
and skirts on lower rails. Children's
clothes are £2.99 each.

Oxfam

152 Kilburn High Road
Tel: 020 7624 6697
Open: Mon-Sat 10.30am-5.15pm,
Sun 11am-4pm (but can vary)

(map 4)

This is an incredibly busy store,
probably due to its set prices.
Among the bargains all jackets
are £3.99, coats only £4.99 and
dresses, tops and trousers all sell for
£1.99 each.

Other charity shops in this area:

Cancer Research UK

187 Kilburn High Road
020 7625 8515
Open: Mon-Sat 9.30am-5.30pm
Sun 12pm-5pm

(map 4)

Pdsa

198 Kilburn High Road
Tel: 020 7328 9632
Open: Mon-Sat 9.30am-5.30pm,
Sun dependent upon staff

(map 4)

Relief Fund for Romania

231 Kilburn High Road
Open: Mon-Sat 10am-5pm, Sun
11am-4pm

Charity Shops • North

Camden Mind

Cuddle Me!

Camden Mind

Trinity Putney

Cricklewood NW2

Tube: Colindale

Bosnia Herzegovina Community Charity Shop
129 Cricklewood Broadway
Tel: 020 8450 5392
Open: Mon-Sat 9am-7pm, Sun 10am-4pm

This cramped charity shop has a great selection of clothes, bags, books and accessories. The pricing policy is simple with all bags going for £1.50, and tops for only £1 each. A great little charity shop, well worth a visit.

St. John's Wood NW8

Tube: St John's Wood

Octavia
53 St John's Wood High Street
Tel: 020 7586 9493
Open: Mon-Sat 10am-6pm, Sun 12pm-5pm

A brilliant charity shop, as are all in this particularly up-market area. The stock is of an excellent quality, with many designer clothes including Joseph and Fenn Wright Mason. Women's suits are great and will set you back about £30, men's suits are equally good. The shop also stocks some upholstery, kid's clothing and CDs are £2. The staff are friendly making this an enjoyable place to shop.

Other charity shops in this area:

Oxfam
61 St. John's Wood High Street
Tel: 020 7722 5969
Open: Mon-Sat 9.30-5.30, Sun 12am-4pm

Charity Shop
53 St John's Wood High Street
Tel: 020 7586 9493
Open: Mon-Sat 10am-6pm, Sun 12pm-5pm

Scope
139 Kilburn High Road
Tel: 020 7624 7798
Open: Mon-Sat 9am-5pm

St John's Hospice
86 St. John's Wood High Street
Tel: 020 7449 9791
Open: Mon-Sat 11am-4pm

Wembley HA9

Tube: Wembley Central

Oxfam
405 High Road
Tel: 020 8900 8482
Open: Mon-Sat 9.30am-5.30pm

Traid
Unit 12, 13 Central Square
Tel: 020 8900 1317
Open: Mon-Sat 10am-6pm, Sun 11am-5pm

West London

Chelsea SW10

Tube: Sloane Square

Britsh Red Cross
67 Old Church Street
Tel: 0207 352 9329
Open: Mon-Wed, Fri 10am-5.30pm,
Thur 10am-7pm, Sun 1-6pm
This is a great charity shop which often receives donations from its classy neighbours Manolo Blahnik and Catherine Walker. Designer wear is plentiful, with labels including Chanel, Prada, Gucci and Christian Dior, to name but a few. The store sometimes holds designer evening sales, once opened in 2004 by fashion journalist Isabella Blow.

Cancer Research UK
393 King's Road
Tel: 020 7352 4769
Open: Mon-Sat 9.30am-5.30pm,
Sun 11.30-4.30pm
This has a very good range of seasonal gear, including a lot of good quality high street knitware with brands such as Boden, Topshop and Zara. Casual menswear is plentiful, videos are £1 and greeting cards start at 99p.

Oxfam
123A Shawfield Street, King's Road
Tel: 020 7351 7979
Open: Mon-Sat 10.30am-5.30pm
This is a fantastic little charity shop solely dedicated to clothes. Situated just off the King's Road, it is unsurprisingly full of designer-wear and well worth a visit. There is a neat little window showcase just outside the shop displaying accessories and very good quality shoes, such as Manolo Blahnik and Prada. The rack of women's party and prom dresses included a Belville Sassoon one on a recent visit. Women's suits are priced at around £35, and include Whistles, Jaegar and L.K Bennett. There are also numerous men's blazers and dinner jackets.

Oxfam
432 King's Road
Tel: 020 7351 6863
Open: Mon-Sat 10am-6pm,
Sun 12noon-5pm
This is another Oxfam store in Chelsea, very similar to the one in Shawfield Street. Designerwear is plentiful with brands such as Nicole Farhi, Joseph, Armani and Conran and there are quite a few nicely displayed jeans. There is a high quality range of bric-à-brac and valuables, which are displayed in glass cabinets and a good stock of books, with some vinyl records, CDs and videos. Items are kept on hold until the end of the day and items can be purchased from the window on Mondays.

Other charity shops in this area:

Octavia
303 King's Road
Tel: 020 7352 8606
Open: Mon-Sat 10am-6pm,
Sun 12pm-5pm

Trinity Hospice
389 King's Road
Tel: 020 7352 8507
Open: Mon-Sat 10am-4.30pm

Fulham SW6

Tube: Fulham Broadway/Parsons
Green

FARA
841 Fulham Road
Tel: 020 7371 0141
Open: Mon & Tue: 10am-6pm
Wed-Sat: 9am-7pm Sun: 11am-5pm
This charity shop has a good range
of women's trousers, skirts and
coats with labels expected from the
area such as Jigsaw and Boden. On
a recent visit a men's dinner suit
was going for £50 and a woman's
Brora cashmere jumper for £40.

FARA
325 North End Road
Tel: 020 7385 4949
Open: Mon-Fri 9.30am-5.30pm,
Sat 10am-6pm, Sun 11am-5pm
A good rummage is needed to
find some serious bargains, but the
clothes are good quality and priced
fairly. There are quite a lot of shoes
and a wall of bric-à-brac.

Other charity shops in this area:

Cancer Research UK
350 North End Road
Tel: 020 7381 8458
Open: Mon-Sat 9.30am-6pm,
Sun 11am-5pm

FARA
297 New King's Road
Tel: 020 7736 2833
Open: Mon-Sat 10am-6pm,
Sun 11am-5pm

FARA Kids in Fulham
Tel: 020 7013 0744
662 Fulham Road
Open: Mon-Sat 9.30am- 5.30pm,
Sun 11am- 5pm

Trinity Hospice
785 Fulham Road_
Tel: 020 7736 8211_
Open: Mon-Sat 9.30- 4.30,
Sun variable: ring to see.

Geranium Shop for the Blind
817 Fulham Road
Tel: 020 7610 6986
Open: Mon-Sat 9.30am-5pm,
Sunday 12pm-4.00pm

Octavia
654a Fulham Road
Tel: 020 7384 9663
Open: Mon-Sat 10am-6pm

South Kensington SW5

Tube: South Kensington

Octavia

309 Fulham Road, SW10
Tel: 020 7352 7986
Tube: South Kensington
Bus: 14, 345
Open: Mon-Sat 10am-6pm,
Sun 12noon-4pm

This charity shop has a fair amount of designer labels among the more usual high street names. There is a rack of party dresses, boxes of scarves going for £3 as well as the usual attractive new houseware. On a recent visit there was a £50 leather men's jacket and a £100 Moschino suit.

Octavia

3 Bute Street
Mon-Sat 10am-6pm,
Sunday 12pm-5pm

This is a small but very good charity shop with lots of designer labels from the up-market neighbourhood. The window is always very well dressed, and you don't have to wait to buy from it. There is a £1 T-shirt box and a good range of jewellery., CDs and books.

Octavia

*Tube: South Kensington/
Knightsbridge*
211 Old Brompton Road
Mon-Sat 10am-6pm, Sunday
10am-5pm

This is one of the best charity shops in London, located halfway between the V&A and Harrods. There is a wide selection of the very high quality household goods and gifts from the charity on shelves in the middle, with clothes around the side. The store is big, with donations from surrounding stores and quite a lot of clothes are discounted. They have a wide range of women's and men's clothing all colour-coded, seasonal and well-displayed, with labels including Paul Costello, D&G and Versus. Stock includes vintage dresses and suits for both sexes, with a good men's suit going for around £20. Downstairs has a cosy atmosphere with mood lighting where you can sit and read before you buy one of the good selection of books. Vinyl records are £1, some paperbacks are discounted to 50p and there is a good kids' section.

Kensington W8

*Tube: High Street Kensington &
Notting Hill Gate*

Octavia

(map 7)

*57 Kensington Church Street
Tel: 020 7937 5274
Open: Mon-Sat 12pm-5pm,
Sun 10am-6pm*

This small charity shop is crammed with good quality clothes and many designer labels and Keira Knightley's Oscar gown was sold for thousands on Ebay after being displayed in the window here. The shop has a fine selection of men's shirts, and women's suits go for about £25. The books and shoes are located at the back, hardbacks are £2 and paperbacks £1.

Oxfam

*202B Kensington High Street
Tel: 020 7937 6683
Open: Mon-Sat 10am-5.30pm, Sun 12pm-5pm*

All stock is of high quality and colour coded, with well displayed shoes above the rails. A Belville Sassoon evening dress was only £230. The shop has recently in-troduced a Traidcraft wall of hand-crafted jewellery, as well as selling Fairtrade and Traidcraft food and goods. Greeting cards start at 99p and there is a good selection of books, including some hardback editions found in the glass cabinets.

Other charity shops in this area

Trinity Hospice

*31 Kensington Church Street
Tel: 020 7376 1098
Open: Mon-Fri 10am-6pm,
Sat 10am-5pm, Sun 11am-5pm*

Geranium

*8A Earl's Court Road
Tel: 020 7795 6166
Open: Mon-Sat 10am-5pm*

Octavia

*266 High Street Kensington
Tel: 020 7602 6043
Open: Mon-Sat 10am-6pm,
Sun 1pm-6pm*

Bayswater/Paddington

Tube: Bayswater/Queensway

Octavia

*178 Queensway
Tel: 020 7221 8582
Open: Mon-Sat 10am-6pm, Sun 12pm-5pm*

This is a small but well organised and busy branch with a particularly good selection of paperback fiction. There are good quality trinkets, vinyl records for £1.25 and kids' clothes for 50p. A coat will set you back about £10.

Trinity Hospice

158 Queensway
Tel: 020 7229 8291
Open: Mon, Wednesday, Thursday
10am-6pm, Tue 10am-4.45pm,
Friday-Saturday 10am-5pm,
Sunday 12pm-5pm.
Sun 11am-5pm

A traditional charity shop with lots of clothing, shoes, books and bric-à-brac. The store is probably the largest charity shop in the area and is always busy with locals sifting through the stock for bargains. Bags are £1 each, Kids' shoes are £2 and babies clothes go for 50p.

Other charity shops in this area :

All Aboard

3 Porchester Road
Tel: 020 7229 0048
Open: Mon-Fri 9.30am-5.30pm
(Fri closes earlier)

All Aboard

12 Spring Street
Tel: 020 7262 5955
Open: Mon-Thur 10am-6.00pm,
Fri 10.00am-3.00pm,
Sun 11noon-4pm

Sue Ryder

27 Praed Street
Tel: 020 7262 6108
Open: Mon-Sat 9am-5pm

Traid

61 Westbourne Grove, W2 (map 6)
Tel: 020 7221 2421
Open: Mon-Sat 10am-6pm

Notting Hill W11

Tube: Notting Hill Gate

Notting Hill Housing Trust

59 Notting Hill Gate (map 7)
Tel: 020 7229 1476
Open: Mon-Sat 10am-7pm,
Sun 1pm-6pm

With a prime location right next to Notting Hill tube station, this is a small charity shop but with very good quality stock. Common to all Notting Hill Housing Trust charity shops is the array of beautiful trinkets and bric-à-brac made to go in the shops – this one includes photo frames, lanterns and crockery. Labels include Whistles, Boden and Karen Miller.

Trinity Hospice

20 Notting Hill Gate
Tel: 020 7792 2582
Open: Mon- Saturday 10.30-5.30

This is a good charity shop to find clothes, books and bric à brac. There are lots of shoes situated below the rails and kids' clothes and bric-à-brac goes for 50p.

Oxfam

144 Notting Hill Gate
Tel: 020 7792 0037
Open: Mon-Sat 10am-5.30pm

This is a fantastic although quite small Oxfam store. It sells mostly high quality clothes, some designer, and has a good selection of shoes.

Other charity shops in this area:

Marie Curie
114 Ladbroke Grove, W10
Tel: 020 7229 9512
Open: Mon-Sat 9am-5.00pm

(map 6)

Oxfam
245 Westbourne Grove
Tel: 020 7229 5000
Open: Mon-Sat 10.00am-6.00pm

(map 6)

Oxfam Bookshop
170 Portobello Road
Tel: 020 7727 2907
Open: Mon-Thurs 10am-6pm, Fri-Sat 10am-6.30pm, Sun 12noon-5pm

(map 6)

Shepherd's Bush W12

Tube: Shepherd's Bush

Age Concern
110 Uxbridge Road
Tel: 020 8749 9888
Open: Mon-Sat 10am-5pm

(map 5)

This is a very good charity shop and one of the few to stock small items of furniture as well as the usual mix of books, clothes, CDs and bric-à-brac. Videos are £1 and there is a good range of menswear and upholstery in the back.

FARA
84 Uxbridge Road
Tel: 020 8743 7799
Open: Mon-Sat 10am-6pm, Sun 11am-5pm

(map 5)

A fairly typical charity shop, with books, clothes and videos and a lot of bric à brac in the window. The staff are also very friendly.

Traid
164 Uxbridge Road
Tel: 020 8749 1437
Open: Mon-Sat 10am-6pm, Sun 11am-5pm

(map 5)

Another fabulous Traid store, although a bit on the sparse side. The rails are all colour coded and there is a good range of evening dresses, and there is also a small range of bric-à-brac. Exclusive to Traid is a label called Remade, where clothes are customised by up-and-coming fashion designers. The designs are all unique and very cool, but will set you back about £20.

Other charity shops in this area:

Octavia
76 Askew Road
Tel: 020 8740 4878
Open: Mon-Sat 10am-6pm, Sunday 12pm-5pm

(map 5)

Hammersmith W6

Tube: Hammersmith

Books for Amnesty

139 King Street
Tel: 020 8746 3172
Open: Mon-Sat 10am-6pm

This store houses dozens of good quality books, including a shelf of recent publications and some old hardbacks too. For all budding scientists there are separate shelves for chemistry, physics and biology and there is a whole wall of children's books with plastic chairs to sit in. Vinyl records are £1, DVDs £3 and videos go for £2.

Wishes (Cancer Research UK)

108 King Street
Tel: 020 8746 3215
Open: Mon-Sat 9.30am-5.30pm,
Sun 11am-4pm

This store is dedicated to cards and all celebratory paraphernalia, and is deceptively similar to Clinton's and other card shops. The range is top-notch and you are bound to find what you want.

The Red Cross Shop

152 Shepherd's Bush Road
Tel: 020 7602 3534
Open: Mon-Sat 10.00am-5.00pm

Situated on the link road between Hammersmith and Shepherd's Bush, this is a good little charity shop with a range of clothes, books and bric à brac. There's also a £1 basket.

Traid

119 King Street
Tel: 020 8748 5946
Open: Mon-Sat 10am-6pm &
Sun 11am-5pm (am yet to confirm times)

This is a very trendy charity shop with lots of retro clothing, especially at the back where you will find rails of women's dresses. The shop feels similar to the Rokit shops, a must for all vintage addicts.

Other charity shops in this area:

British Heart Foundation

127 King Street
Tel: 020 8563 8851
Open: Mon-Sat 10.00am-6.00pm

Cancer Research UK

123A King Street
Tel: 020 8563 0440
Open: Mon-Sat 9.30am-5.30pm &
Sun 11am-5pm

Oxfam

87 King Street
Tel: 020 8846 9276
Open: Mon-Sat 10.00am-5pm,
Sunday 12pm-5pm

Charity Shops ● West

313

Chiswick W4

Tube: Turnham Green

Barnardos

72 Turnham Green Terrace
Tel: 020 8994 9931
Open: Mon-Sat 9am-5pm

The speciality here is children's clothes and toys, although there are a fair few clothes for adults. Vinyl records are £2 and CDs £2.50.

Cancer Research UK

392 Chiswick High Road
Tel: 020 8994 4391
Open: Mon-Sat 9.30am-5.30pm &
Sun 12noon-5pm

This is a well stocked shop with all kinds of goods. On a recent visit there were loads of boots and coats for sale, with a fair few hats and a rack of dresses, some of which were vintage. DVDs are £3, CDs £2 and videos £1.

Cancer Research UK

278 Chiswick High Road
Tel: 020 8742 2501
Open: Mon-Sat 9.30am-5.30pm &
Sun 11am-5pm

This store has a good range of clothing, with knock-offs from the local high street including a rack full of Gap on a recent visit. There are lots of scarves and some vintage dresses with CDs towards the back.

Octavia

46 Turnham Green Terrace
Tel: 020 8995 8864
Open: Mon-Sat 10am-6pm &
Sun 12pm-5pm

Another gem from Octavia (formerly the Notting Hill Housing Trust), the quality of the clothes is good and there are the usual in-house knick-knacks but with an emphasis on throws and cushions.

Oxfam

190 Chiswick High Road
Tel: 020 8994 4888
Open: Mon-Sat 10am-5.30pm &
Sun 12noon-5pm

This is a tidy and well-lit store, with a good selection of women's clothes. Children's toys are well laid out on a table in the back, along with men's clothes and books.

Trinity Hospice

25 Turnham Green Terrace
Tel: 020 8742 3036
Open: Mon-Sat 10am-5pm

A bit of a rummage is required to unearth some finds, but once done you will find some up-market labels such as Nicole Farhi and Jaeger. There is a good range of bric-à-brac, including lots of crockery. Downstairs is small but you will find books and vinyl records.

Ealing W5

Tube: Ealing Broadway

Oxfam Books

1 The Green
Tel: 020 8567 2152
Open: Mon-Fri 10.00am-6pm, Sat 9.30am-6pm, Sun 12noon-5pm

This is a busy shop with a good collection of books in the usual categories. There is a shelf of first editions which will be of interest to collectors, a shelf dedicated to medicine for budding medics and a kids' section.

Oxfam Music

15 The Green
Tel: 020 8840 8465
Open: Mon-Sat 10am-5.30pm, Sun 1pm-5pm

This store had a fantastic amount of music, with not a B*witched or Spice Girls in sight. 99% of CDs are new and unused, some coming from radio stations and recording studios. There are 12 inch vinyl records in their original plastic wrapping, two walls of videos and some DVDs, sheet music for most instruments and you can buy three singles for 99p. In addition there is a top class display of DVD, CD and cassette players for around £30, all of which have been tested. There is local delivery service for a nominal fee and 30 day guarantee.

YMCA

16 Bond Street
Tel: 020 8832 1638
Open: Mon-Sat 10am-5pm

This store has two shops surrounding the local YMCA. The one on the left sells books, vinyl records and videos. The one to the right sells clothes, including kids' and has a good vintage and designer rail.

Other charity shops in this area:

Cancer Research UK

66 The Mall, Ealing Broadway
Tel: 020 8840 1197
Open: Mon-Sat 9.30am-6pm & Sun 11am-5pm

Octavia

40 High Street
Tel: 020 8567 8003
Open: Mon-Sat 10am-6pm, Sun 12.00pm-6pm

Oxfam

34 New Broadway
Tel: 020 8579 6532
Open: Mon-Sat 9.30am-5.30pm, Sun 12pm-5pm

Sue Ryder

2 Bond Street
Tel: 020 8840 0570
Open: Mon-Sat 9.00am-4.30pm

South London

Brixton SW2

Tube/Rail: Brixton

Barnardos
414 Brixton Road, SW9
Tel: 020 7274 4165
Open: Mon-Sat 9am-5pm
This large store offers a great selection of clothing, toys, books, records and CDs. The stock is well priced and there are always discount rails with items reduced to clear.

Traid
2 Acre Lane
Tel: 020 7326 4330
Open: Mon-Sat 10am-6pm,
Sun 11am-5pm
This is a typical Traid store stocking an eclectic mix of retro, casual clothing and designerwear. The charity has been deservedly hailed by Japanese and British Vogue for its label TRAIDremade, where young designers revamp old clothes into trendy glories.

Tooting SW17

Tube: Tooting Broadway

Octavia
36 High Street Tooting
Tel: 020 8767 3431
Open: Mon-Sat 10am-6pm, Sun
12pm-5pm

Oxfam
245-247 Upper Tooting Road,
London , SW17 7TG
Telephone: 020 8682 3500
Open: Mon-Sat 9.30am-5pm
(depending on staff avaliabilty)

Barnes SW13

Rail: Barnes Bridge

Octavia
3 Barnes High Street
Tel: 020 8878 6170
Open: Mon-Sat 10am-6pm, Sun
12pm-5pm

Putney SW15

Tube: East Putney
Rail: Putney

Oxfam
149 Putney High Street
Tel: 020 8789 3235
Open: Mon-Sat 9.30am-5.30pm,
Sun 11am-5pm
This shop is larger than it looks on the outside, and boasts plenty of stock. Books and Oxfam's own goods are situated at the front,

(map 8)

clothing is further back with a very good children's rail, and a great range of menswear. A wall is crammed with bric-à-brac, including cutlery for 39p. Videos sell for £1.

Cancer Research UK
127 Putney High Street
Tel: 020 8788 9305
Open: Mon-Sat 9.30am-5.30pm,
Sun 11am-5pm

This is a well-sized shop, with a good range of stock. The best feature is the retro rail, some of which could only be worn as fancy dress. If you rummage hard enough, vintage lovers are bound to find something worthwhile.

Other charity shops in this area:

Octavia
288 Upper Richmond Road
Tel: 020 8788 5763
Open: Mon-Sat 10am-6pm

⓪ map 8

Trinity Hospice
147 Putney High Street
Tel: 020 8780 0737
Open: Mon-Sat 10am-5pm

⓪ map 8

British Heart Foundation
65 Putney High Street
Tel: 020 8780 5611
Open: Mon-Wed 9.30am-5pm,
Wed- Sat 9.30am-6pm,
Sun 11am-4pm.

⓪ map 8

Wandsworth/ Southfields SW18

Tube: Southfields
Rail: Wandsworth Town

Salvation Army Charity Shop
209 Wandsworth High Street
Tel: 020 8871 1812
Open: Mon-Fri 10.30am-5.30pm,
Sat 11am-5pm

⓪ map 8

This is an excellent charity shop extending over two shop fronts and with a large back room. Unlike many charity shops this one sells electrical equipment that has been checked, and also has a large selection of furniture.

British Heart Foundation
153-155 Wandsworth High Street
Tel: 0844 499 4175
Open: Mon-Sat 9.30am-5pm

⓪ map 8

This very unusual charity shop specialises in furniture and electicals with TVs, washing machines, dishwashers and sofas occupying a great deal of the ground floor, with the first floor dedicated to beds and desks. A great place to go if you are looking to set up home on a budget, they have some attractive two seater sofas for as little as £60.

Other charity shops in this area:

Oxfam
4 Replingham Road
Tel: 020 8870 2676
Open: Mon-Sat 10am-5.00pm

FARA
(map 8)
551 Garratt Lane
Tel: 020 8947 8308
Open: Mon-Fri 10am-6pm, Sun 10am-4pm

Trinity Hospice Bookshop
(map 8)
208 Upper Richmond Road
Tel: 020 8785 3201
Open: Mon-Sat 10am-6pm

FARA
261 Wimbledon Park Road
Tel: 020 8785 0505
Open: Mon-Sat 10am-6pm, Sun 12noon-5pm

Youth Education Sport
(map 8)
292 Merton Road
Tel: 020 8877 3149
Open: Mon-Sat 11am-5pm

Clapham SW11
Rail: Clapham Junction

Ace of Clubs
53 St John's Road
Tel: 020 7978 6318p
Open: Mon-Sat 10am-5pm, Sun 12pm-5pm

The first of a cluster of charity shops just across from Clapham Junction railway station, this is a nice, cheap shop with constantly updated stock. Clothes are a mixed bag, and the toys and bric-à-brac around the window are difficult to resist a rummage through. Some books sell for 10p, and there is a facility to recycle your old phones.

Scope
69 St John's Road
Tel: 020 7801 0746
Open: Mon-Sat 9.30am-5.30pm

Just across the road from Ace of Clubs, this is also worth a visit. Perks include brand new DVDs, £1 jewellery and new shoes as a part of Scope's equality range.

Trinity Hospice
40 Northcote Road
Tel: 020 7924 2927
Open: Mon-Sat 10am-5pm

Known locally for its outlandish window displays during most public holidays, the clothes often reflect the young, trendy volunteers. This is one of the nicest charity shops in the area.

Other charity shops in this area include:

British Heart Foundation
62 St John's Road
Tel: 020 7978 4237
Mon-Sat 9.30am-5pm

Cancer Research UK
83 St John's Road
Tel: 020 7223 5349
Open: Mon-Sat 9am-5pm

FARA
254 Battersea Park Road
Tel: 020 7924 5575
Open: Mon10.00am-6.00pm, Sun 11am-5pm

Balham SW12

Tube/Rail: Balham

British Heart Foundation
184 Balham High Road
Tel: 020 8675 5401
Open: Mon-Sat 9.30am-5pm Sun 10.00am-3pm

Salvation Army Charity Shop
38 Balham High Road
Tel: 020 8675 3809
Open: Mon-Fri 10am-4.30pm

Streatham SW16

Rail: Streatham

Oxfam
23 Streatham High Road
Tel: 020 8769 1291
Open: Mon-Sat 10am-6.00pm, Sun 11am-4pm

This Oxfam shop specialises in furniture and electrical goods. They have three qualified electricians to check the quality and safety of all electrical goods including computers. The selection of furniture is also extensive, with anything from a 60s coffee table to a three-piece suite. The shop also stocks music and books.

Other charity shops in this area:

All Aboard
83 Streatham High Road
Tel: 020 8769 9410
Open: Mon-Fri 10am-6pm & Sun 10am-4pm

Cancer Research UK
65 Streatham High Road
Tel: 020 8677 3940
Open: Mon-Sat 9am-6pm, Sun 11am-3.00pm

Oxfam
7 Astoria Parade, High Road
Tel: 020 8769 0515
Open: Mon-Sat 9.30am-5.00pm

East London

Whitechapel E1

Tube: Aldgate East/Liverpool Street/Shoreditch

Spitalfields Crypt Trust Shop

26-28 Toynbee Street
Tel: 020 7377 9893
Open: Mon-Fri 10am-6pm, Sun 10am-4pm

This is quite a good little charity shop, with low prices but very few quality clothes. However, there are very reasonably priced fragrant oils for £1 and handmade soap.

Spitalfields Crypt Trust Shop

34-36 Watney Market
Tel: 020 7791 0200
Open: Mon-Sat 10am-5pm

Located just off Commercial Road, this is a sister branch to the above, and well worth checking out.

Dalston E8

Rail: Dalston Kingsland

Oxfam

570-572 Kingsland Road
Tel: 020 7923 1532
Bus: 149 from Liverpool Street tube, bus 76 from Waterloo
Open: Mon-Sat 9.30am-5.20pm, Sun 12pm-6pm

This Oxfam, by far the biggest Oxfam in London, is so much like a small supermarket that there are even shopping baskets for the use of customers. There is even a local blog called 'Dalston Oxfam Shop', where the anonymous blogger describes and rates tapes bought from the shop. Towards the front of the shop there are big wooden crates full of stock at rock bottom prices. CD albums and 12 inch records are 99p and 7 inch records sell for 29p. To the left of the door there is the books section with all books selling for 59p. There are racks full of men's and women's clothes, which are all £2.29. Towards the back are children's clothes, good quality hats, linen and top-notch stock displayed in glass cabinets.

Hackney E8 & E9

Rail: Hackney Central

Community of Reconciliation and Fellowship

407 Mare Street, E8
Tel: 020 8985 7356
Open: Mon-Sat 9.30am-4.30pm

This is a medium sized charity shop, stocked with vinyl records, underwear, kids' toys and bric-à-brac. The clothes are not very fashionable but are cheap with most garments sold for £2-£3.

Bethnal Green E3

Tube: Bethnal Green

Sudana

51 Roman Road
Tel: 020 8981 1225
Open: Tues-Fri 12am-6pm, Sat 12noon-5.30pm (closed Sunday and Monday)

Attached to the Buddhist centre next door, this packed little shop never fails to produce some cracking bargains, if you rummage long enough.

Charity Shops • East

Other charity shops in this area:

Salvation Army Charity Shop

Cambridge Heath, 70 Mare Street, E8
Tel: 020 8985 4410
Open: Mon-Fri 10am-4pm, Sat 10am-1pm

Scope

4 Morning Lane, E9
Tel: 020 8985 5825
Open: Mon-Sat 9.30am-5.30pm

Outer London

Richmond TW9

Tube/Rail: Richmond

Cancer Research UK
1 Hill Street
Tel: 020 8940 4581
Open: Mon-Sat 9.00am-5.00pm,
Sun 10.30am-4.30pm
The best in the area for modern, stylish clothes at moderate prices. A collection of nice little handbags, some vintage, range from £2-£3. The occasional cashmere sweater makes an appearance on the women's rails, priced around £8.

Marie Curie
1 Lichfield Terrace (on Sheen Road)
Tel: 020 8940 1800
Open: Mon-Sat 9.30am-5.00pm
The clothes in this shop are smart and of exceedingly good quality. Much of the stock is designer, with labels such as Armani, Chanel and Chloe. There are designer handbags including Mulberry, and wonderful shoes. Prices range between £60 and £90, depending on the quality and type of clothing. The staff are dedicated to raising funds for this worthwhile charity, which funds nurses' visits to cancer patients along with many other things.

Oxfam
6 The Quadrant
Tel: 020 8948 7381
Open: Mon-Sat 9.30am-6pm
(open Sundays depending on staff availability)
This Oxfam is no longer dedicated to new stuff, instead you are more likely to find a typical Oxfam shop full of a large selection of books, clothing and Oxfam's organic fairtrade Traidcraft products.

Twickenham TW9

Rail: Twickenham

The Mind Shop
386 Richmond Road
Tel: 020 8891 2295
Open: Mon-Sat 9.30am-4.45pm,
Sun 11am-5pm

Octavia
394 Richmond Road
Tel: 020 8891 6819
Open: Mon-Sat 10am-6pm,
Sun 12.30pm-5.30pm

Oxfam
46 King Street
Tel: 020 8892 4605
Open: Mon-Sat 10am-5.00pm

324...Clothing
325...Household Goods
327...Out of Town Shopping Villages

Factory Shops

Factory Shops

The term factory shop has become synonymous with good value and for that reason quite a number of outlets describe themselves as such without actually having any link with a factory or particular manufacturer. The factory shops featured below are all in one way or another the genuine article and more importantly all offer good quality at below high street prices.

Clothing

The Burberry Factory Shop
29-53 Chatham Place, E9
Tel: 020 8328 4287
Rail: Hackney Central
Tube: Bethnal Green
Open: Mon-Sat 10am-6pm, Sun 11am-5pm

The famous Burberry Factory Shop has been expanded and improved in recent years despite the closure of the factory which stood alongside the shop and has now moved to the Far East. It could be argued that it is not strictly a 'factory shop' anymore, but the thousands of customers that visit the store every year seem untroubled by the factory's closure and are more interested in the discounts to be found within this large and well organised warehouse space. On a recent visit the store had men's duffel coats for £249.99 (reduced from £570) and stylish ladies' rain coats for £199.99 (reduced from £410). For those with less money to spend there were men's shirts for £34.99 (reduced from £130) and wool skirts for £29.99 (reduced from £39.99). The shop offers a wide range of Burberry products with kids' clothing, accessories and perfumes also available at a discount. This is the largest and most popular factory shop in London and well worth making the trip to Hackney to visit.

Clarks Factory Shop
See main entry in the Shoes, Boots and Bags section (page 95).

Timothy Everest
Bespoke tailor by appointment only
32 Elder Street, Spitalfields, E1
Tel: 020 7377 5770
Website: www.timothyeverest.co.uk
Tube: Liverpool Street
Open: Mon-Fri 9am-6pm, Sat (telephone appointment)

Timothy Everest create garments that are traditional with a contemporary twist. Their quality bespoke men's suits are cut from a pattern made to the customer's measurements and are then hand sewn and finished. They sell their suits for about half the price of big name Savile Row equivalents, with a two piece starting from around £1,800.

Household Goods

Chomette
307 Merton Road, SW18
Tel: 020 8877 7000
Website: www.chomette.co.uk
Tube: Southfields
Bus: 39, 156
Open: Tues-Fri 10am-5pm

map 8

This factory outlet next to the main Chomette warehouse is small but well stocked with a wide range of porcelain cookware and tableware, cutlery, glass, non-stick cookware and kitchen knives. The company supplies quality names such as Pillivuyt porcelain and SKK cookware to hotel and retail outlets and sells direct to the public at considerable discounts. Slight seconds and discontinued lines are sold at even greater discounts and they have regular seasonal sales. The shop is not far from Villeroy & Boch and worth visiting.

The Curtain Fabric Factory
See main entry in the Curtains section (page 163).

Poetstyle Ltd

Unit 1 Bayford Street Industrial Units,
Bayford Street, Hackney, E8
Tel: 020 8533 0915
Tube: Bethnal Green
Rail: London Fields
Open: Mon-Fri 8am-5.30pm, Sat 10am-5pm, Sun 10am-2.30pm

Jack Cohen's grandfather started this family upholstery business in the late 19th century. The company has survived all these years by offering great quality furniture at a very reasonable price. The showroom is in the middle of the factory so you can see the latest designs and also get a view of the sofas, sofa beds and armchairs being made in their work-shop. Customers can specify the dimensions of the furniture, choose from Poetstyle's own range of material or supply their own fabric. Sofa beds start from £560. Poetstyle also offer a great value refurbishment service. A price list and brochure is available on request.

Price's Patent Candle Co

100 York Road, SW11
Tel: 020 7924 6336
www.prices-candles.co.uk
Rail: Clapham Junction
Open: Mon-Sat 9.30pm-5.30pm, Sun 11am-5pm

This famous candlemaker's has been going for a hundred years and al-though the Bicester-based firm has several factory shops, this is the only London one, with overstock and end of lines discounted by up to 75%. As well as church candles, fragrance candles, floating candles and outdoor candles, the shop sells accessories such as bowls and lamps.

Villeroy & Boch

267 Merton Road, SW18
Tel: 020 8875 6006
Tube: Southfields
Open: Daily 10am-5pm

map
8

This famous china, glassware and cutlery manufacturer has 8 outlets for seconds and discontinued stock. This London branch has recently been fully refurbished and extended to double its original size. Some of the designs and patterns are pretty bold but they do have simpler stuff. There are also special purchases such as a patterned plate for £4.95 (reduced from £16.95) and a box of 4 wine glasses for £23 (originally £46). Prices are about half of what you'd pay in a London department store but check every piece you buy for flaws. The store also has regular summer and winter sales.

Out of Town Shopping Villages

Bicester Village

50 Pingle Drive, Bicester, Oxon
Tel: 01869 323 200
Website: www.bicester-village.co.uk
Car: 2 miles from Junction 9 M40
Rail: Bicester Town (from Oxford) Bicester North (London-Birmingham);
courtesy shuttle bus Thurs-Sun
Open: Mon-Fri and Sun 10am-6pm, Sat 9.30am-6pm

This huge discount village has over 100 stores offering savings of up to 60% on the previous season's branded goods, so don't expect to find the very latest fashions. Bargains are nevertheless to be had in any number of stores depending on the time of year and what they happen to have in stock. Expect to find at least 25% discount on regular prices and often a lot more. Outlets include: Calvin Klein, Diesel, Hugo Boss, Samsonite, L.K. Bennett and Molton Brown. The centre can get packed at week-ends, especially between 1pm and 3pm, but there are plenty of distractions from the shopping including Starbucks and Carluccio's. When the car park's full they offer a park and ride at a local school.

Freeport Braintree Designer Outlet

Charter Way, Chapel Hill
Braintree, Essex CM7
Tel: 01376 348 168
www.freeport-braintree.com
Rail: Freeport Braintree Station (from Liverpool Street)
Car: M11 take junction 8, east on A120
Open: Mon-Fri 10am-6pm, Sat 9am-7pm, Sun 10am-5pm

This Essex discount village has over 80 shops selling leading brands at up to 50% discount. Labels available include Burberry, Versace, Nike and Mexx and there are also high street discount outlets for Next and M&S. As well as fashion there are also plenty of discounted homeware stores with Le Creuset and Villeroy & Boch both offering their products at a discount. Those interested in discounted hi-fi equipment should look out for the Bose store which offers the full Bose range with some considerable savings to be found.

the galleria

Comet Way, Hatfield, AL10
Website: www.galleria.co.uk
Car: A1(M) between junctions 3/4
Rail: Hatfield, then local buses (10 mins)
Open: Mon-Fri 10am-8pm, Sat 10am-6pm, Sun 11am-5pm

This huge shopping centre straddling the A1 motorway, which markets itself as a discount centre, has a number of outlets specialising in discounted fashion, furniture and homeware. The outlet stores include Amanda Wakeley, Ghost, Pringle, Claire, Bijoux, TK Maxx, Tog 24, Choice and Donnay with many offering discounts of up to 50%. Newest outlets include Marks & Spencer and Reebok. There are also some regular stores like Waterstones, Superdrug, Body Shop and Oasis. On weekends and Bank Holidays, which get pretty crowded, there are often children's activities, plus a UCI cinema and, for those who get impatient with partners, numerous cafés and restaurants.

330...Fashion and Textiles

332...Ceramics

332...Lighting

333...Furniture

334...Clocks

334...Accessories

335...Workshop Open Days

Independent Designers

Fashion and Textiles

Helena Allon

Tel: 020 8341 7595
M: 07947 965 734
Helena.allon@btinternet.com
Open: Fri 11am-6pm (Exmouth Market, EC1); Sat 10am-4.30pm
(Broadway Market, E8)

Helen Allon make their own distinctive range of women's casual clothing which they sell direct to the public at Exmouth and Broadway markets at considerably below comparable store prices. The range of clothing includes blouses, shirts, skirts, trousers, coats and dresses with prices from as little as £10. The new range of men's shirts are proving popular and they are about to launch a mail order catalogue – phone or e-mail to order a copy.

from marissa v.

34 Hoxton Street, N1
Tel: 07748 636 984
www.marissav.com
Open: By appointment and Sat at Broadway Market

This Hackney-based company offers a great range of stylish women's casual clothing and bags at very competitive prices. Their website is easy to use and shows all the latest designs with prices and you can visit them on Saturdays when they have a stall on Broadway Market (see page 353). The clothing is great value with tops starting from around £20 and a good choice of dresses for £40 – a great place to find original women's fashion on a budget.

Prillywear

Studio E2J, Cockpit Arts Cockpit Yard , Northington Street, WC1
Tel: 020 7242 2887
www.prillywear.com
Open: by appointment

Prilly Lewis specialises in knitted and felted fabrics making unique pieces including coats, jackets, dresses and accessories. Visits to her studio are welcome where you can see her work and enjoy savings buying direct from the designer.

SINE
Cockpit Yard, Northington Street, WC1
Tel: 020 7916 8916
Open: By appointment

This small workshop makes knitwear to order from 100% natural fibres: cashmere, camel hair, silk and cotton. All garments are made to order, so you can choose the yarn and design. Prices start at £50 and go up to as much as £300, but given the quality of the clothes and the prices charged for similar items in smart boutiques, this is still great value. Phone in advance to book an appointment.

Smooth Delight
Broadway Market, E8
Tel: 07768 797784 (Cressida)
Cressida23@hotmail.com
www.smoothdelight.co.uk
Open: Sat 10am-4pm

Cressida has been selling her stylish range of colourful, embroidered dresses from Broadway Market (see page 353) for quite a few years now and has built up quite a following among the local community. The dresses are all 100% cotton and made to a very high standard by an individual dressmaker and represent fantastic value at between £20 and £45. If you are looking for something unique Cressida will also undertake commissioned work, although this costs a good deal more. Take a look at her stall on Broadway Market on Saturdays or look out for the website which is soon to be up and running.

Ceramics

Caroline Bousfield Gregory
Workshop, 77A Lauriston Road, E9
Tel: 020 8986 9585
www.carolinebousfield.co.uk
Open: Tues-Wed, Fri-Sat 10.30am-5.30pm, and by appointment

Caroline has been making and selling her own unique stoneware pots, plates, cups and other more unusual items since 1975. Her work has a matt or semi-matt finish and can be used in the oven and dishwasher. Prices start from £5 and go up to £100 for larger more elaborate pieces, with things like a hand-made tea pot for as little as £20.

People Will Always Need Plates
17 Morgan Court, Battersea High Street, SW11 3HU
www.peoplewillalwaysneedplates.co.uk
Open: by appointment

Founded by Hannah Dipper and Robin Farquhar, People Will Always Need Plates offer high quality, stylish and original plates, mugs and tea towels. Take a look at their website to see the full product range. Customers collecting from their workshop will receive a 10% discount and they offer a 50% discount on end-of-line products and slight seconds at various shows throughout the year, details of which are sent to those on their mailing list.

Lighting

Extraordinary Design Ltd
311 Chase Road, Southgate, N14
Tel: 020 8886 9020
info@extraordinarydesign.com
Website: www.extraordinarydesign.com
Mail Order Service

Extraordinary Design create contemporary lighting products to order, but formerly manufactured lighting for stores such as John Lewis and Heals. They now have a large stock of end-of-line lights which are available to the public at 50% of the original retail price. There are lots of interesting designs to choose from with prices starting from as little as £10 and going up to over £100 for one of their more elaborate lighting designs. Give them a call to arrange a time to visit their workshop.

Helen Rawlinson

The Chocolate Factory,
Unit 5, First Floor, Farleigh Place, N16
Tel/Fax: 020 7503 5839
E-mail: helen_rawlinson@yahoo.co.uk
Website: www.helenrawlinson.com
Open: By appointment
Mail Order

Helen Rawlinson designs and makes fantastic lamps with beech wood stems and hand printed shades in a variety of sizes, colours and designs. Her lamps sell in a number of smart stores, but can be purchased by mail order from her workshop at a discount with up to 50% reductions on many samples and seconds with lamps starting from £48. Helen's workshop can also be visited during the Chocolate Factory open days (see page 336).

Furniture

Alison Cooke

390A Hackney Road, E2
Tel/Fax: 020 7613 3063
Website: www.alisoncooke.co.uk
Open: By appointment

This workshop offers contemporary upholstered furniture and beanbags at very competitive prices considering the quality and originality of their products. Prices start from £150 for a large beanbag. Take a look at Alison's website to see all the available designs and colours.

Daniel Spring

158 Columbia Road, E2
Tel:020 7923 3033
www.springmetalbeds.com
Open Sunday 10am - 2.30pm (showroom), or by appointment

RCA trained Daniel Spring has been designing and manufacturing metal beds since 1990. The beds are handmade in polished iron or stainless steel at his workshop in Hackney and tailored to the clients' requirements with standard dimensions used as a template. Prices start from around £600, but given the quality of the beds this represents excellent value. Visit his showroom or take a look at the website which shows all his designs.

Unto This Last

230 Brick Lane, E2
Tel: 020 7613 0882
www.untothislast.co.uk
Tube: Liverpool Street or Old Street
Open: Daily 10am-6pm

Unto This Last is a unique company making their own range of furniture and selling it from their showroom on Brick Lane at prices considerably below equivalent high street stores. For more information see the review in the furniture section (page 198).

Clocks

Russell Callow

7 Sunbury Workshops,
Swanfield Street, E2 7LF
Tel: 020 7729 1211
E-mail: info@russellcallow.com
Website: www.russellcallow.com
Open: By appointment

Russell Callow restores and sells 20th century clocks. There's a wonderful range of unusual timepieces at his workshop; from the kind found on railway platforms, to 70s designs and massive industrial clocks. His clocks are often used by fashion or interior design stylists so there is a possibility you have seen some of his stock within the pages of the glossy style mags. Despite the authentic exteriors, all clocks are fitted with quartz mechanisms which are guaranteed for two years. Prices start from only £35.00

Accessories

Lucky Bird

unit 2 Padangle House
270 Kingsland Rd, E8
Tel: 07813 707205
Open: Sat 9am-4pm (Broadway Market, E8)

Kim Jenkins makes bags, accessories, prints and cards using recycled material. The products are witty and original and are sold at a very reasonable price with handmade bags for £10-20. Look out for her stall at Broadway Market.

Melissa Simpson

Zeal House, 8 Deer Park Road, SW19
Tel: 020 8542 6700
Website: www.melissasimpson.co.uk
Open: Mon-Fri 10.30am-6pm

Melissa's collection of hand-made leather briefcases, handbags and accessories are both simple and contemporary, ranging from bridle leather bags edged with colour to casual bags using the softest, tactile leathers. Visitors to the workshop can not only see how the bags are made, but have the opportunity to purchase samples and seconds at up to 50% discount and receive a 10% discount on the current collection. Prices range from £14 to £800.

Workshop Open Days

401 1/2 Workshops

401 1/2 Wandsworth Road, SW8 2JP
Website: www.401studios.org
Rail: Wandsworth Road, Tube: Stockwell
Open: Mid-November

This group of workshops holds an annual open weekend in November, showcasing the clothing, jewellery, ceramics, glass and metalwork produced by the thirty artisans occupying the site. Designer bags, paintings, furniture, beautifully crafted sculptural vessels and enamelled gold bowls are some of the objects to peruse. It's not exactly prime bargain hunting territory, but the items on sale are unusual and beautiful with some work available at trade prices. Send them an e-mail via the website to find the dates for the next sale or look out for the banner outside the studios in November.

Archway Ceramics Open Studios

410 Haven Mews, 23 St Paul's Way, E3
Tel: 020 8983 1323
Open: 2nd weekend of December & July, 11am-4pm
Admission Free

Featuring the work of its resident artists and designers, this twice-yearly open studio is dedicated entirely to the world of ceramics ranging from contemporary, functional homeware to more figurative, sculptural pieces with prices starting from £10. Visitors can purchase discontinued lines, samples and seconds at up to 60% off the retail price.

Artists at Home
Over 50 Open Studios in Chiswick,
Hammersmith and Shepherds Bush, W4, W6, W11, W12
Tel: 0208 743 5030 or 07956 953 153 for illustrated studio guide
www.artistsathome.net
Tube: Hammersmith, Turnham Green, Chiswick Park
Open: Mid-June
Admission Free

An annual artistic highlight in West London attracting visitors from far and wide. Artists at Home is a great opportunity to browse for and purchase original art and design at studio prices and to meet the artists. There are over 50 artists and craftsmen including painters, potters, photographers, textile designers, sculptors and jewellers with prices ranging from a few pounds to several thousand. Although AAH is only once a year, individual artists can be contacted at any time via the website.

The Chocolate Factory
Farleigh Place, Stoke Newington, N16
Tel: 020 7503 5839 / 020 7503 7896
Website: www.chocolatefactory.org.uk
Rail: Rectory Road
Open: November-December and July

This north London studio collective opens its doors to the public twice a year. Within its walls can be found painting, sculpture, ceramics, lighting and fashion. Most items are sold for 20% below the retail price and there are usually quite a few end of lines, and slight seconds for much larger discounts. Visitors are welcome at other times but it is advisable to contact the artists and makers first in order to avoid a wasted journey (numbers can be found on the website).

Creekside Artists
Unit A110-114, Faircharm Trading Estate, 8-12 Creekside, SE8
www.creeksideartists.co.uk
Tube: Greenwich DLR or Deptford Bridge (Mainline) DLR/Deptford Mainline
Open: Regular events throughout the year

Creekside Artists collective runs a shared studio for artists, sculptors, photographers, printmakers and textile designers and regularly runs open studios where resident artists can sell their work direct to the public. Take a look at the website to find out about the next event.

East London Design Show

Tel: 020 8510 9069
Website: www.eastlondondesignshow.co.uk

Now a major biannual event in June and December, the East London Design Show profiles the best in contemporary fashion, accessories, furniture, lighting, jewellery, photography and other household goods. The show is always well attended and has for the last few years found residents in the recently renovated Shoreditch Town Hall. Many designers use the show to launch products and it is a great opportunity to buy direct from the maker. The venue, dates and a full list of exhibitors can be seen on the website.

Great Western Open Studios

Lost Goods Building, Great Western Road, W9
Tel: 020 7221 0100
Tube: Westbourne Park
E-mail: office@greatwesternstudios.com
Open: Twice yearly, 1st weekend of June and December

Previously a British Rail lost property store, the aptly named Lost Goods Building now houses around 160 fine and applied artists and designers including ceramicists, painters, furniture makers, jewellery and textile designers, to name just a few. These twice-yearly open studio events provide the opportunity for visitors to check out what's on offer from some of london's most talented artists and designers and pick up a bargain among the samples, seconds, and end-of-lines available.

Iliffe, Pullens & Peacock Yard Open Studios

Iliffe Street, Crampton Street & Amelia Street, SE17
Tel: 020 7701 2422
Tube: Kennington, Elephant & Castle
Open: First weekend of December

In the run-up to Christmas the workshops based in the yards close to the Elephant & Castle open their doors to the public. The yards are home to many disciplines including photography, metalwork, ceramics, painting, jewellery, fashion and furniture makers with the artisans displaying their work and selling to the public at considerable discounts. As well as some reasonable bargains the yards have music, food and wine to make the experience as much a social event as a chance to find some bargains.

Made in Clerkenwell

Craft Central
33-35 St John's Square, EC1
& 21 Clerkenwell Green, EC1
Tel: 020 7251 0276
Website: www.craftcentral.org.uk
Tube: Farringdon
Open: Bi-annual weekend event held in June and November or December
(check website for exact dates and times)

These open weekends are a great opportunity to meet some of the craftspeople supported by Craft Central in the Clerkenwell area. With around 70 designers and makers participating, visitors can meet designers in their studios and buy or commission work directly. Expect to see a diverse range of work from contemporary designs using new technologies to more traditional craftswork. Fashion, jewellery, silversmithing, lighting and textiles are among some of the disciplines represented with prices starting from only £10 and going up to several thousand.

Mazorca Projects 'Hidden Art'

Shoreditch Stables, 138 Kingsland Road, E2
Tel: 020 7729 3301
E-mail: info@hiddenart.co.uk
Website: www.hiddenartlondon.co.uk/openstudios
Open: Held over two weekends in the Winter

Since 1993 this annual Hidden Art Event has celebrated the art and design of east London by opening local studios to the public and offering access to unique designs in the weeks before Christmas. Call or e-mail for more information about the event including a free map revealing the whereabouts of studios that are normally only open by appointment.

Workshop Sales

St Thomas More Hall,
Lordship Lane, East Dulwich
Tel: 02392 510 119
www.theworkshopsale.co.uk
Open: Biannual sales in the summer and winter

Over 30 local designers and makers display and sell their work at this biannual sale. The winter sale is particularly popular with lots of bargains to be found and a great selection of food and mulled wine to make the shopping a festive experience. Take a look at their website to find details of their next sale.

Junk Shops

Junk Shops &
Second-hand Furniture shops

This chapter features many of the best junk shops in London as well as some of the better value retro furniture stores which tend to have more interesting collectable furniture at a higher price. As well as the stores reviewed here take a look at the Auctions (page 276) and Charity Shops (page 287), which are also excellent places to find good value second-hand furniture.

North

Back in Time
93 Holloway Road, N7
Tel: 020 7700 0744
www.backintimeuk.com
Tube/Rail: Highbury & Islington
Open: Mon-Sat 10am-6pm

Back in Time is a smart retro furniture store with a wonderful selection of sofas, tables, chairs and lamps from the 1950s to the 80s. The store is not really a bargain outlet with the large three seater sofa in the front of the store being sold for £1,200 and a teak and steel 50s coffee table for £225, but the quality and design of the stock make this a reasonable price to pay and certainly cheaper than in similar West End retro shops. The 50s leather armchair with teak legs was a good deal for £240. Well worth a visit if you're in search of stylish retro furniture for a reasonable price.

D & A Binder
101 Holloway Road, N7
Tel: 020 7609 6300
www.dandabinder.co.uk
Tube/Rail: Highbury & Islington
Open: Tues-Sat 10am-6pm

This shop specialises in traditional shop fittings, some of which can look good in the home. Most of the stock consists of traditional glass display cabinets – the sort you find in ancient gentlemen's outfitters – but they occasionally sell more practical items of furniture such as desks and picture frames. If you visit the shop don't miss the large back room where many of the larger items are kept.
Also at: 34 Church Street NW8, Tel: 020 7723 0542 Open: Tues-Sat 10am-6pm

Cliford's Antiques

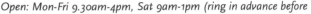

15 Long Lane, N3
Tel: 020 8343 0084
Tube: Finchley Central
Bus: 82, 125, 260
Open: Mon-Fri 9.30am-4pm, Sat 9am-1pm (ring in advance before visiting)

A quirky, cluttered shop with a reasonable range of furniture, glassware and knick-knacks. It's a fun shop to potter around, but the opening times are irregular to say the least and it is best to phone before making the effort to visit.

The Cobbled Yard

1 Bouverie Road, Stoke Newington, N16
Tel: 020 8809 5286

and

Unit 1 Bouverie Mews,
Bouverie Road, Stoke Newington, N16
Tel: 020 8442 3322
www.cobbled-yard.co.uk
Rail: Stoke Newington
Open: Wed-Sun 11am-5.30pm

This large yard just off Stoke Newington Church Street, has a great deal of charm and enough good quality used and antique furniture to make it worth a visit. Unlike many similar businesses, The Cobbled Yard has a very attractive and easy-to-use website which shows all the latest stock. The Art Deco two seat sofa for £250 was excellent value, but there is smaller bric-à-brac here for those with less money to spend. Just opposite the Cobbled Yard, in Bouverie Mews, the business has opened a second shop which offers a greater selection of antique and retro furniture and displays the larger items such as sofas. The store also offers an upholstery and restoration service.

The Junk Yard

121 Marton Road, N16
Tel: 020 7254 9941
Rail: Stoke Newington
Open: Daily 10.30am-5pm

This ramshackle junk yard offers furniture, electrical goods and bric-à-brac and is a firm favourite with many of the Stokey locals. On fine days the larger items of furniture and the occasional washing machine or fridge are put out on the pavement to encourage passers-by. The CDs are kept inside and sold for as little as £2 and the small selection of books are even cheaper. A great shop, well worth a visit if you're in the area and don't forget about The Cobbled Yard just a few minutes away (see page 341).

Mr All Sorts

191 Northchurch Road, N1
Tel: 020 7359 1791
Tube: Highbury & Islington
Open: Mon-Sat 10am-6.30pm

Mr All Sorts has been trading from this small rather run-down shop just off Essex Road for over 30 years. The stock is a mix of furniture, pictures, mirrors, bric-à-brac and a small selection of books. On a recent visit a simple wooden fireplace was £150 and a modern sink with pedestal was £75. On fine days the stock extends onto the pavement where the owner can often be found sunning himself. A little further along towards Islington there is a small architectural salvage yard, The Architectural Forum, which is worth a visit (see page 272).

A. J. McGovern & Company

221 Belsize Road, Kilburn, NW6
Tel: 020 7328 7812
Train: Kilburn High Road
Open: Mon-Sat 9am-5.30pm

(map 4)

McGovern's has been trading in second-hand furniture from this small warehouse since the 1960s but does little to advertise its services with just a few pieces of furniture placed on the pavement to entice passing trade. Inside there are lots of bargains with a recent visit unearthing a solid wood cot (with clean mattress) for £40, a smart three seat cloth sofa for only £150 and an enormous Stagg wardrobe for £295 which was originally £1,300. If you're looking to furnish a home on a budget, McGovern's is one of London's best second-hand furniture shops and well worth taking the trouble to visit.

Ooh-La-La!

147 Holloway Road, N7
Tel: 020 7609 0455
Tube/Rail: Highbury & Islington
Open: Tues-Sat 10am-6pm

This shop sells quality second-hand and collectable furniture, but also has a small selection of clothing and bric-à-brac. The store is not cheap by junk shop standards, but compared to more stylish shops just 10 minutes walk away on Upper Street there are still plenty of savings to be found. On a recent visit they had a large set of butcher's scales in the window for only £55 and a great selection of unusual and collectable lamps from £25. It's a great shop in which to browse with stock ranging from genuine antiques to early 70s retro. The clothes are reasonably priced and there are always garments reduced to clear.

Past Caring

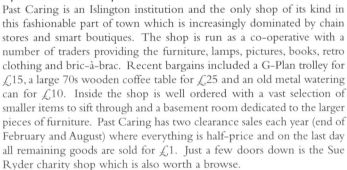

54 Essex Road, N1
Tube: Angel
Rail: Essex Road
Open: Mon-Sat 12am-6pm

Past Caring is an Islington institution and the only shop of its kind in this fashionable part of town which is increasingly dominated by chain stores and smart boutiques. The shop is run as a co-operative with a number of traders providing the furniture, lamps, pictures, books, retro clothing and bric-à-brac. Recent bargains included a G-Plan trolley for £15, a large 70s wooden coffee table for £25 and an old metal watering can for £10. Inside the shop is well ordered with a vast selection of smaller items to sift through and a basement room dedicated to the larger pieces of furniture. Past Caring has two clearance sales each year (end of February and August) where everything is half-price and on the last day all remaining goods are sold for £1. Just a few doors down is the Sue Ryder charity shop which is also worth a browse.

West

L.H. Cook Furnishers

289 Portobello Road, W10
Tel: 020 8969 3458
Tube: Ladbroke Grove
Open: Fri-Sat 8.30am-5pm

This established shop sells a mix of new and used furniture as well as second-hand fridges and washing machines. A good part of the stock is cheap and cheerful modern furniture, but they usually have a few more interesting items such as the large 1940s wardrobe found here recently for only £40. The selection of new pine mirrors were also great value for only £40 each.

The Furniture Gallery

136 Shepherds Bush Road, W6
Tel: 020 7602 4777
Tube: Shepherd's Bush
Open: Mon-Sat 11am-6pm

This small second-hand furniture shop does have some nice furniture but is not cheap with Art Deco chests sold for £145. The furniture is well presented, clean and fully restored so this does represent reasonable value.

Golborne Furniture
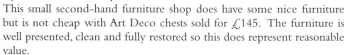

99 Golborne Road, W10
Tel: 020 8969 8399
Tube: Ladbroke Grove
Open: Mon-Thurs 9am-4pm, Fri-Sat 7am-6pm

This family-run junk shop has been selling furniture, pictures and bric-à-brac on Golborne Road for over 30 years. The shop is best visited on a Saturday when the Portobello market is in full swing with several other junk dealers selling their wares on the street. There are several other second-hand furniture stores on the street, but this is the most down to earth and cheapest.

The Cobbled Yard

Victoria Park Furniture Shop

& ACCESSORIES
020 7033 4045

Brick Lane Market

Ollies

69 Golborne Road, W10
Tel: 07768 790 725
Tube: Westbourne Park
Open: Tues-Sat 10.30am-5.30pm

(map 6)

This shop sells more designer retro than junk, but is still worth having a look around when you're in the area. The furniture is very well chosen and sold at a reasonable rather than a bargain price.

Les Couilles du Chien

65 Golborne Road, W10
Tel: 020 8968 0099
Tube: Westbourne Park
Open: Mon-Thurs 9am-5.30pm, Fri 8am-5.30pm, Sat 9.30am-5.30pm

(map 6)

This funky shop offers a good range of 20th century furniture, ornaments and lighting. The stock is collectable and therefore prices are a good deal higher than the genuine junk shop, but the place is still worth a visit if you're in the area.

South

Bambino's
32 Church Road, Crystal Palace, SE19
Tel: 020 8653 9250
email: andy.bambino@yahoo.co.uk
Rail: Crystal Palace
Open: Thurs-Sat 12noon-6pm
This traditional junk shop offers a real mix of things from vintage leather jackets to funky retro furniture and smaller items of bric-à-brac. Recent discoveries here included an army of male shop mannequins for £65 each and a fabulous leather Chesterfield sofa for only £175. If you have a more limited budget they have lots of smaller knick-knacks to sift through for as little as £1.

Cosmic Gaze
148 Maple Road, Penge, SE20
Rail: Penge West
Open: Tues-Fri 10.30m-4.30pm, Sat 10am-5pm (closed Wed)
This shop doesn't have a sign, but is easy to spot with its regular pavement displays of furniture, chandeliers and bric-à-brac. This is a very good junk shop and worth making an effort to visit given that Maple Road boasts several other junk shops.

The Junk Shop
9 Greenwich South Street, SE10
Tel: 020 8305 1666
Website: www.spreadeagle.org
Rail: Cutty Sark
Open: Daily 10.30am-6pm
This junk shop is an old-fashioned establishment full of a cluttered mix of furniture, pictures and other decorative items. In recent years they have acquired the stock of second-hand and antiquarian books from the now closed Spread Eagle Bookshop, which has added to the appeal and chaos of the place. In the basement there is even more furniture and bric-à-brac to sift through and on fine days the yard is open – where the larger items of architectural salvage are kept. There are always bargain to be found from books for just a £1 to a large mahogany bookcase for only £220.

East

Bacon Street Junk Shop

16-22 Bacon Street, E1
Tube: Liverpool Street
Open: Daily 9am-4pm

This large junk shop has all kinds of things for sale from its dark railway arch lock-up, just off Brick Lane. Like all the stores on Bacon Street, there are no signs to indicate the name of the shop and the store makes little attempt to advertise itself. The atmosphere of the place is dark and cluttered with piles of things to rummage through and plenty of unusual bargains to be discovered. The 60s coffee table was a great buy for £15, there are piles of books for only 50p each and old picture frames for just a few pounds. This is a great place to potter around and well worth a visit particularly as there are several other junkshops on the street (see below).

Bacon Street Junk Shop

14 Bacon Street, E1
Tube: Liverpool Street
Open: Daily 9am-4pm

This is a more open plan warehouse than the junk shop next door and tends to have a lot more office equipment with desks for around £30 and lots of steel filing cabinets for £25.

Dublin Jim

64 Sclater Street, E1
Tel: 07973 742 585
Tube: Liverpool Street
Open: Mon-Fri 9.30am-5.30pm

This lock-up at the far end of Sclater Street and is easily seen on fine days because Jim and his colleagues take the opportunity to sun themselves on the furniture that is displayed on the street The stock is limited but there are enough bargains here to make it worth a visit if you're in the area. A recent bargain included solid wood doors for only £15 each and a reasonable looking office chair for only £20.

The Furniture Cafe

202 Brick Lane, E1
Tel: 020 7613 3009
www.thefurniturecafe.co.uk
Tube: Liverpool Street
Open: Tue-Sun 10.30am-5.30pm

This second-hand furniture store on Brick Lane is particularly strong on Scandinavian-designed sofas and other items of furniture from the 60s and 70s. On a recent visit they had two beautiful chests for £70 and £90 each and a decent 2-seat leather Chesterfield for only £300. The basement is where all the best sofas are on display with a very fine leather sofa and chair for £800 which is considerably below the prices in smarter parts of town. A great place to find retro classics at a reasonable price and the only shop of its kind that also serves a mean cappuccino.

Lazy Days

21 Mare Street, E8
Tel: 07816 323 848 (Charlie), 07957 984 611 (Paul)
Tube: Bethnal Green
Open: Mon-Fri 9am-5pm, Sat 9am-2pm

This junk shop has been going for over 18 years, and is a great place to find all kinds of furniture for the home and office. Recently they sold a modern set of table and chairs for only £20 and occasionally have some interesting items of furniture and other unusual things like golf clubs. The shop is best visited on fine days when the stock is displayed on the wide pavement outside.

Lost and Found

115b Brick Lane, E1
Tel: 020 7375 2339
Tube: Liverpool Street
Open: Sun 9am-4pm

(map 12)

A small lock-up that trades in bikes, furniture and bric-a-brac on a Sunday – when Brick Lane market is in full swing. The stock is fairly small, but there are usually a few interesting things such as an industrial floor sander which was recently found here for only £70.

J.C. Second-Hand Furniture

12A Gales Garden, Bethnal Green, E2
Tel: 07956 933 832
Tube: Bethnal Green
Open: Mon-Fri 7am-6pm, Sat 10am-6pm

This archway lock–up is one of several second-hand furniture shops in this narrow alleyway, just opposite Bethnal Green tube station. The furniture is generally cheap and cheerful to cater for the local market, but there are usually a few interesting things to be found here such as the modern Muji steel office shelving which was only £30. While you're here visit Tom, Dick and Harry's Furniture next door (see below).

Tom, Dick & Harry's Furniture

500 Bethnal Green Road, E2
Tel: 020 7613 2230
Tube: Bethnal Green
Open: Mon-Fri 9am-5.30pm

The old stainless steel kitchen units are placed on ramshackle display on Bethnal Green Road, but most of the furniture and the shop's entrance is on the narrow alleyway called Gales Garden. There is nothing fancy to be found here, but they are good for basic items of furniture and often have professional catering equipment.

Victoria Park Furniture Shop

211a Victoria Park Road, E9
Tel: 07956 897 529
Tube: Bethnal Green
Open: Tue-Wed, Fri-Sun 10.30am-5.30pm

This is a fantastic little furniture shop with a regular turnover of interesting kitchen units, chairs, cupboards and tables. The shop has not yet decided upon a name and can be recognised by the piles of furniture that are displayed on the pavement just by Lauriston roundabout. A 70s steel and leather chair was found here recently for only £20 and there are always similar bargains to be found.

Markets

Markets

Alfies Antique Market, W2
13-25 Church Street, Marylebone
Tube: Edgware Road
Open: Tues-Sat 10am-6pm

Alfies is the UK's largest indoor antique market with over five floors of antique, vintage and retro goods supplied by nearly 100 dealers. There are enough bargains here to make it worth a visit and there is a roof-top restaurant should you feel peckish.

Bermondsey, SE1
Bermondsey Square, (between Abbey Street,
Bermondsey Street and Tower Bridge Street)
Tube: Borough/London Bridge
Rail: London Bridge
Open: Fridays 5am-1pm

Bermondsey Market is the largest antiques market in the capital and attracts antique dealers from across Europe. Members of the public are welcome, but you should be prepared to get there before dawn to see the market in full swing. Most of the dealers know the value of their stock and you are unlikely to find fine antiques at a huge discount; savings are more likely on the lower value bric-à-brac to be found here. If you do go early, take a torch.

Brick Lane, E1& E2
Brick Lane (north of Buxton Street), Bethnal Green Road (from Brick
Lane to Commercial Street), Cheshire and Sclater Street, Truman Brewery
(Sunday Upmarket) – see map for details
Tube: Aldgate East, Liverpool Street and Old Street
Open: Sunday 6am-1pm

(map 12)

Brick Lane Market is always changing and recent building work has forced many of the itinerant traders onto the lower part of Brick Lane and it is here that some of the best bargains in bric-à-brac, bikes, books, clothing and electrical goods can be found. The eastern end of Cheshire Street is also one of the best parts of the market with lots of second-hand stalls and the excellent Beyond Retro warehouse at the far end of the street (see page 358). The Sunday Upmarket is held in the Truman Brewery and is a great place to find independent jewellery and fashion designers selling their wares. The Bagel Bakery at the top of Brick Lane is always popular for refreshments as is Coffee @ Brick Lane which is just a few doors down.

Brixton, SW9

Brixton Station Road, Pope's Road, Atlantic Road,
Electric Road and Electric Avenue
Tube/Rail: Brixton
Open: Mon-Sat 8am-5.30pm, Wed 8am-1pm

For those more interested in bargain hunting than food shopping, Brixton Station Road is the best part of this market. The most interesting part of the street is after the junction with Pope's Road, where all the second-hand stalls are located.

Broadway Market, E8

Broadway Market, London Fields
Rail: London Fields
Open: Sat 9am-4.30pm

This market has taken off in recent years as a food market and has expanded to include lots of second-hand clothing and books. One of the best things about the market is the number of independent fashion designers selling their clothing and accessories to the public at very competitive prices. The second-hand clothing stalls at Broadway Market are among the best in London. If you want a rest from the crowds there are lots of cafés on the street and London Fields – just north of the market – is a great place to relax when the weather is fine.

Camden, NW1

Camden High Street
(North of Camden Town tube)
Tube: Camden Town, Chalk Farm
Open: Sat-Sun 9am-5pm (all parts of the market),
Thurs-Fri 9am-5pm (about half the market)

Camden is not just one market but several, each with different opening hours and each specialising in different merchandise. The market opposite Inverness Street is called Camden Market and is a good place to find cheap new and used clothes; it is also open on Thursday and Friday if you want to avoid the weekend crush. Camden Lock is another major part of the market and has stalls selling anything from books to designer and retro clothing. Prices can be high, but if you hunt around you can usually find some interesting things for less than you might expect. The most interesting part of the market for the determined bargain hunter is the Stables Market which is situated at the most northern end of the High Street and is only open at the weekends. It is here that the majority of the junky second-hand and retro clothing can be found.

Camden Passage, N1

On the junction of Essex Road and
Upper Street, opposite Islington Green, N1
Tube: Angel
Open: Wed 7am-2pm, Sat 8am-4pm (Antiques),
Thursdays 10am-4.30pm (Books)

This market is not in Camden, but Islington. The antiques market is not as cheap as Bermondsey Market, but it's usually possible to pick a few bargains. The best place to look is along the passage outside the Camden Head pub, where traders sell bric-à-brac on the pavement. The book market on Thursdays is small with just a few regular stalls, but lots of bargains.

Greenwich, SE10

Greenwich Church Street, Stockwell Street, Greenwich High Road
Rail/DLR: Greenwich
Open: Sat-Sun 9.30am-5pm
Wed-Fri 9am-5pm (Crafts Market within the Charter Market)
Thurs 9.30am-5pm (Collectables Market within the Charter Market)

Greenwich is a huge market and one of the best for books, furniture, fashion and bric-à-brac. It is not as fashionable or as busy as Camden and for that reason it's generally a little cheaper than its north London rival. The best parts of the market are the Antiques Market on Greenwich High Road and the Central Market on Stockwell Road both of which are good for second-hand things.

Kingsland Waste, E8

Kingsland Waste, Kingsland Road (between Forest and Middleton Road)
Rail: Dalston Kingsland
Open: Sat 9am-5pm

This market is a bit rough and ready with lots of junk, used electrical goods and books sold on an unprepossessing stretch of Kingsland Road. Despite the lack of scenery, this is good bargain hunting terrain.

Leather Lane, EC1

Leather Lane between Clerkenwell Road and Greville Street
Tube: Chancery Lane, Farringdon
Open: Mon-Fri 10.30am-2pm

Leather Lane is one of London's lunch-time markets, much frequented by the office workers of Clerkenwell. There are no second-hand goods sold here, but lots of contemporary smart and street fashion at below shop prices. If you can, visit in the morning before it gets too busy.

Merton Abbey Mills, SW19
Off Merantun Way, behind the Savacentre, South Wimbledon
Tube: Colliers Wood
Open: Sat-Sun 10am-5pm, Thurs 6am-12pm (antiques and collectables)

This weekend market is a pleasant place to visit with the river Wandle flowing by and a good few places to eat and drink. Besides the entertainment value there are also quite a few independent designers who sell their clothing or jewellery here at below the usual price. If you're looking for antiques, visit on a Thursday when the market is given over to antiques and collectables.

Petticoat Lane, E1
Middlesex Street and Wentworth Street, and adjacent streets and lanes
Tube: Aldgate, Aldgate East, Liverpool Street
Open: All streets Sun 9am-2pm

Petticoat Lane is a vast market, but doesn't sell any used goods which makes it less interesting than nearby Spitalfields and Brick Lane markets. Still if you're on the hunt for new street fashion, shoes, bags or leather goods this is a useful place to visit.

Portobello, W11
Portobello Road (from and including Golborne Road to Chepstow Villas)
Tube: Ladbroke Grove, Notting Hill Gate
Open: Sat 8am-5.30pm (Antiques), Mon-Sat 9am-5pm (General Market),
Sun 9am-1pm (Second-hand)

Portobello Road is at its most crowded and generally most expensive south of the Westway as most tourists approach it from Notting Hill tube station. To avoid the worst of the crowds and find the best bargains try approaching the market from Ladbroke Grove station. The best of the bric-à-brac, used clothing and second-hand books can be found in the narrow streets running alongside the Westway and under the canopy at the junction with Portobello Road. If you still have the energy walk north along Portobello Road to Golborne Road where there are lots of junk shops and more stalls selling bric-à-brac.

Roman Road, E3
Roman Road (from St Stephen's Road to Parnell Road)
Tube: Mile End
Open: Tues, Thurs and Sat 8.30am-5.30pm

Roman Road is a great value East End market which is at its busiest and best on a Saturday. Look out for the stall at the far end of the market which specialises in slight seconds from established labels like French Connection.

Spitalfields Market, E1
West side of Commercial Street between Folgate and Brushfield Street
Tube: Liverpool Street
Open: Sun 11am-3pm (main Sunday market)

The back part of this market is being redeveloped, but the front part is still a massive indoor space housed in an atmospheric purpose-built Victorian iron building. Despite the reduced size of the market there is still a wide range goods to be found here including organic food, designer and vintage clothing, second-hand furniture and bric-à-brac. Sunday is the best time to visit, when the market is in full swing.

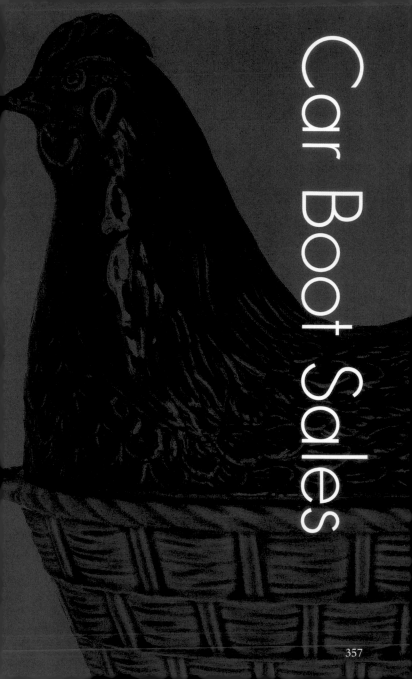

Car Boot Sales

Car Boot Sales

North

Earls Mead School, Broad Lane, N22
Sundays 7am-1pm (6am set up)
250 pitches
Contact: Giant Boot Sales
Tel: 020 8365 3000

Holloway, N7
Seven Sisters Rd (behind McDonalds)
/ and opposite Odeon Holloway
Saturdays 8am-4pm, Sundays 10am-
2.30pm
100 pitches
Tel: 01992 717198

Kilburn, NW6
St Augustine's School,
Kilburn Park Road
Saturdays 11am-4pm, (set up 8am)
100 pitches
Tel: 020 8440 0170

Nightingale School, Bounds Green Rd
Bounds Green, Tottenham, N22
Sundays 7am-1pm (6am set up)
250 pitches
Contact: Giant Boot Sales
Tel: 020 8365 3000

Tottenham, N17
Tottenham Community Sports Centre,
Tottenham High Road
Thursdays from 7am
55 pitches
Contact: Countryside Promotions
Tel: 01992 468 619
www.countrysidepromotions.co.uk

Wood Green, N22
New River Sports Centre,
White Hart Lane
Fridays from 6am
60 pitches
Contact: Countryside Promotions
Tel: 01992 468619
www.countrysidepromotions.co.uk

West

Chiswick, W4
Chiswick Community School,
Burlington Lane
First Sunday of month (except Jan),
8am-1pm (set up from 7am)
200 pitches
Tel: 020 8747 0031

Christ Church C of E School
New Broadway, Ealing, W5
75 pitches
Tel: 07764 995 896

South

Battersea , SW8
New Covent Garden Market,
Nine Elms Lane, Battersea
Sundays 8am-2.30pm (set up 6am)
250 pitches
Tel: 07972 092017

Battersea Technology Centre, SW8
Battersea Park Road
Every Sunday 1.30pm-5pm
Tel: 07941 383 588

Harris Academy
Southwark Park Road,
Bermondsey, SE16
Sundays 10am
200 pitches
Tel: 020 8309 5696

Meridian Sports Club Car Boot Sale
Meridian Sports Club, Charlton Lane,
London, SE7
Saturdays from 7am
150-200 pitches
Tel: 020 8856 1923

Wimbledon Stadium
Plough Lane, Wimbledon, SW17
Saturdays from 7am
Tel: 01932 355 538

East

William Morris School Car Boot Sale
Foley Lane, Billet Road,
Walthamstow, E17
Sundays from 6am
Tel: 07932 919 707

Out of Town

Ardleigh Green Car Boot Sale
Ardleigh House,
42 Ardleigh Green Road,
Hornchurch, Romford, RM11
Saturdays from 8am
Tel: 07931 270 181

Bishop Stortford, CM23
Bishop Stortford Town Centre,
Sundays from 7am
130 pitches
Contact: Countryside Promotions
Tel: 01992 468 619
www.countrysidepromotions.co.uk

Field End School
Field End Road, Ruislip, Middx, HA4
9PQ
Alternate Sundays 7am-1pm
300 pitches
Contact: Irene Calver
Tel: 020 8561 4517

Flamingo Park Car Boot Sale
Flamingo Park (A20),
Sidcup, Kent BR7
Sundays (April-Aug) 11am
pitches: 300
Tel: 020 8309 1012

Harlow
Pinnacles Industrial Estate,
Harlow, Essex
Sundays from 10.30am
320 pitches
Contact: Countryside Promotions
Tel: 01992 468 619
www.countrysidepromotions.co.uk

Hatfield
Birchwood Sports Centre, Longmead,
Hatfield, Herts
A1, Junction 4, then follow signs
Sundays from 10.30am
320 pitches
Contact: Countryside Promotions
Tel: 01992 468 619
www.countrysidepromotions.co.uk

Hayes, Middlesex, UB3
Hayes & Yeading FC,
Church Road, UB3
Every Wednesday & Friday
8am-2pm (set up 7am)
70 pitches
Tel: 020 8573 2075

Hounslow, Middlesex
Hounslow West Station Car Park
Saturday 7.30am-2pm (set up 7am) /
Sunday 7.30am-2pm (set up 7am)
75-150 pitches
Contact: Bray Associates
Tel: 01895 639912

Hounslow, Middlesex
Hounslow Heath Garden Centre,
Staines Road, TW4
Sundays & Bank Holidays,
6am-approx 1pm
250 pitches
Tel: 020 8890 3485

Middlesex Showground
Park Road, Uxbridge, UB8 1PS
Alternate Sundays 7am-1pm
300 pitches
Contact: Irene Calver
Tel: 020 8561 4517

North Weald / Harlow, Essex
From M11 junction 7, take A414 Road
to North Weald,
near Talbot round about
Saturdays 10.30am-2pm
150 pitches
Contact: Countryside Promotions
Tel: 01992 468 619
www.countrysidepromotions.co.uk

Pear Tree Car Boot Sale
Pear Tree, Brentwood Road (A128),
Bulphan,
Grays, Essex, RM14
Saturdays from 7am
Tel: 07765 121179
www.peartreebootsale.co.uk

Shepherton Car Boot Sale
New Road, Shepperton, Surrey
Saturdays 7.30am
Tel: 07807 609 283
www.sheppertoncarboot.co.uk

Waltham Abbey
Upshire Road, Waltham Abbey, Essex
M25, Junction 26,
then follow signs to Upshire
Sundays from 10.30am
475 pitches
Contact: Countryside Promotions
Tel: 01992 468 619
www.countrysidepromotions.co.uk

Wanstead Rugby Club Car Boot Sale
Wanstead Rugby Club
Roding Lane North, off Woodford
Avenue
Buckhurst Hill, Wanstead, Essex
Saturdays from 7am
Tel: 01279 871 117
Country Group

Welwyn Garden City
Stanborough Road,
Welwyn Garden City, Herts
A1, Junction 4, then follow signs
Sundays from 10.30am
150 pitches
Contact: Countryside Promotions
Tel: 01992 468 619
www.countrysidepromotions.co.uk

Pawnbrokers

Pawnbrokers

The traditional pawnbrokers just sell watches and jewellery, but there are also quite a number of more modern pawnbroker businesses that buy and sell a much wider selection of electronic and houshold goods and on some occasions bikes. In this chapter all the more general London pawnbrokers have been listed and reviewed. They are always good places to find bargains and all stores offer some kind of returns policy should the item prove faulty.

Cash Converters
www.cashconverters.co.uk

Branches at:

417 Bethnal Green Road, E2
Tel: 020 7729 4937

286-292 Camberwell Road, SE5
Tel: 020 7277 4424

141-145 Kentish Town Road, NW1
Tel: 020 7482 2000

315 Kilburn High Road, NW6
020 7624 4555

127 Fore Street, Edmonton, N18
Tel: 020 8345 5900

292-294 Lewisham High St, SE13
Tel: 020 8690 9800

159 High Street, Penge, SE20
Tel: 020 8776 5544

797-801 High Road, Leyton, E10
Tel: 020 8558 7776

180 The Grove, Statford, E15
Tel: 020 8536 1514

194 King Street,
Hammersmith, W6
Tel: 020 8741 8850

43B Goldhawk Road,
Shepherd's Bush W12
Tel: 020 8576 6111

12-14 St James St,
Walthamstow, E17
Tel: 020 8521 5550

33-35 Hare Street, Woolwich, SE18
Tel: 020 8316 0989

Open: Times vary, most branches are open Mon-Sat 10am-5.30pm

Cash Converter stores are run on a franchise basis and therefore the style of the shop, the range of second-hand goods on offer and the guarantee varies from store to store. Most shops offer a reasonable range of second-hand cameras, electronic goods, sports equipment and bikes. A recent visit to the branch in Kilburn discovered a quality Teak separates hi-fi system for only £274.99.

Cash Exchange

352 Holloway Road, N7
Tel: 020 7609 2022
Tube: Holloway Road
Open: Mon-Sat 10am-5.45pm

This large shop offers a wide variety of second-hand valuables at very competitive prices. Items on offer include hi-fis, bikes, musical instruments, computers, camcorders, mobile phones and cameras. All goods come with a two month guarantee.

Cash Express

158 Uxbridge Road, W13
Tel: 020 8840 1400
Tube: Northfield or Ealing Broadway
Open: Mon-Sat 10am-5.30pm

Formerly a branch of Cash Converters, this shop offers a good selection of hi-fis, TVs, bikes, cameras and much more.
Also at:
165 Camberwell Road, SE5
Tel: 020 7708 3296

Cash XChange

303 Kilburn High Road, NW6
Tel: 020 7625 1298
Tube: Kilburn
Open: Mon-Sat 10.30am-6.30pm

map 4

This is one of the best pawnbrokers in London to find all manner of cameras, computers, hi-fi separates, TVs, videos and power tools. The shop is large and a little dingy, but packed with interesting things at very reasonable prices. On a recent visit a boxed Xbox 360 with one game was only £174.99 and a 5 megapixel Sony digital camera was a mere £64.99. They also have a large collection of CDs with an offer of 2 CDs for £5 and 6 CDs for only £10. A great shop for second-hand bargains. Just a few doors down is a small branch of Cash Converters which is also worth visiting (see page 362).

Money Store

228 North End Road, SW6
Tel: 020 7381 6046
Tube: West Brompton or West Kensington
Open: Mon- Sat 10am-5.30pm

This former branch of Cash Converters has changed its name but continues to sell a reasonable range of hi-fis, TVs, cameras, mobile phones and musical instruments.

Enfield Exchange

9-10 Savoy Parade, Southbury Road,
Enfield, EN1
Tel: 020 8366 5520
Rail: Enfield Town
Open: Mon-Sat 9.30am-5.30pm

This shop offers a good selection of bikes all of which are slight factory seconds, computers and computer games, hi-fis, cameras, TVs and musical instruments. The shop also loans money on goods and offers a cheque-cashing facility.

General Index

1920s–1970s Crazy Clothes Connection 10, **55**
20/20 Optical Store **118**
20th Century Theatre 10, 72
21st Century Retro **54**
295 10, **57**
331 12, 33, **34**
401 1/2 Workshops **335**

A

A & K Warehouse Ltd 6, **201**
A-One Fabrics 9, 187
A.M. Leather Fashion 16, **34**
Abbott's **156**
Absolute Vintage 16, **59**
A D Jones Ltd **140**
Age Concern 6, 9, 293, 301, 312
Air Baltic **259**
Air Berlin **259**
Air Comet **259**
Alan's Records **239**, 241
ALDO Sale Shop 6, 91
Alexander Furnishings **160**, 181
Alfies Antique Market **352**
All Aboard 8, 15, 295–297, 302, 311, 319
Allon, Helena **330**
Allsop **286**
Alma Home **194**
Amnesty International Book Sale **235**
Andrew Jose **129**
Andrews & Robertson **286**
Anerley Frock Exchange **87**, 210
Any Amount of Books 4, **225**
Aperture Photographic 4, **248**
Apricot 4, **22**
Architectural Forum, The **272**
Architectural Reclaim **275**
Architectural Salvage **274**
Archive Second-hand Books & Music 230
Archway Ceramics Open Studios **335**
Arena Electronics 17, 114, 116
Artists at Home **336**
ask 17, 114, 115
Askew Paint Centre 9, **171**
Atlantic Clothing 6, 8, 9, 13, **28**
Atlantic Silk Fabric **188**
A to Z Fabrics 9, 187
Audio Gold **109**, **239**
Audio T **109**
Aurigny **260**
Austrian Bedding Co **148**
Autumn Down **150**

B

Back in Time **340**
Bacon Street Junk Shop **348**
Bainbridge's **283**
Bambino's **347**
Bang Bang 4, **76**, **77**, 81
Barbarella Shoes **97**
Barber Green **181**
Barclays for Bikes **221**
Bargain Bedstores **143**
Bargain Bookshop, The **235**
Bargain Centre 7, **184**
Bargain Tile Centre **141**, **159**
Bargain Wallpapers **171**
Barnard Marcus **286**
Barnardos 14, 296, 314, 316
Bathroom Discount Centre 13, **138**
Bathstore 13, **138**
Battens Carpets & Wood Floors **151**
Battersea Vintage Fashion, Accessories and Textiles Fair **63**
BCA Auctions **285**
Beanos **246**
Beats Workin' 16, 241, **247**
Beauty Base **125**
Beauty Collection **126**
Beds Ltd **145**

Bedtime Superstore **144**
Bellows 12, **274**
Bermondsey Market **352**
Berty & Gerty 6, 44, **48**
Berwick St Fabric Stores 4
Berwick Street Cloth Shop 182
Beyond Retro 4, 16, **36**, **60**
Bhopal Fabrics 16, **188**
Bicester Village **327**
Big Bed & Pine Co **143**, **193**
Big Table Furniture Co-op Ltd **145**
Bike Station, The **221**
BJ Computers 6, **101**
Blackmans Shoes 16, **95**
Blackout II 4, **36**
Bleetman Opticians **122**
Blondie 16, **59**
Bloomsbury Book Auctions **284**
Blue Audio Visual 7, **109**
Bohemia **197**
Book & Comic Exchange 11, **232**
Bookends 4, **225**
Bookhouse **226**
Bookmongers **233**
Books for Amnesty 6, 9, **300**, **313**
Books Ink **230**, 235
Bookthrift **232**
Book Warehouse 4, 9, 11, 15, **226**
Borders Books and Music 4, **236**
Borovick Fabrics Ltd 182
Frank G. Bowen Ltd **283**
Boznia Herzegovina Community
Charity Shop 8, 295, 306
Bradleys Curtain & Linen Centre **149**
Brains 17, 114, 116
Brick Lane Bikes 16, 217, **221**, **223**
Brick Lane Market **352**
Brill **236**
British Bathroom Centre **136**
British Computer Fairs **103**
British Designers Sale **72**
British Heart Foundation 6, 9, 12, 13,
14, 296, 301, 313, 317, 319
Britsh Red Cross 307
Brixton Market **353**
Broadway Market **353**
Broadwick Silks 182
Brondesbury Architectural
Reclamation **274**
Browns Labels for Less **64**
Bucks Warehouse **196**
Buildbase **167**
Burberry Factory Shop **324**
Burge and Gunson **139**
Burt & Mary 16, **60**
Buyers & Sellers 10, **177**

C

C & A Electronics 17, 114, 116
Callow, Russell **334**
Camden Contact Lens Centre 6, **121**
Camden Cycles 6, **216**, 217
Camden Market **353**
Camden Passage Market **354**
Camera Care **255**
Camera Club, The **256**
Camera World 4, **248**
Cancer Research Society 8
Cancer Research UK 6-9, 12,-15,
288-322
Carhartt Clearance Store **66**
Caroline Bousfield Gregory **332**
Caroline Charles **65**
Carpetman, The 12, **155**
The Carpetstore 9, **154**
Carpet Tile Centre 14, **151**
Carpet Warehouse **156**
Cash Converters 6, 8, 9, **362**
Cash Exchange **363**
Cash Express **363**
Cash XChange 8, **363**
Casino **53**
Cass Art 4, 7
Catwalk **77**
Cenci **58**

Centaur Auctions **277**
Central Park **24**, **28**, 33
CES **175**
CHA CHA CHA **53**
Chamberlaines **216**
Change of Heart **80**
Changing Curtains **160**
David Charles **68**, 211
Cheapo Cheapo Records Ltd **4**, **237**
Chelsea Removals **12**
Chi Chi Ra Ra **58**
Children's Society, The **8**, 302
Chiswick & West Middlesex Auctions **279**
Chocolate Factory, The **336**
Choice **29**, 211
Chomette **12**, 203, **325**
Chris Stephens Ltd **136**, **168**
Church Street Bookshop **231**
Ciclos Uno **223**
Citybeds Ltd **146**
Clarks Factory Shop **91**, **95**, 324
Classical Music Exchange **11**, 245
Classic Textiles **9**, 187
Cliford's Antiques **14**, **341**
Clive Emson Property Auctioneers **286**
Cloth House **182**
Cloth Shop, The **10**, **163**, 183, **186**
Cobbled Yard, The **341**, 345
Colour Centre **170**
Colourwash **13**, **137**
Community Charity Shop, The **8**, 302
Computer Games Exchange **11**, **106**
Computer Precision **7**, **101**
Computer Warehouse (Macs) **102**
Alison Cooke **333**
Cooker Centre Ltd **177**
Corcoran & May **165**, 190
Cornucopia **37**
Cosmic Gaze **347**
Countrywide Property Auctions **286**

Creekside Artists **336**
Criterion #2 Tiles **13**, **158**
Croydon Powertool Centre **174**
Crusaid **291**
CSN Curtains & Blinds Ltd **162**
Curtain Exchange, The **163**
Curtain Fabric Factory **13**, **163**, 325
Curtain Factory Outlet **14**, **161**
Curtain Mill Ltd **165**
Cutting Bar **133**

D

D & A Binder **340**
Daniel Galvin **129**
Data Serve **104**
Dave's DIY **171**
David Oliver Designer Outlets **24**
David Richards & Sons **201**
Davina **97**
Decathlon **218**, **257**
Decoy **24**
Dell Outlet **104**
Mr C. Demetriou DIY **167**
Denny's **4**, **200**
Dentons Catering Equipment **203**
Designer Sales UK **71**, **73**
Designer Showroom Sale **67**
Designer Warehouse Sales **69**
Designs on Her **80**
Deuxieme **13**, 81, **84**
De Ver Cycles **218**
Dialabike **215**
Diamond Merchants **139**
Digital Centre, The **17**, 114, 116
Dingwall Motor Auctions **285**
Direct Dance Wear **257**
Discount Appliance Centre **180**
Discount Bathroom Warehouse **141**
Discount Carpets **155**
Discount Decor **171**
Discount Shoe Sales **90**
Ditchfields **222**

Dollar Promotions **247**
H Dourof & Sons Ltd **156**
Dreamland Linen **150**
Dreamsport 9, **95**
Dress Box, The **84**
Dresser, The **84**
Dress for Less 7, **79**, 81
Drivers Norris **286**
Dublin Jim 16, **348**
Duffer of St George Sample Sale **73**
Dwell Clearance Shop **196**
Dynasty Designer Wear **85**
Dynasty Menswear **85**

E

E.D. Elson Ltd **167**
East End Cosmetics **127**
East London Design Show **337**
Easyjet **260**
Edwardes 217, **219**
Edwin Evans **286**
Empee Silk Fabrics Ltd **184**
Emporio Home **191**
Emporium, The **58**
Enfield Exchange **363**
Episode 6, 44, **51**
Epra Fabrics 16, **164**, **189**
Epsilon Computers 17, 114, 116
Everything Cycling **222**
Excel **260**
Exclusivo **82**
Extraordinary Design Ltd **332**
Eye Warehouse, The **121**

F

Fabric World **165**
Factory Monaco **25**, 33
Factory Outlet 11, 14, **25**, **29**
Fancy Curtains **164**
FARA 9, 12-13, 40, 292, 308, 312, 318-319

FARA Kid's Charity 13
Farz Design 8, **25**
Fashion East **74**
Fashion Made Fair **74**
Keith Fawkes **231**
Felt **85**
Film Plus **252**
Flashback 7, **240**
Flight Centre 6, 12, 13, 15, **264**
Flybe **260**
FPD Savills **286**
Freeport Braintree Designer Outlet **327**
Frock Market 12, **88**
Frock Me! **63**
from marissa v. **330**
Funky Town 50
Furniture Café, The 16, **349**
Furniture Gallery, The 9, **344**
Futon Company **192**

G

Games Planet 9, **106**
Gamestation 6, **105**
A. Gatto & Son 12, **172**
Gemini Shoes **98**
General Auctions 12, **281**
Geranium Shop for the Blind 13, 291, 308, 310
German Wings **261**
Ghost Ltd **70**
GHS Technology 17, 114, 116
Gill & Hoxby **174**
Glotech **175**
Gloucester Road Bookshop **232**
Going Abroad **264**
Golborne Furniture 10, **344**
Golds Factory Outlet 15, **26**
Gray & Lowe 9, **154**
R.F. Greasby **281**
Great Western Open Studios **337**
Greenwich Auctions Partnership **281**
Greenwich Market **354**

Index

Gultronics 17, 114, 116

H

Haggle Vinyl 7, **240**
Half Price Bathrooms **142**
Handmade & Found 7
Hani Wells Carpets **154**
Hansens 13, **202**
Hardwick Textiles **189**
Harold Moores Records & Video 4, **237**
Harp Electronics 17, 114, 116
Heal's Warehouse Sale **193**
Hcales Cycles **222**
Help the Aged 6, 301, 302
Henry Pordes Books Ltd 4, 227, **228**
Hi-Fi Surplus Store 17, 114, 115
Hinds, John **205**
Honest Jon's Records 10, **244**
Hornsey Auctions Ltd **277**
Hot & Cold 10, **178**
House Hospital, The **275**
Husen Moda 15
Hussain Fabrics **190**

I

Iceland Clearance Centre **179**
Iceland Express **261**
Ideabright 13, **172**
Iliffe, Pullens & Peacock Yard Open
Studios **337**
I Mark **93**
Impact Power Tools Ltd **174**
Ink Factory, The 104
Insight 13, **86**
Intoxica Records 10, **244**
Ixia Leather Sofas **193**

J

J.C. Second HandFurniture **350**
Jacobs Digital 4, **249**
Jami 15, 297

Jasper Conran End of Season Sales **67**
Jersey Vogue **190**
Jessops 4, 9, 12, **249**
Jimmy Choo **93**
John Frieda **128**
Jo Jo Maman Bébé 15, **208**, 210
Joseph Clearance Shop **66**
Judd Two **228**
Junior Style **69, 208**
Junk Shop, The 347
Junk Shop &
Spread Eagle Bookshop, The **234**
Junk Yard, The **342**
Just Beds **146**

K

Kamla 17, 114, 115
King of Cotton **150**
Kingsland Waste Market **354**
Kitchen Tech 9, **178**
Kitchen Warehouse 16, **204**
Kojak 16, **34**
KVJ 16, **112**

L

L.A. **29**
L.H. Cook Furnishers 10, **344**
L.W. Carpet Warehouse **155**
L'Homme Designer Exchange **79**
L'Oréal Technical Centre **134**
Laden Showroom, The **66**
La Scala **86**, 211
LASSCO **272**
Laurel Herman **82**
Lazy Days **349**
Leather Lane Market **354**
Lee's Cameras **254**
Leebanks Carpet Centre **152**
Leon Jaeggi & Sons 4, **200**
Les Couilles du Chien 10, **346**
R G Lewis Ltd 4, **250**

Leyland Paint 6, **170**

Leyland SDM 13

Lezley George **74**

Lillywhites 4, **23**, **258**

Linen Cup**boa**rd, The 4, **148**

Linen Mill, The **149**

Little Book of Furniture Ltd **198**

Little Trading Company, The **210**

Litvinoff and Fawcett **147**

LK Bennett Clearance Store **65**, **94**

Lloyds International Auction Galleries **282**

Loft, The 4, **80**

Lombok Clearance Store 13, **194**

London Bicycle Repair Shop **220**

London Camera Exchange 4, **250**

London Camera Repair Centre **255**

London Camera Shop 10

London Domestic Appliances **176**

London Fashion Weekend **70**

London Hospice, The 14

London Picture Centre, The 13, **206**

London Plumbing & Heating Supplies **141**

London Power Tools & Fixings **173**

London Scenes & Framing Ltd **205**

London Vintage Fashion, Textiles, & Accessories Fair **63**

London Warehouses Ltd **196**

Lords Home Care 10, **202**

Lost and Found 6, 16, 45, **49**, **349**

Lots Road Auctions 13, **280**

Lotus Leaf **26**

Louis Féraud **68**

Love Vintage 4, **37**

Lucky Bird **334**

M

M & S Supplies Bathroom Centre **138**

Mac's Cameras 9, **253**

Macmillan **129**

Made in Clerkenwell **338**

Magnet Discount Warehouses Ltd **176**

Maison du Monde **195**

Manheim Motor Auctions **285**

Manolo Blahnik International Ltd **93**

Maplin 6, 9, 12, **113**

Marcet Books **233**

Marie Curie 7, 8 10, 294, 297, 312, 322

Marshmallow Mountain 4, **38**

Martin's Fabric **162**, **184**

Martin Barnett Furniture Ltd **191**

Mary Shoes **97**

Matalan **26**

Maxx Outlet **27**

Mazorca Projects 'Hidden Art' **338**

MBA 17, 114, 115

A. J. McGovern & Company **342**

W M McGovern 8

MDC Music & Movies 4, **237**

Mend-a-Bike 13, **216**, 217, **223**

Meridiana **261**

Mermaid Fabrics **164**, 190

Merry-Go-Round **211**

Merton Abbey Mills Market **355**

Micro Anvika 17, **101**, 114, 115

Microglobe 4, **251**

Microworld 2000 17, 114, 115

Mind 6, 301, 304, 322

Misco 104

Miss Cardini **98**

MK One 9, 12, **31**

Moda 16, **35**

Modern Age Vintage Clothing 6, **52**

Modern Computers **102**

Monarch **261**

Money Store **363**

Monica **27**

M.P. Moran & Sons Ltd 8, **168**

Mordex 16, **35**

Morgan 4, **100**, **251**

Mr All Sorts **342**

Mr Cad **253**

Mr Scher's Spectacle Shop **123**

Index

Mr Toppers **130**

Music & Video Exchange 4, 6, 11,
238, 241, **242**, **245**, **246**

Musical Images 4, **108**

Musical Vision 17, 114, 116

My Back Pages **234**

My Travelite **261**

N

N & C Tile Building Materials **168**

N & C Tile Style **137**, **159**

n-genious 17, 114, 116

Nasseri Fabrics **190**

Nelly Duff **205**

New Era Optical **122**

Next To Choice 15, **27**

Nicholas Camera Company 6, **251**

Nicky Clarke **128**

Niki **262**

North London Auctions 14, **278**

North London Hospice 14, 15, 295–
298, 300

Norwegian **262**

Norwood Ravenswood 15, 295, 297

Notting Hill Books **232**

Octavia 9, 11–13, 293, 302, 306,
308–322

Nu-Line Builders Merchants 10, **169**

O

Observatory, The **59**

Ocean Books **231**, **243**

Office 4, **90**

Old Hat 13, 45, **56**

Ollies 10, **346**

On the QT 71, **72**

On Your Bike **215**

Ooh-La-La! **343**

Open Space 16, 33, **35**

Optical World **121**

ORT 14, 295

Out On The Floor 6, 241, **243**

Oxfam 4, 6–15, 40, 225, 288–322

Oxfam Original 4, 90

P

Pages 4, **200**

Pandora **86**

Pandora's Box 7, **201**

Parkins **283**

Past Caring 7, **343**

Paul Smith Sale Shop 4, **64**

Pdsa 8, 302, 303

Pedal It **215**

People Will Always Need Plates **332**

Perlie Rides **223**

Personal Computer Solutions **102**

Peter Jude 15, **162**

Petticoat Lane Market **355**

Photocraft **252**

Photomarket **253**

Photo Optix **252**

Pili & Mili 10, **31**

Pixies **210**

Plumbcraft Ltd **140**

Plush Floorings Ltd **152**

PNR Audiovision 17, 114, 116

Poetstyle Ltd **197**, 199, **326**

Pop Boutique 4, **38**

Portobello Market **356**

Pot Luck **204**

Power Giant **180**

Price's Patent Candle Co **326**

Prillywear **330**

Primark 8, 9, 12, **31**

Process Supplies **256**

Purple Bee 11, **32**

Putney Flight Centre 12

Q

Quinto 227, **228**

Quinto of Great Russell Street **229**

Index

R

Radio Days **39**

Rat Records **246**

Rawlinson, Helen **333**

RDC 104

Recycling **220**

Red Cross Shop 9, 313

Reflections 12, **140**

Reject Pot Shop 6, **202**

Relief Fund for Romania 296, 303

Rellik 10, **56**, 61

Resurrection Recycle Boutique **82**

Retro Clothing 11, **57**

Retro Home & Jewellry 11

Retro Man 11, **57**

Retromania **40**, 292

Retro Sofas **195**

Retro Woman 11, 57

Retro World 6, **50**

Revival Records 4, **238**

Revive **89**

RGA Appliances Ltd **180**

Ribbons & Taylor **54**

Richer Sounds 4, 13, **107**

Richmond & Surrey Auctions **280**

R K Photographic **254**, 256

Rokit 4, 6, 16, **40**, 45, **51**, 61, **62**

Rokit Clearance 6, **50**

Rolls & Rems **185**, 188

Roman Road Market **356**

Rosans & Company **284**

Rosebery's **282**

RSPCA 12, 298

Rub-a-Dub-Dub **209**

Russell & Chapple 4, **181**

Ryanair **262**

S

S & M Myers **152**

S.J. Carter Electrical Tools Ltd **172**

Sally Hair and Beauty 14, 15, **125**

Salou **86**

Salvation Army Charity Shop 4, 7, 12, 290, 294, 317, 319, 321

Salvation Army Charity Shop/Cloud 9 4, **290**

Salvo Fair **275**

Sam Greenberg 4, **42**, 61

Samuel King 17, 114, 116

Satellite Electronics 8, **110**

Savers Health Home & Beauty 6

Schools Connect Auction 103, **278**

Scope 6, 8, 295, 298, 301, 303, 306, 318, 321

SCP Ltd **192**

Screwfix Direct **169**

Seconda Mano 7, **83**

Second Look, The **88**

Second Tread **96**

Secret Sample Sale **75**

Sendean Camera Repair **255**

Sequel **89**

Sew Fantastic 7, **185**

Shantel AV Ltd 14, **110**, **176**

Shasonic 17, 114, 116

Shaukat Fabrics **94**, **149**, **186**

Shaw Leather Goods **96**

Shaya 13

Shepherd's Bush Eye Centre 9

Shoe Centre For Men **92**

Shoe Express 4, **91**

Shoe Zone 12, 14, **92**

The Shop 16, **62**

Shyamtronics 17, 114, 115

Sid's **94**

Sign of the Times **87**

Silverfields Chemist **127**

Simply Outgrown Nursery Equipment & Toys **209**

Simpson, Melissa **335**

SINE **331**

Sister Ray 4, **239**

Skoob Russell Square **229**

SkyEurope **262**

Smith, Francis **280**
Smith Bros **220**
Smooth Delight **331**
Sofas to Go **195**
Soho Original Bookshop 4, 8, **229**
Soho Silks 182
Sony Centre 17, 114, 116
Soul & Dance Exchange 11
Southgate Auction Rooms **278**
South London Fabric Warehouse **166**
South Molton Drug Store **127**
Soviet Carpet and Art Galleries **153**
Spatial Audio & Video 17, 114, 116
Specsavers Opticians **118**
Spex in the City 4, **118**
Spitalfields Crypt Trust Shop 320
Spitalfields Market Market **356**
Sports World 4, 12, 13, **258**
Sport Teck Ltd **96**
Spring, Daniel **333**
Stage & Screen 11, 245
Stanley Productions **113**
STA Travel **265**
Stelios 87
Sterling **262**
St John's Hospice 306
Stone Zone **158**
Stratford Computer Fair **103**
Student Travel Centre **265**
Sue Ryder 7, 291-294, 300, 301, 315
Sun Hill Electric **179**
Sunrise Digital 17, 114, 116
Super Design Ltd 9
Superfi London 6, **110**
Supreme Hair Design **134**
Swim, Bike, Run 13, **218**

T

Taurus Beds **144**
Teletext **266**
Textile King 182, 183
Thameside Motor Auctions **285**

Thames Motor Auction 13
Thea 6, **50**
the galleria **328**
The Girl Can't Help It **53**
Thomas Cook **266**
ThomsonFly **263**
G. Thornfield Ltd **206**
Tile Superstore 12
Timothy Everest **325**
TK Maxx 9, **32, 65**
Tlon Books **233, 234**
Tom, Dick & Harry's Furniture **350**
Toni & Guy **130, 131**
Toni Textiles 9, 187
Topps Tiles 12, 13, **157**, 158, 159
Top Value Drug Store **126**
Torpedo Blue 16, 61, **62**
Tottenham Court Road PC Market **104**
Toucan Tools Co. **173**
Traid 9, 10, 298, 303, 306, 311, 312, 313, 316
Transavia **263**
Travelwise **266**
Travel Zone 9, **94**
Trevor Sorbie **131**
Trinity Hospice 11-13, 292, 310, 311, 317, 318
Trinity Hospice Bookshop 12, 318
Truman Brewery 16
Truth Trading Ltd 16, 35
TV4U 8, **111**
Twice as Nice **88**
Twinkled 4, **43**, 44
Two Agent See **75**
C W Tyzack **173**

U

U.K. Textiles 9, 187
Uniqlo 23
University Vision **119**
Unsworths Booksellers **230**
Unto This Last **198**, 199, 334

Up the Video Junction 6
Uttam London Ltd 11, **32**

Youth Education Sport 12, 318

Z

Z. Butt Textiles 16, **189**
Zaga Shoes 6, **92**
Zoom Airlines **263**

V

Victoria Park Furniture Shop 345, **350**
Vidal Sassoon **131, 133**
Villeroy & Boch 12, 203, **326**
Vintage **89**
VIP Events **247**
Vision Express **119**
VLM **263**

W

Walden Books 6, **231**
Walrus **108**
Waterforce **139**
Wellingtons **83**
West End Beds **145**
West End Carpets **151**, 153
What!!! Stores **203**
What Goes Around Comes Around
6, **49**
What The Butler Wore **43**
Willesden Green Architectural Salvage
274
Willmotts **286**
Wishes (Cancer Research UK) 313
Wizzair **263**
Workshop Sales **338**
World's End Bookshop 13, **233**
WOW Retro 4, **46**

X

X Electrical 9, **111**

Y

Yemmy Textiles & Fashion **188**
Yes Domestic Appliances **177**
YMCA 293, 315

Index

Order our other Metro Titles

The following titles are also available from Metro Publications. Please send your order along with a cheque made payable to Metro Publications to the address below. Postage and packaging free.

Alternatively call our customer order line on 020 8533 7777 (Visa/Mastercard/Switch), Open Mon-Fri 9am-6pm

Metro Publications
PO Box 6336, London N1 6PY
info@metropublications.com
www.metropublications.com

London's Parks and Gardens
Nana Ocran
£6.99 ISBN 1-902910-19-2

London's Monuments
Andrew Kershman
£7.99 ISBN 1-902910-25-7

London's City Churches
Stephen Millar
£6.99 ISBN 1-902910-24-9

London's Cemeteries
Darren Beach
£6.99 ISBN 1-902910-23-0

Veggie & Organic London
Russell Rose
£6.99 ISBN 1-902910-21-4

Book Lovers' London
Lesley Reader
£8.99 ISBN 1-902910-26-5

Museums & Galleries of London
Abigail Willis
£8.99 ISBN 1-902910-20-6

London Architecture
Marianne Butler
£8.99 ISBN1-902910-18-4

London Market Guide
Andrew Kershman
£6.99 ISBN 1-902910-14-1

London Theatre Guide
Richard Andrews
£8.99 ISBN 978-1-902910-28-4

Food Lovers' London
Jenny Linford
£8.99 ISBN 1-902910-22-2